*Praise for* SAINTS PRESERVED

"Long before there were cameras and videos to record for posterity, relics had become the visible reminder of great, heroic, and holy lives—remembrances of heroes of the faith. *Saints Preserved: An Encyclopedia of Relics* gives an account of the lives of those heroes and provides renewed inspiration for Christians everywhere who face many of the challenges that were a part of the lives of the saints."

—CARDINAL DONALD WUERL, coauthor of *The Mass* and author of *The Catholic Way*

"Relics are an often misunderstood part of the Catholic devotional life. Derided as either superstitious or just plain 'gross,' they are in fact an important reminder of the physicality of the saints. The saints were not mythical creatures or legendary personages, but flesh-and-blood men and women who walked the earth, ate and drank, wore clothes, wrote letters, and lived entirely human lives. Thomas Craughwell's new book provides readers with a comprehensive guide to the most important relics in the Church and where they can be found, and venerated. His book is simply one of a kind."

—JAMES MARTIN, S.J., author of *My Life with the Saints* and *The Jesuit Guide to (Almost) Everything*

"Sacred Scripture tells us that 'Precious in the eyes of the Lord is the death of His holy ones' (Psalms 116:15). These holy men and women, boys and girls, whom we know as saints, are therefore precious to the Catholic Church. Thomas J. Craughwell has rendered an honorable service to the Church and the world with his new book, *Saints Preserved*—a lively and captivating account of three hundred resplendent saints and their holy relics, which we venerate with devotion to this day."

—PATRICK MADRID, author of *Search and Rescue* and
*Does the Bible Really Say That?*

"Honoring relics was one of the distinguishing marks of early Christianity. A practice rooted in Scripture, it was a universally popular devotion. Thomas Craughwell helps us recover this important element of our tradition. He shares a fascination born of love, the deep familial love that made a family of the first-century Church, and can renew our sense of family in the Church of the twenty-first century."

—MIKE AQUILINA, author of *The Fathers of the Church* and
*Roots of the Faith*

# SAINTS PRESERVED

*An Encyclopedia of Relics*

THOMAS J. CRAUGHWELL

IMAGE BOOKS

*New York*

IMAGE

Library of Congress Cataloging-in-Publication Data
Craughwell, Thomas J., 1956–
Saints preserved: an encyclopedia of relics/Thomas J. Craughwell.—1st pbk. ed.
  p.   cm.
Includes bibliographical references (p. 307).
1. Relics—Encyclopedias.   I. Title.
BX2315.C73 2011
235'.2—dc22          2010050870

ISBN 978-0-307-59073-2
eISBN 978-0-307-59074-9

*Book design by Lauren Dong*
*Cover photography: (top) relics of Saint Geminianus in crypt of*
*Cathedral of Modena © Alinari Archives/Corbis; (left) Saint Suaire exhibition*
*at the Dome in Turin © Alberto Pizzoli/Sygma/Corbis*

First Edition

147429898

*For my friends and fellow relic-hunters
the Carlson Family, the McCaffrey Family,
Msgr. Ignacio Barreiro, and Msgr. Richard Soseman*

# Contents

*Acknowledgments*  *ix*

*Introduction*  *xi*

LIST OF RELICS  *1*

*Bibliography*  *307*

# Acknowledgments

My first word of thanks goes to my friend and editor, Gary Jansen, the godfather of this book. I am especially grateful to my friend Msgr. Ignacio Barreiro, who has led me through churches and catacombs and monasteries throughout Rome and the surrounding countryside to venerate some of the Catholic Church's most sacred relics. And my thanks to Ann Gladwin, administrator of the Ladyewell Shrine in England; Father John Fitzpatrick, S.A.C., rector of the Church of San Silvestro in Capite in Rome; Father Alex Kirsten, S.J., director of the Martyrs' Shrine in Midland, Ontario; Rev. Knut Andresen of the Nidaros Cathedral, Norway; and Susan Wolff at the National Shrine of St. Odilia in Onamia, Minnesota, all of whom were kind enough to interrupt their day to answer questions from a complete stranger. A special thank-you to Maggie Carr, the gold standard among copyeditors. Finally, my thanks to my friend John Thornton for suggesting the title of this book.

# Introduction

Anyone who thinks that the cult of relics of the saints is itself a relic of the Middle Ages should log on to eBay. On any day of the week the online shopper will find a thriving business in the sale of relics, ranging from dust from the tomb of Christ to splinters of the True Cross to bone fragments of countless saints.

Among the faithful, relics have an enormous appeal. In 1999–2000, when relics of Saint Thérèse of Lisieux (1873–1897), popularly known as the Little Flower, traveled across the United States, millions turned out to touch or kiss the reliquary. The scene was repeated in 2003, when a tiny fragment of the cloak that bears the miraculous image of Our Lady of Guadalupe was carried from parish to parish throughout the country.

Believers will go out of their way to see famous relics. An online search of Catholic travel companies turns up dozens of itineraries designed specifically to visit churches that exhibit renowned relics, such as the incorrupt body of Saint Bernadette in her convent's chapel in Nevers, France, and the basilica in Padua, Italy, where Saint Anthony lies buried.

Though many of the most famous relics like Padre Pio's gloves and Saint Francis of Assisi's tunic are associated with saints, relics are not limited to the Catholic and Orthodox churches. Buddhists venerate the teeth of the Buddha; Islam venerates the sword, the robe, and even strands from the beard of Mohammed. In ancient times, when a farmer or an excavation crew unearthed dinosaur bones, the Greeks and Romans took them for the remains of the Titans, or a legendary hero such as Theseus.

Even secular society prizes relics: at the Abraham Lincoln

Presidential Library and Museum in Springfield, Illinois, I saw crowds press around a display case that contained the gloves Mary Todd Lincoln wore to Ford's Theatre, stained with the blood of her assassinated husband. No doubt morbid curiosity plays a part, but I believe the desire to see Mary Lincoln's bloodstained gloves represents something deeper—the longing to have a physical connection with one of the greatest men, and one of the most tragic moments, in American history. It is that same longing to connect on a physical and not just a spiritual level that draws the faithful to the tombs of the saints, the houses where they lived, the altars before which they prayed, even the prisons where they were tortured.

In the Catholic Church relics fall into one of three categories: a first class relic is the physical remains of a saint, such as bones, hair, and blood; a second class relic is a personal possession of a saint, such as clothing, devotional objects, handwritten letters, even furniture; and a third class relic is an object, such as cloth or a holy card, that is touched to a first class relic.

Reverence for the remains and belongings of saints is rooted in Sacred Scripture. In 2 Kings 13:20–21 we read of a dead man being restored to life after his corpse touched the bones of the prophet Elisha. In Mark's Gospel we find the story of a woman who suffered from a hemorrhage for twelve years and was cured when she touched the hem of Christ's garment (Mark 5:25–34). And the Acts of the Apostles recounts how Christians touched handkerchiefs and other cloths to the body of Saint Paul; when these cloths were given to the sick or the possessed, "diseases left them and the evil spirits came out of them" (Acts 19:11–12).

Even in times of persecution the early Christians made an earnest effort to recover the remains of the martyrs so they could be given a proper burial and their martyrdom commemorated annually with Mass celebrated at their tombs. A letter from about the year 156 AD describes the martyrdom of the elderly bishop of Smyrna, Saint Polycarp. His body had been burned, but the Christians of Smyrna searched among the ashes for any trace of the saint that had not been consumed by the flames. "We took up his bones," the anonymous author of the letter wrote, "which are more valuable than precious stones and finer than refined gold, and laid them in a suitable place, where the Lord will permit us to gather ourselves together, as we are able, in gladness and joy, and to celebrate the birthday of his martyrdom."

After Emperor Constantine legalized Christianity in the Roman Empire, great basilicas were built over the tombs of Saints Peter, Paul, and Lawrence, to name only a few. In 386 Saint Ambrose discovered the relics of the protomartyrs of Milan, Saints Gervase and Protase, and had them enshrined in his church where the faithful could venerate the relics and ask for the martyrs' intercession. In *City of God,* Book 22, Saint Augustine bears witness to the many miracles that were wrought by the newly discovered relics of Saint Stephen. According to Augustine, in Tibilis, during a procession with a relic of the protomartyr, "a blind woman entreated that she might be led to the bishop who was carrying the relics. He gave her the flowers he was carrying. She took them, applied them to her eyes, and immediately saw."

There was always the danger, of course, that some Christians in their enthusiasm might treat the saints as if they were little gods and the relics as if they were magical. Saint Jerome, in his letter to Riparius, writes of the proper veneration of saints and relics: "We do not worship, we do not adore [saints], for fear that we should bow down to the creature rather than to the Creator, but we venerate the relics of the martyrs in order the better to adore Him whose martyrs they are."

During the Middle Ages a pilgrimage to a shrine was a popular expression of religious devotion as well as a kind of vacation or road trip. Journeys to the Holy Land, Rome, or Compostela in Spain could be dangerous (Saint Bridget of Sweden was shipwrecked on her pilgrimage to Jerusalem), but there were many shrines closer to home where one could venerate relics. Cathedrals, monasteries, and convents began to build up impressive relic collections, the better to attract throngs of pilgrims. Pilgrims were an important asset to local economies: they needed food and lodging; they would make gifts to the church; they would purchase a badge, a holy card, or some other souvenir to recall their journey. In time, aristocrats began to amass private relic collections to which they gave the public access on certain days of the year. In Wittenberg, Frederick the Wise kept his collection of thousands of relics in the Wittenberg Castle Church. It was on the door of that church in 1517 that Martin Luther nailed his ninety-five Theses, an early step in the religious revolution known as the Protestant Reformation.

The Protestant reformers attacked the veneration of relics, but the Catholic bishops at the Council of Trent responded by explaining and defending the practice, saying, "The holy bodies of holy martyrs and of others now living with Christ—which bodies were the living members of Christ and 'the temple of the Holy Ghost' [1 Corinthians 6:19] and which are by Him to be raised to eternal life and to be glorified are to be venerated by the faithful, for through these [bodies] many benefits are bestowed by God on men." Nonetheless, during the Reformation period vandals smashed countless shrines, burning or otherwise destroying the relics they contained. In Lutheran Scandinavia such violence was rare; typically the relics of a saint were removed from a shrine and buried in an unmarked grave in the same church. As a result, the relics of Saint Bridget and her daughter, Saint Catherine of Sweden, as well as the relics of the martyred king Saint Eric, have survived. In England, Scotland, and Wales the reformers destroyed almost every shrine, but in recent years some Anglican bishops have attempted to restore the shrines in their cathedrals. In Winchester Cathedral, for example, a small contemporary shrine marks the spot where the shrine of Saint Swithun stood during the Middle Ages. The shrine is empty; all of the saints' bones were destroyed during the Reformation. But at St. Alban's Abbey a bone of the martyr lies within the new shrine, the gift of the Catholic archbishop of Cologne who had a relic of Saint Alban in one of the churches of his archdiocese.

As a rough estimate, the Catholic Church venerates about forty thousand saints. Most of these are local holy men, women, and children, virtually unknown outside the region where they lived and died. To try to catalog the location of the relics of all of these saints would require the labor of several lifetimes. And to track down the tiny fragments of saints' bones, the snippets from saints' clothing, would be impossible. So I have been obliged to narrow my focus. This volume contains approximately 350 entries of the Catholic world's most important, interesting, unusual, or rare relics. Most but not all of the entries describe the relics of saints. I have included Old Testament relics such as Noah's Ark and the Ark of the Covenant (said to be hidden in a church in Ethiopia); Holy Land relics such as the house where Jesus, Mary, and Joseph lived and the stairs from Pontius Pilate's palace; relics of Jesus Christ, including the Manger, the True Cross, the Shroud of Turin, the Crown of Thorns, Veronica's Veil, the Pillar of the Scourging, and the Holy Sepulcher; relics of the Virgin Mary such as her veil (at Chartres Cathedral), her portrait (Poland's Black Madonna and Mexico's Our Lady of Guadalupe), and her belt (at Prato Cathedral). For easy reference, the book is arranged in an A–Z format. Each entry includes the location of the relic, its history, a brief biography in the case of a saint, and the feast day.

The relics of all saints and blesseds of the United States (current at the time of this book's publication date) are included, as well as the relics of many saints and blesseds of Canada and Latin America. I have also included entries for the two largest relic collections in America, Maria Stein in Ohio and St. Anthony's Chapel in Pittsburgh.

Every year Maria Stein and St. Anthony's Chapel welcome many visitors, who tend to be an amalgam of the devout and the curious. Probably very few have the level of enthusiasm for relics their ancestors knew during the Middle Ages, when monasteries, convents, cathedrals, and even nobles and kings succumbed to a kind of relic-collecting mania. The craving to possess an important, even an exceptional relic, led to all types of abuses, from theft, to relic peddling, to the manufacture of bogus relics—hence the multiple heads of Saint John the Baptist. Sadly, some churches claimed to possess relics that were spurious at best and at worst sacrilegious—a feather of the Holy Spirit, for example, or the shield of Saint Michael the Archangel. Such "relics" I have not included. In most cases the churches that possessed these items disposed of them or retired them long ago.

Nonetheless, some of the relics included in this book may raise eyebrows. It is true that not all relics that are still publicly venerated can be authenticated with 100 percent certainty. But if these relics are well known and the church that possesses them has not put them away, I felt that they ought to be included here.

Every Catholic church and chapel contains at least one relic—it is a requirement of the Church under canon law that every altar consecrated for the celebration of Mass must contain the relic of at least one saint, preferably a martyr. This requirement links even the most contemporary church with the earliest practice of the Church, when priests offered Mass using the sarcophagus of a martyr as the altar. In addition to the fragmentary relic in the altar, most churches possess other relics, which are sometimes brought out for veneration on a saint's feast day. On a recent Good Friday it was my privilege to venerate a relic of the True Cross—one of the treasures of the Church of St. John the Evangelist in Stamford, Connecticut.

In some cases years after a saint's death, his or her grave was opened and the body found to be in a remarkable state of preservation. Generally speaking, the term applied in such a case is "incorruptible." However, incorruptibility is often in the eye of the beholder. Gazing upon the bodies of some of these saints, the terms "mummified," "embalmed," or "desiccated" may also come to mind. The body of Saint Bernadette is usually described as incorrupt, and her face is exquisitely beautiful. But the case becomes more complicated when one learns that the saint's actual face has darkened over time, and so it has been covered with a lovely, utterly lifelike wax mask. The translation of the body of Blessed Pope John XXIII from his sarcophagus in the grottoes beneath St.

Peter's into a side chapel of the basilica set off a debate over whether his body was supernaturally incorrupt, or whether it had been embalmed at the time of his death. The question has never been resolved definitively. It is possible that Blessed Pope John's body is so well preserved because it had been enclosed inside three coffins, and then sealed in a stone sarcophagus.

No one should feel uneasy visiting a shrine or venerating a relic. In many respects it is similar to visiting the grave of a beloved member of the family, or cherishing a family heirloom—but on a much higher level. The shrine or relic is a physical link with someone who was so faithful to God in this life that he or she is now glorified in the Kingdom of God forever. Bringing out Grandma's china for Christmas dinner stirs the emotions and makes us feel connected once again to someone we loved but who has since died. Relics work in the same way but more intensely, because in the case of sacred relics the connection is not only to someone we love but to someone who was genuinely holy.

# SAINTS
# PRESERVED

**The Aachen Relics (first century).** According to Charlemagne's biographer, Einhard, in 800 the patriarch of Jerusalem sent a monk to Aachen with four extraordinary relics for the newly crowned Holy Roman Emperor: the dress the Blessed Virgin Mary wore when she gave birth to Jesus Christ; the Infant Jesus's swaddling clothes; the loincloth Christ wore as he hung upon the cross; and a towel in which was wrapped the head of Saint John the Baptist. All four relics are kept in a golden chest that was made for them in 1238; the reliquary is on display in the Treasury of Aachen, Germany's Aachen Cathedral and the Shrine of St. Mary. Once every seven years the relics are exposed for public veneration; the next exposition will be held in 2014.

Aachen's Kornelimünster, or Church of St. Cornelius, has three precious relics: the cloth Christ tied around his waist when he washed the feet of his apostles at the Last Supper; the shroud in which Saint Joseph of Arimathea wrapped the body of Jesus for burial (this shroud is different from the much more famous Shroud of Turin); and the sudarium, or the cloth that was laid over the face of Jesus at the time of his burial.

**Saint Afra (died 304).** The bones of Saint Afra are preserved in a simple stone sarcophagus in the crypt of the Basilica of St. Ulrich and St. Afra in what is present-day Augsburg, Germany. The church is an important historic site: in 1555 the Peace of Augsburg was signed here, putting an end to religious warfare in Germany and establishing the right of individual princes to choose if they would be Catholic or Lutheran. The basilica is split between the Catholic half dedicated to Saint Afra and the Lutheran half dedicated to Saint Ulrich.

Before her conversion to Christianity, Afra had been a prostitute in Augsburg's temple of Venus. During Emperor Diocletian's persecution of the Church she was arrested. "You were a prostitute," the judge reminded her. "The God of the Christians will reject you."

"Not so," Afra replied. "Jesus Christ forgave the adulterous woman because her repentance was sincere. And he will forgive me, too."

The judge sentenced Afra to be suffocated. Guards took her to an island in the middle of the Lech River, bound her to a stake, and built a large smoky fire around her. She choked to death in the fumes.

Saint Afra is the patron saint of converts and is one of the patron saints of Augsburg. Feast day: August 7.


**Saint Agatha (died c. 250).** The majority of Saint Agatha's bones are enshrined in a chapel in the Cathedral of Catania. During volcanic eruptions of Mount Etna, which overlooks the city, Saint Agatha's veil has been removed from her shrine and carried in procession through the streets; it is said that through the prayers of the saint, the city has been spared from disaster several times, including in the twentieth century.

Both Palermo and Catania on the island of Sicily claim to be Saint Agatha's birthplace, but there is no reliable documentation to settle the question. In fact, there is no reliable biography of this saint at all. The only thing we know for certain is that a Christian woman named Agatha was martyred in Catania about the year 250 and that immediately after her death she was venerated first by her fellow Sicilian Christians, and then by Christians throughout the Roman Empire. In the Roman Canon of the Mass she is invoked along with six other female martyrs.

The legend of Saint Agatha, which dates from about the sixth century, tells us that she was beautiful, wealthy, and the daughter of a noble family. When a consul named Quintianus asked to marry her, Agatha refused, explaining that she had consecrated her virginity to Jesus Christ. Angry and humiliated that he had been rejected, Quintianus had her arrested and tortured. At one point, the torturer sliced off Agatha's breasts. Guards carried her unconscious and half dead to a prison cell where Saint Peter appeared and healed her. When the prison guards reported to Quintianus that Agatha was alive and that her breasts had been restored, he condemned her to be rolled over red hot coals until she died. That is the basic legend of Saint Agatha; there are other versions.

Saint Agatha is invoked against breast cancer and all diseases of the breast, volcanic eruptions, and all natural disasters. She is the patron saint of wet nurses and bell makers, and she is one of the patron saints of Sicily. Feast day: February 5.


**Saint Agnes (died 304).** A chapel in the Church of St. Agnes in Agone in the Piazza Navona preserves Saint Agnes's skull. The majority of her bones are kept in a silver casket under the high altar of the Basilica of St. Agnes on Rome's Via Nomentana.

During Emperor Diocletian's empire-wide persecution of Christians, Agnes was arrested and arraigned. She was about thirteen years old at the time, the child of a family of Christians who lived in Rome. It is likely that by the time Agnes was taken, her parents had already been martyred.

The judge who presided over her case threatened to burn her alive if she did not renounce Christianity and sacrifice to the Roman gods. Agnes refused. Since she was a virgin, the judge sent her to serve in the temple of the goddess Vesta, which was tended only by virgins, but Agnes would not perform any function in a pagan sanctuary. Finally, in the arena that stood on what is now Rome's Piazza Navona, the judge had Agnes exposed naked to the jeering crowd, then beheaded.

Saint Agnes is the patron saint of chastity and innocence, of engaged couples, of the Girl Scouts, and of the sodality of the Children of Mary. She is almost always represented with a lamb: this emblem represents her purity and is also a pun on her name— the Latin word for lamb is *agnus*. Feast day: January 21.

**Saint Alban (died c. 290).** On December 6, 1539, commissioners of Henry VIII arrived at the Abbey of St. Alban to strip the buildings of all their valuables. They carried off all items of gold, silver, gilt, iron, brass, and lead, as well as altar cloths, tapestries, and the church bells. The shrine of Saint Alban was smashed, but there is no record of what became of the relics. There is documentation that the looters emptied some of the tombs and burned the remains; it's likely that the bones of Saint Alban ended up on the pyre. In the late twentieth century the abbey clergy decided to rebuild Saint Alban's shrine, using the rediscovered pieces of the smashed original remains along with new materials. Since they had no relic, they approached the archbishop of Cologne in Germany, where relics of Saint Alban were preserved in Cologne's Church of St. Pantaleon. The Anglican clergy hoped the Catholic archbishop would authorize the transfer of one of these bones to the Abbey of St. Alban's. In 2002 an auxillary bishop of Cologne came to the abbey with a shoulder bone of the saint, which he laid inside the shrine. Today the shrine of Saint Alban is once again a destination for pilgrims, both Anglicans and Catholics. The thigh bone of Saint Alban, also from the Church of St. Pantaleon, is preserved in the Roman Catholic Abbey of St. Michael at Farnborough, England.

Late in the third century, during a period of anti-Christian persecution in Britain, Alban, a young pagan, sheltered a Christian priest named Amphibalus. During the weeks he hid in Alban's house, Amphibalus explained his faith to Alban; in time, Alban asked to be baptized.

Sometime later the authorities of Alban's town, Verulamium, ordered a house-to-house search for Christians. As soldiers approached Alban's house, the young man helped Amphibalus escape, then threw on the priest's cloak. When the soldiers entered Alban's house they demanded to know who he was. "My name is Alban," he said, "and I worship the only living God." The soldiers arrested him.

Before the magistrate, Alban repeated his statement that he was a Christian. He admitted that he was not a priest, but would not say where Amphibalus was. And he refused to save his life by sacrificing to the Roman gods. The magistrate sentenced Alban to death.

The guards escorted Alban out of the city to Holmhurst Hill, where they stripped and flogged him then cut off his head. Not long afterward the Romans arrested Amphibalus and beheaded him, too.

Saint Alban is venerated as England's first martyr. By 429 there was a shrine over Alban's grave, which eventually was replaced by the great abbey church that dominates the town of Saint Albans today.

Saint Alban is the patron saint of refugees and converts. Feast day: June 22.


**Saint Albert the Great, also known as Albertus Magnus (1206–1280).** The remains of Saint Albert the Great lie in a large, plain stone sarcophagus that dominates a tiny crypt beneath the Church of St. Andrew in Cologne.

One of the great minds of the Middle Ages, Albert is best known for teaching theology to Saint Thomas Aquinas. In addition to theology, Albert's interests extended to all the natural sciences; in fact, he wrote forty books on the subject, always arguing that for true scientists, "experiment is the only safe guide." In this he was ahead of his time; most "men of science" in thirteenth-century Europe still relied on ancient "authorities" who made absurd claims, for example, that barnacle geese were hatched out of trees. Albert wrote in response, "The aim of natural science is not simply to accept the statements of others, but to investigate the causes that are at work in nature."

Tragically, during the last years of his life Saint Albert suffered from a form of dementia.

Saint Albert the Great is the patron saint of scientists, particularly natural scientists. Feast day: November 15.

**Saint Alexander Briant or Brian (1556–1581).** As is true of most of the English martyrs of the Reformation period, very few relics of Saint Alexander Briant survive. One exception is his missal, with prayers written in the martyr's own hand on the flyleaves at the back of the book. It is said that Catholics purchased the saint's little wooden cross from the churlish Anglican minister who snatched it out of his hands during his trial; the cross is preserved at the English College in Rome.

Alexander Briant was eighteen years old when he abandoned his studies at Oxford University and crossed the English Channel to enter the English seminary at Douai in France. In 1578 he was ordained a priest, and in 1579 he was sent back to his homeland to minister in secret to Catholics while trying to bring Anglicans back to the Catholic faith. For two years he managed to elude the priest-hunters, but in April 1580 he was arrested in London and imprisoned in the Tower.

In addition to the usual questions Queen Elizabeth's government put to captive priests—In whose house did he say Mass? Who attended? Whose confessions had he heard? Who had he reconciled to Rome?—Father Briant's interrogators in the Tower also wanted to know the whereabouts of another Jesuit missionary to England, Father Robert Persons, who had taught Briant when he was at Oxford. As punishment for his refusal to cooperate, Father Briant was stretched on the rack for two days in succession. In a letter smuggled out of the Tower by a friend, Briant told the Jesuit superiors on the Continent that as the torture began he fixed his mind upon the Passion of Christ and felt no pain until the session ended. Then he asked to be admitted to the Society of Jesus. The Jesuits accepted him at once, although it is not certain if Father Briant ever learned that he had been received into the society.

On November 21, 1581, Briant and six other priests were escorted into Westminster Hall for trial. Briant held in his hand a tiny wooden cross he had made in his cell. An Anglican minister snatched it away from him. "You may tear it from my hands,"

Father Briant told the clergyman, "but you cannot tear it from my heart."

Father Briant and his fellow priests were convicted on a trumped-up charge of having sworn to assassinate Queen Elizabeth. On December 1 Briant, Saint Edmund Campion, and Saint Ralph Sherwin were dragged on hurdles through the streets of London to Tyburn, where each was hanged, disemboweled, and quartered. Alexander Briant was the last to die; he was twenty-five years old.

Feast day: December 1.

**Saint Alexander Nevsky (1220–1263).** Russia's Communist government confiscated the relics of Saint Alexander Nevsky (along with the magnificent silver sarcophagus in which the relics had been enshrined) in 1919 when they shut down the St. Alexander Nevsky Lavra, or monastery, and executed twenty of the monks. The saint's relics were put on display in an antireligion museum in St. Petersburg, while the sarcophagus, which had been commissioned by Tsar Peter the Great, was exhibited as a work of art at the Hermitage Museum. In 1989 the Russian government authorized the transferal of Saint Alexander's relics from the museum back to Holy Trinity Cathedral in the St. Alexander Nevsky Lavra, where they were enshrined in a new sarcophagus. The original shrine was not returned and remains in the Hermitage.

Saint Alexander was prince of Novgorod and grand duke of Vladimir during one of the most difficult periods in Russia's history. In 1236 the Mongols invaded, laying waste to every major city and town in what is now Russia and the Ukraine, and killing or enslaving tens of thousands of men, women, and children. Princes such as Alexander's father, Yaroslav II, hoped to stop the slaughter and destruction by acknowledging the Mongol Great Khan as their overlord from whom they received the authority to rule their domains. But the khans were suspicious of the princes who still exercised great influence over the people of Russia. In

1243 the Great Khan invited Yaroslav to visit him at his capital in Mongolia, and there Yaroslav was poisoned. Some years later the Khan invited Alexander to his court, but Alexander declined.

In 1240 the Swedes invaded Russia. On the banks of the Neva River, Alexander and his army took the invaders by surprise and destroyed them. To commemorate this victory the prince was given the surname "Nevsky," which means "of the Neva."

Alexander's most famous victory occurred two years later. The Teutonic Knights, a German military order that was carving out an empire for itself in Eastern Europe and the Baltic, besieged the city of Pskov. Alexander met the knights at Lake Peipus. It was the first week of April but the lake was still frozen. The battle was a stalemate until Russian cavalry reinforcements arrived; at the sight of them, the knights retreated across the frozen lake. But the ice was not thick enough to bear the weight of the armored men and their warhorses. The ice split open, swallowing up about four hundred knights. The Battle of the Ice was immortalized by Sergei Eisenstein in his 1938 film, *Alexander Nevsky.*

In 2008 the Russia news service Interfax conducted a poll among its readers to learn who Russians regarded as their greatest national hero: Alexander Nevsky took first place with 2,011,766 votes.

Saint Alexander Nevsky is the patron saint of soldiers and the protector of Russia's borders. Feast day: November 23.


**Saint Alexius.** The body of Saint Alexius has been lost, but a portion of the staircase under which he lived for seventeen years is displayed in the Church of St. Alexius in Rome.

Although Alexius was a very popular saint in the Middle Ages, we know almost nothing about him. According to legend he was the son of a Roman senator and ran away from home on his wedding day, traveling to Edessa in what is now Turkey, where he lived for many years as a beggar. In a vision Our Lady told him to return home, but when he knocked on the door of his home his family did not recognize him. Without disclosing who he was, Alexius asked permission to live under the front staircase of the house. Seventeen years later, when Alexius died, his family found him holding a scroll that revealed his identity.

Saint Alexius is the patron saint of panhandlers. Feast day: July 17.

**Saint Aloysius Gonzaga (1568–1591).** It was the custom among the Jesuits of Rome to wrap the body of a deceased brother in a shroud and lay it in the bare earth. When Aloysius Gonzaga died, his spiritual director, Saint Robert Bellarmine, was so convinced that the young man was a saint that he persuaded his superiors to place Aloysius's body in a coffin so it could be found easily and moved to a proper shrine after his canonization. The relics of Saint Aloysius are preserved in a side altar of the Church of St. Ignatius in Rome. The bones of Saint Robert lie in an adjacent altar.

For centuries it has been conventional to portray Aloysius as a frail, effeminate, doe-eyed youth. He was in fact a headstrong boy with a bit of a combative streak. The Gonzagas were one of the warrior clans of Renaissance Italy, and Aloysius channeled the family trait into a determination to become a Jesuit and a saint.

He took a boot-camp approach to sanctity, forcing himself to get out of bed in the middle of the night to pray, never using a cushion but always kneeling on the bare floor, sometimes whipping himself with a leather dog leash if he believed he had committed an especially grave sin.

At age fifteen Aloysius informed his parents that he wanted to enter the Jesuit novitiate. His father, Ferrante, was furious; Aloysius was the eldest son and had been trained to be a marquis and continue the family line. The meeting ended in a tremendous quarrel between father and son. Ferrante and Aloysius's stalemate dragged on for two years until, after one final tantrum, Ferrante relented and gave his son permission to enter the Jesuit novitiate in Rome.

At the novitiate Saint Robert Bellarmine ordered Aloysius to follow the Jesuit routine of prayer and discipline—no more rising in the middle of the night for extra prayers or beating himself with a leash. Like every other novice, Aloysius was assigned charitable work. Often he was sent to help in one of Rome's hospitals, which he detested; the smell of the place, the gruesome wounds and hideous diseases of the patients, the repulsive tasks of emptying chamber pots and changing soiled bedding—all disgusted him. But by exercising his iron will he overcame his repugnance.

It was about this time that an epidemic broke out in Rome. Aloysius was sent out to collect the sick from their homes, or in the streets, or wherever he found them. By now he was a skilled and compassionate nurse, but by spending so much time among the sick he contracted the disease himself and died.

Saint Aloysius Gonzaga is the patron saint of teenagers, of Jesuit students, and of AIDS patients and their caregivers. Feast day: June 21.

**Saint Alphonsus Maria de Liguori (1696–1787).** The saint's remains are preserved in a silver casket in a side chapel of the Basilica of St. Alphonsus, a church that he designed for the Redemptorists in Pagani, Italy. Adjacent to the basilica is a museum that contains many of Alphonsus's personal belongings, including his vestments, his wheelchair, and his harpsichord.

Alphonsus entered the priesthood at a time when there were many priests in the Kingdom of Naples—about 75,000—but not many who were a credit to the calling. In eighteenth-century Italy it was common for younger sons who would not inherit any property from their parents to become priests, then angle for a job in Church administration, where they would enjoy a comfortable income without having to work very hard.

With religious life grown so lax, Alphonsus started a new order, the Congregation of the Most Holy Redeemer, or Redemptorists, to reclaim priests who were living worldly or even scandalous lives, to assist parish priests who were overworked, and to teach the faith to the laity and encourage them to come more often to Mass, to receive the sacraments more frequently, and to devote more time to prayer.

Alphonsus trained his Redemptorists to be skillful preachers and gentle confessors. They traveled from parish to parish, holding missions that lasted several days during which the Redemptorists said Mass, led popular devotions, preached daily, and heard confessions for hours at a time. It was hoped that by the time they moved on the pastor would have learned how to revitalize his parish and to rekindle the religious fervor of the parishioners.

The Redemptorist missions were so successful that bishops throughout Italy wrote to Alphonsus asking him to send some of his priests to work in their dioceses. As the Redemptorists' reputation spread, requests came from Austria, Poland, and Germany.

Saint Alphonsus is the patron saint of religious vocations, moral theologians, confessors, excessively scrupulous people, and those who suffer from arthritis. Feast day: August 1.

**Saint Ambrose (c. 340–397).** Saint Ambrose's body is enshrined in the crypt of the Basilica of St. Ambrose in Milan. He lies between the bodies of Saints Gervase and Protase, the martyrs of Milan whose relics he discovered.

Ambrose was born into a prominent Roman family who had been Christian for generations; he was particularly proud that there was a saint in the family, his great-great aunt Soteris, who died a martyr in 304.

He had a talent for oratory and organizing arguments in a way that was compellingly persuasive, so he became a lawyer. He was practicing in Milan when the bishop died. At the election, held in the city's cathedral, Ambrose climbed into the pulpit to demand that the Catholics of Milan must have an equal voice with the Arians (who were the dominant denomination in the city at the time). When he finished, a child shouted, "Ambrose for bishop!" The crowd took up the cry, and Ambrose was forced to submit to election by popular acclaim.

There were a few problems. He was not a priest. In fact, he had not yet been baptized (it was common practice among Christians at the time to postpone the sacrament for as long as possible so that when they were baptized, all the sins of their life would be washed away). In a week he was baptized, ordained, and consecrated bishop. Ever the good student, Ambrose brought in theologians to deepen his understanding of the Catholic faith so he would not lead the souls entrusted to him into error.

He was a wondrously convincing preacher. When he spoke in praise of a life of consecrated virginity, so many young women became nuns that mothers with marriageable daughters would not take them to Mass at the cathedral if Ambrose was preaching. His most famous success was converting Augustine, an obstinate Manichean who had lived for seventeen years with a woman who was not his wife.

Saint Ambrose is the patron saint of learning; of bees, beekeepers, and candlemakers; and of the city of Milan. Feast day: December 7.

**Saint André Bessette (1845–1937).** In the crypt of Montreal's Oratory of St. Joseph is the Votive Chapel, where crutches, canes, and other apparatus left by individuals who have been healed through the intercession of Saint Joseph are displayed. Behind the statue of Saint Joseph is a black marble sarcophagus in which lie the remains of Saint André Bessette.

André was one of ten children born into a French-Canadian family in Quebec. When he was nine his father, a lumberjack, was killed by a falling tree. When André was twelve his mother died of tuberculosis. The older children went to work, and the younger ones were split among the homes of relatives and friends.

André had virtually no education, so he did manual labor. He worked in construction, as a baker, on a farm, and for four years in a textile mill in the United States. In 1870 he asked the superiors of the Congregation of Holy Cross to admit him to their novitiate to train as a lay brother. Four years later he took his perpetual vows and was assigned as the doorkeeper at the Notre Dame College. He washed the floors and windows, brought in firewood, delivered messages, and screened visitors to the college. There was a tram station across from the college, and commuters became accustomed to seeing the small, thin brother going about his work. Some people stopped to chat with Brother André, and if they mentioned that they had troubles, he recommended that they pray to Saint Joseph. Many of these people returned to say that Saint Joseph had answered their prayers.

It was the dream of Brother André to erect a great church in honor of Saint Joseph on one of the mountains above Montreal. Friends and donors paid to have a small chapel erected in 1904; by 1936 the Congregation of Holy Cross had received sufficient funds to build the grand oratory on Mount Royal, the largest church in Canada and the largest in the world dedicated to Saint Joseph.

Many people came to believe that Brother André was a miracle worker. "People are silly to think that I can accomplish miracles," he said. "It is God and Saint Joseph who can heal you, not I. I will pray to Saint Joseph for you."

Pope John Paul II beatified André Bessette in 1982; Pope Benedict XVI canonized him in 2010. Feast day: January 6.

**Saint Andrew Bobola (1591–1657).** The martyr was buried in the parish church of Janow, Poland, the town where he died. Later the body was moved to the Jesuit church in Pinsk. In 1922 the Soviets confiscated the relics and put them on display in a museum in Moscow. A year later Pope Pius XI, through two American Jesuits, Fathers Edmund A. Walsh and Louis J. Gallagher, petitioned the Soviet government for the return of the relics; the Holy Father's request was granted and then-Blessed Andrew's remains were sent to Rome. Since his canonization in 1938 Saint Andrew's relics have been enshrined in the Jesuit church in Warsaw.

Andrew Bobola was a member of the Polish nobility and

entered the Jesuit novitiate at age sixteen. As a priest he was a gifted preacher, especially skilled at elucidating Sacred Scripture and making Catholic doctrine accessible to laypeople who had little or no education. He was devoted to the Blessed Mother and founded sodalities to encourage love for Mary and compassion for the needy. When an epidemic broke out in Vilnius, the members of Father Bobola's sodalities were among the most active in caring for the sick and the dying. In some parts of Poland there were no resident Catholic priests, so most of the inhabitants had joined the Russian Orthodox Church. Father Bobola went to these regions, established Catholic parishes, and brought many former Catholics back to the faith.

In the 1650s Russian Orthodox Cossacks led by Bogdan Chmielnicki were terrorizing Polish Catholic communities. They targeted Father Bobola as a "soul-hunter" for having brought Poles back to the Catholic faith. In 1657 the Cossacks occupied Janow, massacred the town's Catholics and Jews, and took Father Bobola prisoner. In a butcher shop they flayed the priest alive. An armed force of Poles arrived suddenly, driving the Cossacks out of Janow; they found the Jesuit's body hanging from its feet in the butcher shop.

Saint Andrew Bobola is one of the patron saints of Poland and of the archdiocese of Warsaw. Feast day: May 16.


**Saint Andrew the Apostle (first century).** In 1460 the Turks captured the Greek city of Patras; the governor, Thomas Palaeologos, a member of the Byzantine imperial family, fled to Italy, taking with him Patras's most sacred treasure, the skull of Saint Andrew. It was preserved in the Basilica of St. Peter in Rome from 1464 until 1964, when Pope Paul VI returned it to the Greek Orthodox Church.

Most of Saint Andrew's relics are enshrined in the crypt of the Cathedral of St. Andrew in Amalfi; they were brought here in 1206 by crusaders who had carried off the apostle's relics as a prize during the Sack of Constantinople in 1204. Legend claims that in the fourth century a Greek monk, Saint Regulus, or Rule, arrived in Scotland with a few of Saint Andrew's bones. He built a chapel for the relics; a town sprang up around the chapel and took the name Saint Andrews. Over the centuries a series of successively larger churches were built on the site until 1559, when Protestant extremists destroyed all the altars and sacred images in the cathedral of St. Andrew and burned the saint's relics. The cathedral was abandoned and today lies in ruins. When the Catholic hierarchy was restored in Scotland in 1878, the following year the archbishop of Amalfi presented Archbishop John Strain of Edinburgh with a large piece of Saint Andrew's shoulder bone. In 1969 Paul VI presented Cardinal Gordon Joseph Gray with another relic of Saint Andrew. The two relics are kept in Saint Mary's Cathedral in Edinburgh, in a chapel known as Scotland's National Shrine of Saint Andrew.

The brother of Saint Peter, Andrew was the first apostle to follow Jesus Christ. He was a fisherman. Andrew and Peter had formed a fishing partnership with two other brothers who became apostles, James and John. Saint John's Gospel tells us that it was Andrew who presented to Jesus the boy with the basket of five loaves and two fishes, which Christ multiplied to feed the five thousand.

Tradition says that Saint Andrew carried the Gospel to Byzantium, Russia, Romania, and Greece. At the Greek town of Patras he was tied to an X-shaped cross; he lingered for three days, preaching from the cross until he died.

Saint Andrew is the patron saint of fishermen and fish dealers. Unmarried women pray to him for help finding a husband. He is one of the patron saints of Scotland, Greece, Russia, and the Ecumenical Patriarchate of Constantinople. Feast day: November 30.

**Saint Angela Merici (1474–1540).** Visitors must make an appointment to view the remains of Saint Angela Merici displayed in the Church of Saint Afra in Brescia, Italy. The church is attached to the motherhouse of the Ursuline nuns, who admit visitors and escort them to the church.

For almost all of her adult life Angela lived a quiet, pious life, performing good works. As a girl she had excelled in Latin and biblical exegesis, and she taught catechism to children. In 1535, at age sixty-five, she and twenty-eight associates established the Company of Saint Ursula, popularly known as the Ursulines, dedicated to teaching young girls. Three years later Angela died, but her congregation survived her and flourished. The Ursulines were the first nuns to arrive in the New World, founding schools, orphanages, and hospitals in Canada and Louisiana.

During World War II Allied bombs destroyed the Church of St. Afra, but the body of Saint Angela was not harmed. The church has since been rebuilt, with a museum dedicated to the saint's life.

Saint Angela Merici is the patron saint of schoolgirls, the sick, and the handicapped. Feast day: January 27.


**Blessed Angelico (c. 1395–1455).** Fra Angelico lies buried near the high altar in Rome's Church of Saint Mary sopra Minerva. His paintings can be found in museums around the world, but the largest collection of his work is preserved at the Monastery of Saint Mark in Florence, where virtually every room contains a fresco by the blessed artist.

When Guido di Pietro took his vows as a Dominican friar he received the name Angelico. His superiors discovered that he was a talented artist and put him to work in the scriptorium painting illustrations and decorative borders on manuscripts. Initially Fra Angelico followed the Gothic style, but like other artists in Italy during the fifteenth century, he was strongly influenced by the artistic style of the Italian Renaissance. Soon he was in demand to paint altarpieces and frescoes. In 1447 Pope Nicholas V commissioned Fra Angelico to paint scenes from the lives of Saint Stephen and Saint Lawrence in a tiny chapel in the Vatican Palace.

Fra Angelico was revered in life for his deep faith as well as for his gifts as an artist, and after his death many of the faithful prayed to him as Beato, or Blessed, Angelico. Pope John Paul II made the title official in 1982 when he beatified Fra Angelico.

In 1984 Pope John Paul II formally named Blessed Angelico the patron saint of artists. Feast day: February 18.


**Saint Anne (first century).** According to legend, Saint Maximinus, a disciple of Christ, often identified as the man born blind whom Jesus healed (John 9), carried some of Saint Anne's bones to southern France. These relics are preserved in the Church of St. Anne in Apt. In 1625 a Breton peasant named Yves Nicolazic claimed to have received visions of Saint Anne in which she requested that a chapel be built at Auray in her honor. During the construction the builders uncovered an ancient statue, which they took to be an image of Saint Anne, and they installed it in the completed church. Louis XIII and Anne of Austria gave the church a relic of Saint Anne in thanksgiving for the saint's intercession; after several miscarriages, the queen gave birth to a son in 1643, the future Louis XIV. The shrine of St. Anne de Beaupré in Quebec, Canada, possesses three major relics of Saint Anne: a portion of a finger bone and two portions of a forearm bone.

The Gospels do not mention Saint Anne and Saint Joachim, the parents of the Blessed Virgin Mary. Their story is told in a work called *The Protoevangelium of James,* an apocryphal text written perhaps as early as AD 150. According to the *Protoevangelium,* Anne and Joachim were a childless couple until an angel appeared to them when they were elderly with a message from God that Anne would give birth to a daughter who would be "spoken of in all the world." That daughter was Mary.

By 550 devotion to Saint Anne was well established in the Christian East. Emperor Justinian built a church in her honor in Constantinople. Another church was built in Jerusalem over the remains of an ancient house, which some believe was the home of Joachim, Anne, and Mary. Devotion to Saint Anne spread to the West during the Middle Ages and remains very strong among Catholics to this day.

Saint Anne is one of the patron saints of Brittany, France, and Canada; of women who have difficulty getting pregnant, of expectant mothers, and of women in labor; also of grandmothers, homemakers, and miners (because she gave the world her daughter Mary, who is like silver; and her grandson Jesus, who is like pure gold). Feast day: July 26.

**Saint Anthony of Padua (1195–1231).** Every day crowds of pilgrims throng the tomb of Saint Anthony in the Basilica of Il Santo in Padua, Italy. After praying at the tomb, almost all of them line up to enter the Chapel of the Relics. There, displayed among the relics of countless saints, are some of Saint Anthony's personal belongings, including his Franciscan habit. Over the altar, encased in a crystal urn, is the saint's tongue. Some years after Anthony's death, the Franciscans opened his coffin; only bones remained, but in the skull was Saint Anthony's tongue, intact; its preservation has been understood to be a tribute to the saint's eloquence as a preacher.

Anthony was born in a stone house in Lisbon—it is still standing, just a few steps from the cathedral. As a young man Anthony joined a new religious order, the Franciscans. He asked his superiors to send him to North Africa as a missionary to the Muslims. It was a dangerous assignment; five Franciscan friars had just been executed by the sultan of Morocco. But the Franciscans granted Anthony's request. But as soon as he landed in Morocco, he fell severely ill. After he spent months as an invalid, his superiors recalled him to Portugal. A storm in the Mediterranean blew the ship off course, and Anthony landed in Italy. He made his way to a Franciscan house in Forli in northern Italy, where he was put to work as a housekeeper.

On a day when several men were to be ordained Franciscan priests, the superiors realized that they had failed to assign one of

In 2009 the Franciscans in charge of the Basilica of St. Anthony in Padua, Italy, restored the shrine chapel. Before the saint's remains were placed in the refurbished shrine, they were exposed for five days for public veneration. © Andrea Merola/pool/epa/ corbis

the friars to preach. Anthony was chosen at random. To the surprise of the Franciscans, the bishop, and the congregation, Anthony preached a magnificent sermon. From that day onward he was sent out on preaching missions. As his reputation grew, so did the size of the crowds. Often Anthony preached in city piazzas because the thousands who had come to hear him could not squeeze into any of the churches. Through Anthony's preaching hardened sinners made their first confession in years, enemies were reconciled, and Cathars, a sect intensely hostile to the Catholic faith, were brought back to the Church.

Anthony died at age thirty-six. Immediately afterward so many people testified to miracles wrought through his intercession that Pope Gregory IX declared Anthony a saint less than a year after his death—the fastest canonization on record.

Saint Anthony is the patron saint of amputees and poor people;

he is also invoked to find lost objects. He is also one of the patron saints of Portugal and Brazil. Feast day: June 13.

**Saint Anthony of the Desert (251–356).** At the foot of Al-Qalzam Mountain in Egypt, near the Red Sea, is the Monastery of St. Anthony, founded shortly after the saint's death in 356. It is the oldest continuously inhabited Christian monastery in the world. Saint Anthony's tomb is found inside the monastery church, and about a mile from the monastery, pilgrims climb a cliff almost 2,310 feet above the Red Sea to pray in the cave where Anthony lived.

Anthony was born in a town known today as Kemn-el-Arouse in central Egypt. At age eighteen, when his parents died, Anthony became heir to a large fortune. One day at Mass he heard the priest read this Gospel passage: "If you would be perfect, go, sell what you possess and give to the poor and come follow me" (Matthew 19:21). Anthony took the passage to heart, sold everything, distributed it to the poor, and then went into the desert to live as a hermit.

He had been in the desert thirty-seven years when other men came to him seeking spiritual guidance and the privilege of living near him. Anthony organized these men into the world's first Christian monastic community.

There are stories that demons appeared and physically assaulted Anthony, and that he once traveled deep into the desert to meet the first Christian solitary, Saint Paul the Hermit.

In 352 he left the desert for Alexandria, where he assisted the city's bishop, Saint Athanasius, in refuting the doctrinal errors of an Egyptian priest named Arius. Athanasius would become Anthony's first biographer.

Anthony spent his last years in his cell above the Red Sea. He died at age 105.

Saint Anthony of the Desert is invoked against rashes, skin diseases, epilepsy, and temptation. He is the patron saint of animals, especially pigs, of basket weavers, monks, and gravediggers. Feast day: January 17.


**Saint Antoninus of Florence (1389–1459).** The body of Saint Antoninus lies in a glass casket in a side chapel of the Church of St. Mark in Florence, Italy.

At age sixteen Antoninus entered the Dominican order. He devoted himself to studying theology and mastering the art of preaching, but his superiors observed that Antoninus also had administrative gifts. He was made vicar, or superintendent, of several houses of Dominican friars who had returned to the austere, original ideals of their founder, Saint Dominic. He founded the Monastery of St. Mark in Florence, which became the home of the Renaissance artist Fra Angelico and the fiery Renaissance reformer Savonarola.

In 1446 Pope Eugene IV named Antoninus archbishop of Florence. Antoninus tried to avoid the appointment by claiming ill health, but the pope insisted, finally threatening to excommunicate Antoninus if he did not submit.

In an age when most archbishops lived and acted liked princes, Antoninus lived like a humble friar. He sold off the gold and silver tableware of the archbishop's residence, the expensive furnishings, the stable of horses, and the kennel of hunting dogs and distributed the money to the poor. When he traveled through Florence he went on foot; for longer journeys he kept a mule.

He set an example for other bishops by preaching every Sunday and holy day in his cathedral. After a violent earthquake Antoninus sheltered the homeless and used the archdiocese's funds to build them new houses.

In spite of the demands on his time, Antoninus kept up an intense daily life of prayer. "To enjoy interior peace," he wrote, "we must always reserve in our hearts amidst all affairs, as it were, a secret closet, where we are to keep retired within ourselves, and where no business of the world can ever enter."

Saint Antoninus of Florence is invoked against fever. Feast day: May 10.


**Saint Apollonia (died 249).** Saint Apollonia's skull is preserved in the Church of St. Mary in Trastevere and her arms in the Basilica of St. Lawrence Outside the Walls, both in Rome. Many churches in Europe claim to have one or more of her teeth, including the cathedral in Rab, Croatia; and the cathedral in Porto, Portugal. The greater part of the saint's relics appear to have been lost after the Church of St. Apollonia in Rome was torn down, although they may be in the tiny closed chapel of St. Margaret in Rome's Trastevere neighborhood.

For Saint Apollonia we have a rare firsthand, eyewitness account of her martyrdom, written by her bishop, Dionysius of Alexandria, to his fellow bishop, Fabius of Antioch. When the emperor Decius began persecuting Christians in 250, pagan mobs ran through the streets of Alexandria, attacking Christians in the marketplace, dragging them from their places of business, and breaking into their homes. They dragged their victims outside the city walls where an enormous bonfire had been kindled. Anyone who denied Christ was spared; those who remained faithful were thrown into the flames.

Bishop Dionysius wrote that the mob seized "a wonderful old lady [named] Apollonia." As they drove her out of the city they beat her about the face so severely that all her teeth were broken or knocked out.

At the pyre they threatened her with death if she did not pray to the gods of Rome. Apollonia asked for a little time to make her choice. The mob waited, and in that moment Apollonia leapt into the fire.

Saint Apollonia is invoked against toothache and is the patron saint of dentists. Feast day: February 9.

**Ark of the Covenant.** No, the Ark of the Covenant is not inside a wooden crate amid thousands of other crates in a vast U.S. government warehouse. According to the Ethiopian Orthodox Church, Menelik I, the child of Solomon and the Queen of Sheba, brought the Ark from the Temple in Jerusalem to Ethiopia. After Christianity was introduced to the country by Saint Frumentius in the fourth century, the Ark was moved to the Church of St. Mary of Zion in Axum. Today it is said to reside in the treasury adjacent to the church; only its guardian may see it.

God commanded Moses to build the Ark of the Covenant, a chest 45 inches long by 27 inches high, of acacia wood plated with pure gold, inside and out, with two cherubim, also of pure gold, affixed to the lid of the chest. Inside the Ark, Moses placed the tablets of the Ten Commandments (see Exodus 25:10–22 and 37:1–9). The family and descendants of Kehath of the priestly tribe of Levi were given the privilege of carrying the Ark.

The Ark represented for the Israelites the presence of God. It went before them on their journey to the Promised Land, and it accompanied them when they went into battle. In 953 BC Solomon enshrined it in the Temple he built in Jerusalem.

After 586 BC, when the Babylonians captured Jerusalem and looted and destroyed the Temple, the Ark disappeared from the historical record. There are legends that it was buried on the Temple Mount, or hidden in a cave above the Dead Sea, or was carried to Ethiopia. But no one knows with any certainty what became of it.

**Saint Athanasius (c. 295–373).** After his death Saint Athanasius was buried in Alexandria. At some point his body was moved to Constantinople. During the Fourth Crusade, Venetian crusaders took the relics from Constantinople to Venice, where they were enshrined in the Church of St. Zachariah. When the Coptic Orthodox pope, Shenouda III, visited Rome in 1973, the Roman Catholic pontiff, Paul VI, presented Shenouda with some of the relics of Saint Athanasius; the rest remain in St. Zachariah. Pope Shenouda enshrined the saint's relics in the crypt of the Coptic Orthodox Cathedral of St. Mark in Cairo.

Athanasius was eighteen years old in 313 when Emperor Constantine published the Edict of Milan, which gave Christians the right to worship freely, without fear of persecution. Yet within a few years the Church suffered another crisis, the Arian heresy, whose prophets denied that Christ was the Son of God, the Second Person of the Holy Trinity, and portrayed him instead as a kind of superhero endowed by God with supernatural powers. This teaching was spread by an Egyptian priest named Arius. In 325 several hundred bishops, priests, and deacons met at Nicaea (modern-day Iznik, Turkey) to examine Arius's work. They concluded that it was counter to the Church's understanding of the Trinity and condemned Arius and his unorthodox doctrine.

Nonetheless, Arius continued to promulgate his ideas, and it was Athanasius, by that time the patriarch of Alexandria, who took the lead in refuting Arianism. As Arianism spread among influential members of the imperial court, and even found supporters within the emperor's family, Athanasius, Pope Liberius, Saint Ambrose, and other orthodox bishops found themselves under attack. Emperor Constantius banished Pope Liberius from Rome. Imperial troops threatened to murder Saint Ambrose inside his own cathedral. As for Athanasius, between 335 and his death in 373, the Arians managed to have him exiled from Alexandria on five separate occasions.

Toward the end of Athanasius's life, Emperor Valens, although sympathetic to the Arians, permitted Athanasius to return to his residence in Alexandria and resume his duties as patriarch.

In Orthodox churches on the feast of Saint Athanasius the faithful sing a hymn that praises the saint as a "pillar of orthodoxy [who] refuted the heretical nonsense of Arius."

Saint Athanasius is the patron saint of religious orthodoxy. Feast day: May 2.

**Saint Augustine of Hippo (354–430).** In the last weeks of Augustine's life a Vandal army led by Gaiseric surrounded Hippo. Three months into the siege, Saint Augustine died. Eleven months later the city surrendered after receiving generous terms from Gaiseric: the entire population was free to leave with their possessions; no Vandal would interfere or harm them. When the citizens of Hippo walked out of Hippo, they left the body of Augustine behind in its grave in his cathedral. In 480 Catholics returned to the derelict, half-burned city, opened the grave, and took the relics to Cagliari on Sardinia. In the eighth century, when Saracens conquered the island, Luitprand, king of the Lombards, ransomed Saint Augustine's relics, paying the Saracens the bones' weight in gold. He gave the relics to the Church St. Peter in Ciel d'Oro in Pavia, where they have remained ever since. The relics are encased in a magnificent white marble Gothic shrine adorned with ninety-five statues and fifty bas reliefs. A few of the saint's bones have been moved to a small glass casket for the veneration of the faithful.

Saint Augustine's father was a Roman pagan; his mother, Saint Monica, was a Berber Catholic. He was not baptized as an infant, but he was anointed with sacred oil, and Monica raised him as a Catholic. (It was common in the fourth century to put off baptism until adulthood, when the water of the sacrament would wash away a lifetime of sins.)

When Augustine was in his teens, his parents sent him to study at the university in Carthage—the Harvard of Roman North Africa. There he acquired a mistress (we do not know her name), and together they had a son out of wedlock. Augustine also turned his back on the Catholic faith and joined the Manicheans, a religion whose adherents believed there were two realms—one good, the other evil—that were locked in a perpetual struggle for control of the world. At the time Manicheanism was popular among the intellectual elite of the Roman Empire, and Augustine was ambitious to join this level of society.

For seventeen years Monica prayed that her son would return to the Catholic faith, and in 386, when he was teaching in Milan,

Monica met the man who would prove to be the answer to her prayers. The bishop of Milan, Saint Ambrose, was as intellectually sophisticated as Augustine; furthermore, he was a dynamic, persuasive preacher. After hearing a few of Ambrose's sermons, Augustine agreed to meet him. Through his conversations with Ambrose, one of the most astute minds Christianity has ever known, Augustine was brought back to the Church. Ambrose baptized Augustine and his son at the Easter Vigil in 387.

It was Augustine who synthesized the message of the Gospel with the teachings of the Greek philosophers. His writings on the human will inspired the philosophers Arthur Schopenhauer and Friedrich Nietzsche. In 2003 his theory of the just war was the focus of fresh debate during the invasion of Iraq. After Saint Paul, St. Augustine is Christianity's most influential theologian and a Doctor of the Church.

Saint Augustine is the patron saint of theologians. Feast day: August 28.

**Saint Barbara (died c. 270).** Several places claim to possess the bones of Saint Barbara: the Church of St. Barbara in Cairo, Egypt; the Cathedral of St. Vladimir in Kiev, Ukraine; the Cathedral of St. Mary of the Assumption in Rieti, Italy. The multiple claims tell us just how popular Barbara has been in both the East and the West.

Legend tells us that Barbara was the only child of a wealthy family in Nicomedia, in what is now Turkey. Her father, afraid that Barbara's beauty would attract the attention of unworthy men, housed her in a tower in a remote location until he found a respectable suitor for her. One day, as Barbara sat by the only window in her tower, a man walked by singing a song she had never heard before. She called to him, asking him to explain the song. The stranger answered that he was singing to Jesus Christ, whom he worshipped. Intrigued, Barbara invited the man to come in and tell her more.

The stranger was a Christian priest. Moved by this faith that was so different from the paganism in which she had been raised, Barbara asked to be baptized. Naturally, she kept her conversion secret from her father, but then she committed an indiscretion. Her father, feeling guilty that he had given his daughter only one window, sent a work crew to the tower to add a second. Barbara asked the men to install two more windows so that she would have three—in honor of the Holy Trinity. That request gave her away.

Barbara's father denounced her to the local magistrate, who sentenced her to death. He declared he would execute her himself. With a single blow of his sword Barbara's father decapitated his own child. At the moment Barbara died, lightning fell from heaven, killing her father.

That is the only story we have concerning Saint Barbara; her name does not appear on any of the ancient lists of martyrs; the first time she is mentioned in any surviving text is about the year 700. But by 800 she was widely venerated throughout the Christian world.

Saint Barbara is invoked against lightning and sudden death; she is the patron saint of artillerymen, munitions workers, and manufacturers of fireworks. She is the patron saint of Rieti, Italy; and of Santa Barbara, California. Feast day: December 4.


**Saint Barnabas (first century).** In 478 Anthemios, archbishop of Constanta on the island of Cyprus, had a dream in which Saint Barnabas revealed the location of his long-lost grave. Anthemios went to the spot and found a tomb with the skeleton of a man inside. That skeleton is enshrined in the church of the Monastery of St. Barnabas in Famagusta, Cyprus.

Barnabas is the man who introduced the newly converted Saul of Tarsus, now known as Saint Paul, to the apostles in Jerusalem. Saul had been a ferocious persecutor of Christians, so it was only natural that among some of the faithful his conversion would be met with suspicion. But having Barnabas vouch for him reassured the apostles that Saul's conversion was authentic.

Barnabas came from a Jewish family living in Cyprus. He was among the first Jews to be converted to Christianity after the first Pentecost, and his gifts as an orator had won many converts in Antioch. Among the apostles Barnabas was well respected.

Paul wanted to set out on a missionary journey to Asia Minor (modern-day Turkey) and Barnabas agreed to join him. He brought along his young cousin, John Mark, to act as their assistant and apprentice missionary. Although Paul and Barnabas were close friends and enjoyed great success on their mission, John Mark taxed Paul's patience. Paul came to regard the boy as lazy and unreliable. After their first mission concluded, Paul swore he would never travel with John Mark again. Barnabas became offended, and the two friends split up and apparently had no more contact with each other.

We know that Barnabas took John Mark to Cyprus, but then Barnabas disappears from the historical record. Tradition tells us that Barnabas became the first bishop of the island and was martyred there.

Saint Barnabas is the patron saint of peacemakers and is invoked against hailstorms. He is the patron saint of Cyprus and Antioch. Feast day: June 11.


**Saint Bartholomew or Nathanial (first century).** In 809 the relics of Saint Bartholomew were moved from his tomb in Armenia to Lipari and then in 838 to Benevento in southern Italy. In 983 the Holy Roman Emperor Otto III erected in Rome a church on Tiberina Island in the Tiber River and dedicated it to Saint Bartholomew (known today as San Bartolomeo all'Isola), and he had a portion of the apostle's relics enshrined there. The rest are venerated in Benevento's basilica of St. Bartholomew.

All four Gospels include Bartholomew in their list of the twelve apostles, but only Saint John's Gospel tells us a story about him. (John's Gospel calls him Nathanial or Nathanael. This is not unusual; Peter is also known as Simon and Saint Jude as Thaddeus.)

John tells us that after Philip encountered Jesus he went to tell his friend Nathanial that he had met the Messiah. He found Nathanial resting under a fig tree and in no mood to hear about a messiah from a northern backwater village. "Can anything good come from Nazareth?" he asked. Philip convinced Nathanial to come and see for himself.

As the two friends approached, Christ called out, "Behold, an Israelite indeed, in whom there is no guile!" Confused, Nathanial asked Christ how he knew him. Jesus answered, "When you were under the fig tree I saw you." Astonished, Nathanial exclaimed, "Rabbi, you are the Son of God! You are the King of Israel!" "You will see greater things than these," Christ promised. "You will see the heavens opened and the angels of God descending and ascending upon the Son of Man" (John 1:43–51).

Saint Bartholomew is the patron saint of Armenia, tanners, and anyone who works with leather, as well as butchers and bookbinders. Feast day: August 24.

**Saint Basil the Great (c. 330–379).** The relics of Saint Basil have been scattered across the Christian world. His skull is venerated at the Great Lavra on Mount Athos, Greece.

Basil came from a family of saints: his father, Basil the Elder; his mother, Emmelia; his grandmother Macrina the Elder; his sister Macrina the Younger; and his brothers Gregory of Nyssa and Peter of Sebaste—all are venerated as saints. The family was wealthy, and they used their wealth to assist the needy in Caesarea, their hometown, in what is now Turkey. The principle of putting faith into action was ingrained in Basil and his nine brothers and sisters. When the region around Caesarea suffered a famine, young Basil joined the family's servants in the kitchen, making soup and bread for the hungry.

Basil became a priest and in 370 was consecrated bishop of Caesarea. For many years he had called for a reform of monastic life; now he was in a position to put his ideas into practice.

In the fourth century there were few monasteries or convents as we know them today; most men and women who discerned a call to the religious life lived in the desert as hermits. They had no formal rule of life to guide them, and some of these solitaries adopted penitential practices that ruined their health and in a few extreme cases left them mentally unbalanced. Arguing that humans are "sociable beings, and not solitary or savage," he urged the hermits to come together in communities near or even inside cities and towns. In addition to prayer and contemplation, he encouraged the monks and nuns to open schools, operate hospitals, and take in orphans and the elderly. Eventually Basil's suggestions were written down as a rule that continues to guide most of the communities of monks and nuns in the East.

Saint Basil is the patron saint of reformers and of the province of Cappadocia in Turkey. Feast day: January 2.

**Saint Bede the Venerable (672–735).** At his death in 735 Saint Bede was buried in the cemetery of the monks of St. Peter and St. Paul's Monastery at Jarrow. In 1022 his bones were moved to Durham Cathedral, where they joined Saint Cuthbert's relics in the choir. During the fourteenth century a splendid shrine was erected to Saint Bede in the cathedral's Galilee Chapel; his relics were translated there in 1370. When Henry VIII's commissioners came to Durham in 1540 to shut down the monastery attached to the cathedral, they dismantled Saint Bede's shrine but, uncharacteristically, did not burn his bones; instead they buried them beneath the floor of the cathedral, at the place where the shrine had stood. The tomb in which the saint's relics rest today was erected in 1831. The inscription reads HAEC SUNT IN FOSSA BEDAE VENERABILIS OSSA, which means, "In this tomb are the bones of Venerable Bede."

Bede was seven years old when his mother and father presented him as an oblate to the Benedictines at the Monastery of St. Peter and St. Paul in their town of Wearmouth-Jarrow in northern England. The custom of dedicating a child to the service of God, with the intention that he would be trained for life as a monk, was common at this time. Certainly not all children were suited to monastic life, but Bede took to it easily, both the spiritual life and the intellectual life. Monasteries at this time were the guardians of Europe's intellectual heritage. In their scriptoria monks copied ancient Greek and Roman works, as well as sacred Christian texts, which were carefully preserved in the monastery library. Scholar-monks such as Bede wrote new works that were in turn copied and disseminated among other monastic houses.

During his long career at Wearmouth-Jarrow, Bede studied and wrote about topics ranging from mathematics to music. For his commentary on the Bible he has been named a Doctor of the Church, but he is best known for his *Ecclesiastical History of the English People,* an invaluable work for the study of English society before and during the arrival of Christianity.

During the last days of his life he tried to finish his commentary on the Gospel of Saint John. His last words were, "Gloria Patri, et Filio, et Spiritui Sancto" (Glory be to the Father, and to the Son, and to the Holy Spirit).

Saint Bede is the patron saint of church lectors. Feast day: May 25.

**Saint Benedict (c. 480–550).** On February 15, 1944, more than two hundred Allied bombers dropped more than eleven hundred pounds of explosives and incendiaries on the ancient Benedictine Abbey of Monte Cassino. The reason for the destruction: the Allies were convinced that the Germans were using the mountaintop monastery as an observation station. The bombing destroyed the church and almost all of the abbey, but the relics of Saint Benedict and his twin sister Saint Scholastica survived; so did the abbot, seventy-nine-year-old Dom Gregorio Diamare, several monks, three local farm families, and a group of orphaned children. The abbey has been completely rebuilt, and the relics of Saints Benedict and Scholastica are still in their sarcophagi on opposite sides of the sanctuary in the crypt chapel. Although Monte Cassino has the oldest claim to the relics of Saints Benedict and Scholastica, for centuries the Monastery of St. Benedict in Fleury, France, has claimed that it possesses the saints' bones. At this point it is nearly impossible to determine which relics are authentic. It is possible that at some unknown date some of the relics of Benedict and Scholastica were given to the monks at Fleury.

Benedict was in his early twenties when he withdrew from the world to live inside a cavern in the mountain ravine of Subiaco, about forty-four miles east of Rome. For three years he lived in solitude, deepening his spiritual life and contemplating a new regimen for monastic life.

Since the third century, when the first Christian hermits left their homes to live a life of prayer and penance in the desert, there had been a tendency among some to deprive themselves of food, water, proper clothing, even sleep, all in the hope of drawing closer to the mystery of God. Benedict came to regard these self-imposed penances as extreme, counterproductive to the spiritual life, and even dangerous to an individual's physical and mental health. In place of these practices he drew up a short book known today as *The Rule of Saint Benedict* in which he set out a commonsense routine of physical labor, study, prayer, and rest, with a healthy diet and clothing suitable to the seasons. Men who became his disciples at Subiaco eventually put the *Rule* into practice in what became the first Benedictine monastery. Benedict's twin sister, Scholastica, adapted his *Rule* for women, founding the first Benedictine convent. By the time of his death Benedict had founded a dozen monasteries, including Monte Cassino, where he died.

Saint Benedict is invoked against fever, kidney disease, gallstones, poison, temptation, and the occult. He is the patron saint of monks, spelunkers, schoolchildren, and farmers. He is also one of the patron saints of Europe. Feast day: July 11.

**Saint Benedict Joseph Labre (1748–1783).** Rome's Church of St. Mary ai Monti, Benedict Joseph Labre's personal favorite, has become his shrine. His body lies beneath an altar in the north transept, and the church also preserves his death mask and the rags he wore at the time of his death (he collapsed inside the church and died in a house nearby).

Benedict Joseph Labre was a religious misfit. He longed for a life in one of the more austere monastic orders such as the Carthusians or the Cistercians, but his quirky personality made him unsuitable for life in a religious community. Since he could not be a monk he decided to become a permanent pilgrim. He carried nothing with him, not even food. He did not beg, but relied upon God to inspire strangers to give him something to eat. From his home in France he walked to the great shrines of Western Europe: Compostela in Spain, Paray-le-Monial in France, Assisi, and, of course, Rome. In 1744 he made the Eternal City his home—by "home" he meant the place where he camped out amid the ruins of the Colosseum. Every morning he attended Mass at the nearby Church of St. Mary ai Monti, then spent the rest of the day walking across the city, visiting churches and the tombs of saints.

Benedict Joseph did not bathe, nor wash his clothes, nor buy new clothes. He was infested with lice. He stank. It was not unusual for sextons to bar Benedict Joseph's way when he tried to enter a church, or to drive him out if he had gotten inside.

Eventually living outdoors affected Benedict Joseph's health, and he moved into a homeless shelter, but he kept up his routine of daily Mass and church visitations. On Wednesday of Holy Week, 1783, he collapsed while at Mass in St. Mary ai Monti and died a few hours later.

Saint Benedict Joseph Labre is the patron saint of the homeless. Feast day: April 16.

**Saint Bernadette Soubirous (1844–1879).** In 1909, as part of the process that would lead to her canonization, the body of Bernadette

Soubirous was exhumed from its grave in the burial ground of the Sisters of Charity at Nevers. Among the witnesses were the bishop of Nevers, the town's mayor, and several physicians. In a signed official report Dr. Charles David wrote, "The body is practically mummified, covered with patches of mildew and quite a notable layer of salts, which appear to be calcium salts. The skeleton is complete, and it was possible to carry the body to a table without any trouble. The skin has disappeared in some places, but it is still present on most parts of the body." From its exposure to the air the skin began to turn black, so a plaster cast was taken of Bernadette's face and hands from which wax masks were made. In 1925, after Bernadette's beatification, her body was enshrined in a glass reliquary in the convent chapel; the wax masks were applied to her face and hands at that time. During the exhumation one of the physicians, a Dr. Comte, with the permission of the local bishop and the nuns, surgically removed two of Bernadette's ribs as relics.

As a child Bernadette Soubirous knew extreme poverty, hunger, and humiliation. Asthma and other ailments often kept her away from school, and as a result she was behind the other children in her class. On February 11, 1858, she experienced her first vision of the Blessed Virgin Mary at the grotto of Massabielle on the outskirts of Lourdes, her hometown. Our Lady delivered a simple message to Bernadette: to pray for all sinners, and to have the Church erect a chapel at the grotto as a place of pilgrimage. Instructed by Mary, Bernadette uncovered a spring; many pilgrims who have bathed in the water have been healed of a host of illnesses.

To escape the notoriety generated by her visions, Bernadette joined the Sisters of Charity at Nevers. In the convent she never spoke of her visions unless required to by her religious superiors. She followed the rule of her order faithfully and tried to attract no attention to herself.

Saint Bernadette is invoked against poverty and all illnesses, especially asthma. She is the patron saint of shepherds, the sick, and the town of Lourdes, France. Feast day: April 16.

**Saint Bernard of Clairvaux (1090–1153).** At his death Saint Bernard was buried in the church of Clairvaux Abbey beside the grave of his closest friend, Saint Malachy of Armagh. In 1790 supporters of the French Revolution shut down the abbey and dispersed the monks. The relics of Saints Bernard and Malachy were taken to Troyes Cathedral, where they have been kept together in a reliquary chest ever since.

Bernard lived during the twelfth-century Renaissance. This was an era of great flowering in music and poetry, as well as Gothic art and architecture. It was the time of the rise of Europe's first universities, the age of the Crusades, and the birth of military orders such as the Knights Templars. And it was the time when devotion to the Blessed Mother became nearly universal throughout Western Christendom. Bernard was an enthusiastic participant in all of these new movements.

As a young man he entered the austere Cistercian order, but he found it difficult to remain in his cloister. There were always crises that required his help: doctrinal controversies with Peter Abelard, one of the great intellects of the age; schism within the Church, with two men claiming to be pope; a resurgence of Seljuk Turk activity in the Holy Land that required another crusade. Between emergencies Bernard established new Cistercian monasteries—from Ireland to Sweden to Portugal to Rome.

He was devoted to Our Lady and urged all Catholics to turn to Mary with confidence, assuring them that of all the saints in heaven, no one's intercession was more powerful than Our Lady's.

Saint Bernard is the patron saint of bees, beekeepers, and candlemakers. He is also the patron of the Cistercian order, the French province of Burgundy, and the island of Gibraltar. Feast day: August 20.


**Saint Bernardine of Siena (1380–1444).** The Basilica of St. Bernardine in L'Aquila, Italy, was erected in the fifteenth century to celebrate Bernardine's canonization. Behind a gilded grill within a splendid Renaissance-style white marble mausoleum pilgrims can see the reliquary chest that contains the relics of the saint.

Bernardine of Siena was a Franciscan who promoted reverence for the Holy Name of Jesus. Typical of Franciscan spirituality at this time, Bernardine emphasized the human dimension of Jesus Christ, portraying him as humankind's loving brother and most generous friend. In the sermons he preached—often in piazzas because few churches were large enough to accommodate the crowd—Bernardine appealed for an end to the feuds and petty wars that were tearing apart fifteenth-century Italy. He called upon squabbling families and bitter enemies to make peace with one another. And always, as his sermon reached its emotional crescendo, he would suddenly raise high a wooden placard on which was inscribed in golden letters IHS—an abbreviation for the name of Jesus.

As a young man Enea Silvio Piccolomini (the future Pope Pius II) heard Bernardine preach. He said later that he imagined Saint Paul must have had the same power to touch hearts and move souls.

Saint Bernardine of Siena is the patron saint of advertising professionals because he created the first logo. Feast day: May 20.


**Saint Bibiana (died c. 361).** The relics of Saint Bibiana, along with those of her mother, Saint Dafrosa, and her sister, Saint Demetria, are preserved inside an alabaster urn beneath the high altar of the little Basilica of St. Bibiana in Rome. Inside the church is a column, said to be the one to which the executioners bound her.

Julian, known as the Apostate, was a nephew of Constantine the Great, the first Christian emperor of Rome. By 355, when Julian became emperor, Christianity was the dominant religion in the Roman Empire and the old cult of the Roman gods was fading away. Julian decided to revive ancient Roman worship and drive the Christians out of the imperial government. In some instances Julian's anti-Christianity campaign turned violent. Among the victims was a Roman Christian family, Flavian and Dafrosa and their daughters, Bibiana and Demetria. Flavian died from the effects of torture. Dafrosa was beheaded. Demetria died apparently from shock. Bibiana was tied to a column and scourged to death.

Saint Bibiana is invoked against hangovers. Feast day: December 2.


**Black Madonna of Czestochowa (first documented in Czestochowa, Poland, in 1382).** Legend claims that the evangelist Saint Luke painted this portrait of the Virgin and Child in the house of the Holy Family in Nazareth, using the kitchen table as his canvas. Since it was painted by a saint upon an article that belonged to the Holy Family, this painting is not a typical sacred image or icon but a sacred relic. Saint Helen found the painting in Jerusalem during her pilgrimage to the Holy Land in 326 and had it taken to Constantinople. Gradually the icon made its way to Poland; the earliest reference to it dates from 1382, when it came to the Jasna Góra Monastery outside the town of Czestochowa. The painting, measuring 47.67 x 32 x 1.37 inches, is painted on a wooden panel. The image is a Byzantine-inspired representation of the Virgin Mary as Hodegetria, "She who shows us the way." The Virgin holds the Christ Child in her left arm and with her right hand points to Him, "the way, and the truth, and the life" (John 14:6).

The painting is damaged—two slashes scar Mary's right cheek. On Easter Day 1430 a ragtag band of Hussites broke into the monastery church, seized the gold and silver ornaments on the altar of the Black Madonna, and ripped the icon from its frame. Outside they hacked at the face of Mary with their swords and broke the icon into three pieces.

Polish Catholics recovered the shattered image and it was sent to an artist's studio in Cracow for restoration. Since paint would not adhere to the blend of wax and pigment used by the original artist, the restorers scraped off the ancient image and painted a

According to tradition, Saint Luke the Evangelist painted this portrait of the Virgin and Child on the Holy Family's kitchen table, making the Black Madonna both a relic and an icon. NICOLAS SAPIEHA/ART RESOURCE, NY

copy. To commemorate the assault on the Black Madonna, they drew two slash marks on Mary's cheek with a pen.

In 1655 an army of Swedish invaders besieged Jasna Góra. For forty days the monks defended their monastery until the Swedes retreated. Attributing the victory to Our Lady, Poland's King Jan Casimir crowned the image and declared Our Lady of Czestochowa "Queen and Patron of Poland."

Ever since, the Black Madonna has been the most venerated

image of Mary among Poles. During the Solidarity movement of the early 1980s, Lech Walesa always wore a small reproduction of the icon pinned to his lapel. Pope John Paul II established a chapel in honor of the Black Madonna in St. Peter's Basilica in Rome. When he returned to Poland in 1979, he visited the shrine in Jasna Góra and declared, addressing Our Lady, "Mother, I am yours and all that I have is yours." Then he laid a golden rose on the altar of the Black Madonna.

The Black Madonna is the primary patron saint of Poland. Feast day: August 26.

**Saint Blaise (died c. 316).** The skull and hands of Saint Blaise are venerated in the Church of St. Blaise in Dubrovnik, Croatia. The greater part of his relics are preserved in the Basilica of St. Blaise in Maratea, Italy. They were brought from the saint's tomb in Sivas, Turkey, about the year 730 to save them from desecration during the Byzantine Empire's Iconoclast Controversy.

We know that Blaise was bishop of Sebaste (modern-day Sivas) and that he died a martyr. All the stories told about him are legends. For example, it is said that at his arrest Blaise and his guards saw a wolf running off with a piglet in its mouth, pursued by a poor widow. In a commanding voice Blaise ordered the wolf to drop the pig. To everyone's surprise, the animal did as it was told. The widow recovered her piglet, and the soldiers took Blaise to prison.

That evening the widow visited Blaise in his cell, bringing him food and two tall candles to dispel the gloom. The next morning before the guards came to lead him out to execution, a mother rushed into Blaise's cell, carrying in her arms her son who was choking to death on a fish bone. Picking up the remains of the two candles Blaise formed a cross, placed it against the child's throat, and blessed him. Immediately the bone was dislodged and the little boy's life was saved.

To this day Catholics line up in their churches on Saint Blaise's Day to have their throats blessed with two crossed candles.

Saint Blaise is invoked against all illnesses of the throat. He is the patron saint of Croatia. Feast day: February 3.

**Saint Blandina and the Martyrs of Lyon (died 177).** Some Christians of Lyon recovered the mangled body of Saint Blandina, which her executioners had thrown into the Rhone River. Her relics are enshrined in the Church of St. Leu in Amiens, France. The relics of some of the saints martyred with Blandina, including Saint Photinus, were preserved in the Church of St. Nizier in Lyon, but they were largely destroyed by anti-Catholic mobs during the Wars of Religion in the sixteenth century; the relics that remained were obliterated during the French Revolution. The ruins of the amphitheater where the martyrs suffered still stand in Lyon. The Basilica of St. Martin d'Ainay is built over the martyrs' prison.

A remarkable document, an authentic eyewitness account of the arrest and martyrdom of Saint Blandina and her companions, has survived the centuries. The unknown writer tells of a wave of anti-Christian hysteria that swept through Lyon and Vienne, during which Christians were charged with cannibalism and incest. Dozens of Christians were arrested and condemned to public torture in the amphitheater. The ninety-year-old bishop of Lyon, Photinus, was kicked and beaten to death by a mob. Sanctus, a deacon, and two Christian laymen, Attalus and Maturus, were mauled by wild beasts. Ponticus, a fifteen-year-old boy, was tortured to death. Blandina was scourged, burned with hot irons, then gored to death by a bull.

Saint Blandina is the patron saint of girls and of those who are falsely accused of wrongdoing. She is one of the patron saints of Lyon, France. Feast day: June 2.

**Saint Bonaventure (1221–1274).** In the sixteenth century a mob of Huguenot extremists ransacked the Church of St. Bonaventure in Lyon, France. Among the many precious objects destroyed during the looting of the church was the body of Saint Bonaventure. All that remains are bone fragments and the saint's right arm, preserved in the Cathedral of Bagnoregio, Italy, his hometown.

Bonaventure, an Italian Franciscan theologian and philosopher, "mainstreamed" the Franciscan order. Saint Francis of Assisi had envisioned his friars living like Our Lord and the twelve apostles—never knowing where they would sleep at night or when or where they would get their next meal. But by the time of Saint Francis's death, thousands of men across Europe had joined the new order. It was Bonaventure who realized that Francis's ideal of absolute and total poverty was no longer practical, and that the order would have to modify the original *Rule* if the Franciscans were to survive.

Bonaventure decided that the friars should live in a monastery-type setting but that they should not be cloistered—they would still be active in the world: teaching, preaching, hearing confessions; assisting the poor, the sick, the elderly, and the helpless. Although the order might own property for the support of the friars and their mission, each individual friar—true to Saint Francis's ideal—would own nothing personally.

In order to spread Saint Francis's message that Catholic clergy should be humble, charitable servants of the poor, Bonaventure encouraged his fellow Franciscans to study in the universities, to accept posts as professors and appointments as bishops. Bonaventure himself was named a cardinal. It is Bonaventure's modified vision of the Franciscan order that has endured to this day.

Saint Bonaventure is invoked against disorders of the stomach and bowels. He is the patron saint of Bagnoregio, Italy. Feast day: July 15.

**Saint Boniface (680–754).** After his martyrdom at Dokkum in the Netherlands, the body of Saint Boniface was carried to Fulda Abbey in Germany and buried in the church. The saint's relics lie in a marble tomb in the church's crypt.

Boniface was an English Benedictine monk who wished to become a missionary among the pagan tribes of the area that is now the Netherlands and northern Germany. With the pope's approval he traveled to Germany, where he began his mission with a challenge to Thor, the god of thunder. At what is now the city of Fritzlar stood an ancient oak tree the local people regarded as sacred to Thor. With an axe in his hands, Boniface stood beside the tree, daring Thor to prove he existed and strike him down. To the astonishment of the Germans, Boniface cut down the oak without any sign of displeasure from Thor. He then used the wood to build a chapel (the cathedral of Fritzlar stands on the site today).

As the number of Boniface's converts grew, monks and nuns came from England to help, founding monasteries and convents where they opened schools and hospitals.

At age seventy-four Boniface traveled to Dokkum, where many converts had assembled to receive the sacrament of confirmation. On the day of the ceremony Boniface was attacked by pagan warriors who hacked him to death with swords and axes.

Saint Boniface is the patron saint of brewers and tailors and is one of the patron saints of Germany. Feast day: June 5.


**Saint Brendan (c. 486–575).** Saint Brendan founded a monastery at Clonfert in County Galway, Ireland, and almost certainly was buried there. Over the centuries the monastery and church were destroyed and rebuilt several times, most recently in 1541 by English invaders. Consequently, the location of Saint Brendan's relics is not certain, although they are believed to lie in a grave near the front door of the Church of Ireland Cathedral of St. Brendan.

Brendan is said to be the man who *really* discovered America. One day a wandering monk named Barinthus arrived at the monastery where Brendan was abbot, asking for shelter. The law of hospitality was an absolute among monks, and the stranger was admitted at once. Barinthus claimed that he had just returned from a voyage across the Atlantic Ocean during which he had found a marvelous new land where jewels were strewn on the ground and each tree bore strange but delicious fruit. Intrigued by Barinthus's stories, Brendan decided to cross the sea and visit this wonderful country himself.

With seven handpicked monks, Brendan set sail for the west. The colorful legends of their adventures are told in the *Voyage of Saint Brendan,* which became one of the best-selling books of the Middle Ages. One of the most memorable moments takes place on Easter when the monks find a small island and go ashore to cook their breakfast. When they light their fire, the island moves—they have landed on the back of a whale.

Saint Brendan is the patron saint of navigators, sailors, and whales. Feast day: May 16.

**Saint Bridget, or Birgitta, of Sweden (1303–1373).** Saint Bridget died in Rome, where she had lived for twenty-four years. Her daughter, Saint Catherine, transported her mother's body to Sweden, to Vadstena Abbey, the motherhouse of the Bridgettine order of monks and nuns that Bridget had founded in 1369. Saint Bridget's relics, along with those of her daughter Saint Catherine, are preserved in a wooden chest in the church of Vadstena Abbey. The house where Bridget and Catherine lived is still standing in Rome's Piazza Farnese; it is a convent of Bridgettine nuns.

Bridget's father was the governor and judge of Uppland, and her mother was related to the Swedish royal family and to Saint Ingrid, the first Dominican nun in Sweden. At age twelve Bridget married Ulf Gudmarsson; it was an arranged marriage, but the couple was well suited to each other. Both came from wealthy, well-connected families, and both were pious Catholics. In time Bridget and Ulf had a family of eight children.

In 1341 the couple went on pilgrimage to the shrine of Saint James at Compostela in Spain. By the time they returned two years later Ulf was seriously ill; he died in 1344. After her husband's death Bridget devoted herself to founding a new religious order, the Bridgettines, at Vadstena. She said that every day she received visions of Christ, or the Blessed Virgin, or sometimes both.

In 1349 Bridget left Sweden and moved to Rome; she wanted to live in the city of Saints Peter and Paul and spend the rest of her life praying at the tombs of the city's countless saints and contemplating Rome's extraordinary collection of sacred relics. A year later her daughter Catherine joined her and they spent their days visiting churches and tending the sick and the poor.

Saint Bridget is the patron saint of widows and of Sweden. In 1999 Pope John Paul II named her one of the patron saints of Europe. Feast day: July 23.

**Saint Brigid of Kildare (c. 453–523).** With Saint Patrick and Saint Columba, Saint Brigid is revered as one of the three greatest saints of Ireland. Her mother, Brocca, a Pictish slave and a Christian, was made pregnant by her master, Duhbthach, king of Leinster and a pagan. Some stories say that Brigid was baptized by Saint Patrick, while others say that she only heard him preach. There is no doubt that she was raised a Christian, and that from an early age she had a vocation to the convent.

About the year 468 Brigid, along with seven nuns, founded a convent at Kildare. There she opened the first Catholic school in Ireland, where students were taught the truths of the faith as well as the ancient wisdom of the Celts.

She is said to have been a wonder-worker: her convent's supply of ale never ran out; the cows in the convent dairy produced a lake of milk; she had the power to heal lepers, the blind, the mute, and madmen; and when an unwed mother falsely accused a holy priest of fathering her child, Brigid made the sign of the cross over the newborn and the infant declared who his real father was.

Saint Brigid is buried with Saint Patrick and Saint Columba at Armagh in Northern Ireland. Her skull is enshrined in the Church of St. John the Baptist in Lumiar, Portugal, outside Lisbon. Since 1928 a portion of the saint's skull has been enshrined in the Church of St. Brigid in Killester, Dublin.

Saint Brigid is the patron saint of cattle, dairy workers, nuns, and students. Feast day: February 1.

**Saint Callixtus (died c. 222).** Saint Callixtus was buried in the catacomb he once managed and that bears his name, San Callisto, on the Appian Way. As is the case with almost all of the early martyrs, his remains were moved from the catacombs to a church inside Rome, in his case to the Church of St. Mary in Trastevere, near the place where he was murdered by a Roman mob.

Callixtus was an unlikely choice for pope. At the time of his election there were Romans who remembered when Callixtus had been an unruly slave who belonged to a Christian master. He had been a street brawler and a bankrupt who, through disastrous investment decisions, had lost all the money his master had entrusted to him. For his misbehavior he had been sentenced to work in the mines on Sardinia, but by luck he was saved by a general pardon granted to all Christian convicts.

Back in Rome Pope Saint Victor I took an interest in Callixtus and gradually brought about his conversion. When Callixtus showed himself to be dependable, Pope Zephyrinus placed him in charge of the catacombs where Christians buried their dead. Eventually Callixtus was ordained a priest and became an advisor to Victor's successor, Pope Saint Zephyrinus.

During Callixtus's pontificate a debate raged regarding what to do about Christians who during periods of persecution had renounced their faith to save their lives but who wished to return to the Church. Hard-liners wanted the Church to reject the apostates. But Callixtus took the view that offering forgiveness to penitent sinners was one of the primary functions Christ had granted to His Church. Under Callixtus, former Christians who wished to return were welcomed back after they had done penance.

Saint Callixtus is the patron saint of cemetery workers. Feast day: October 14.

**Saint Camillus de Lellis (1550–1614).** In 1699 the religious order founded by Camillus de Lellis completed the construction of the Church of St. Mary Magdalene, just a few steps from Rome's Pantheon. The Camillians enshrined in the new church the relics of their founder.

At age seventeen Camillus de Lellis left his home in Abruzzi, central Italy, and enlisted as a mercenary. He was an ideal recruit: he stood six feet, four inches tall, was heavily muscled, and he had a violent temper. Camillus was a chip off the old block—his father was also a mercenary. They fought together in wars across Europe, and when no war was being fought they supported themselves as cardsharps and con artists.

Camillus was in his mid-twenties when his life turned sour: his father died, all of his cons failed, he was broke, and he had developed a nasty open sore on his leg that wouldn't heal. He limped to Rome, hoping to find some kind of work, or least better begging opportunities. There he met Philip Neri, the priest who was leading a religious revival in the Eternal City. Philip helped Camillus learn to control his temper; give up gambling, drinking, and chasing women; and return to God. Philip even found a doctor to heal Camillus's leg.

As an outlet for his energy—he was still in his twenties—Camillus decided to open a hospital for the destitute. Philip advised against it, saying Camillus was not yet sufficiently mature in the spiritual life, that he was at risk of backsliding. The disagreement broke their friendship. And Philip was wrong; Camillus did not return to his evil habits but advanced in holiness. Other men who joined him at his hospital became the basis for the Camillian nursing order.

Saint Camillus de Lellis is the patron saint of nurses and all hospital workers, as well as cheats and con men. Feast day: July 14.

**Saint Candida (ninth century?).** In the Church of Whitchurch Canonicorum in Dorset, England, is a stone tomb chest that contains a lead casket bearing the bones of Saint Candida.

Candida is thought to have been a hermit who lived in the neighborhood of Dorset and was killed by marauding Vikings. Several Anglican cathedrals in England have the relics of Catholic saints, but Saint Candida's remains are the only relics of a saint that reside in an ordinary Anglican parish church and that survived the iconoclasm of the English Reformation. Feast day: June 1.

**Saint Canute IV (c. 1042–1086).** Benedictine monks buried the bodies of Saint Canute and his brother Prince Benedict before the high altar of St. Alban's Priory Church in Odense. After Canute's canonization in 1101, his remains and those of Benedict were moved to the new Cathedral of St. Canute in Odense. During the Reformation the Lutheran clergy sealed the crypt chapel containing the relics of Canute and his brother. The crypt was opened again in the 1870s and refurbished to receive pilgrims. In recent years the saint's skeleton was examined by forensic scientists. On his sacrum, the large bone at the base of the spine, they found marks of a stab wound from a spear. The bones showed no other injuries, which is consistent with the account that says that Canute put up no resistance.

Like so many kings of the early Middle Ages, Canute was a man of political ambition and religious devotion. Although he was an illegitimate son of King Sweyn II of Denmark, he inherited the crown after the death of his legitimate half brother.

By ancient tradition Danish kings were weak figures, dependent on the support of the nobles and wealthy landowners and restricted by custom from exercising absolute power over the people. Canute tried to claim that all political power by right belonged to the king. At this time many Danes were nominally Catholic, so Canute became a champion of the Church, demanding a tithe, a tax of 10 percent of an individual's income, for the construction of new churches, monasteries, and hospitals across the kingdom. He welcomed foreign priests who acted as missionaries to the half-heathen Danes, and foreign merchants who expanded Denmark's access to markets overseas.

The peasants resented the tithe, the influence of foreigners at court and the abolition of the old Viking religion. In 1086 they revolted, driving Canute to seek safety in Odense. On a day when he and his brother, Benedict, along with seventeen retainers, went to St. Alban's Priory for confession, a mob of peasants attacked the church. Benedict and the retainers put up a strong defense, but the rebels forced their way inside, hacked Benedict to death, killed all the king's retainers, and ran Canute through with a spear.

Saint Canute IV is one of the patron saints of Denmark. Feast day: January 19.

**Blessed Carlos Rodriguez (1918–1963).** The tomb of Blessed Carlos is found inside the Cathedral of the Sweet Name of Jesus in Caguas, Puerto Rico. Some relics of Blessed Carlos are also preserved in the Cathedral of St. John the Baptist in San Juan, Puerto Rico.

Carlos Manuel Cecilio Rodriguez Santiago is the first Puerto Rican candidate for sainthood. He was a bachelor devoted to the Church, in love with the liturgy, and blessed with a profound desire to bring others to a deeper love of the Catholic faith and the Mass.

He worked at the Catholic University Center in Río Piedras, where he served as a kind of lay missionary to the students and faculty. In addition to trying to draw back those who had drifted away from the faith or had grown lukewarm in their practice of it, Carlos also tried to inspire faithful Catholics to be more fervent. He published a newsletter, *Christian Life Days,* which spotlighted holy days, saints' feast days, and the liturgical seasons, to encourage students and professors to follow the unique rhythms of the liturgical year.

Priests who knew Carlos were sometimes surprised by his ideas about the Mass. In conversation he advocated Mass in the vernacular and urged the laity to attend the ceremonies and Mass of the Easter Vigil—a lengthy liturgy that was sparsely attended in most parishes.

Carlos Rodriguez died of cancer in 1963. Feast day: July 13.


**Carthusian Martyrs (died 1535–1540).** None of the bodies of these eighteen martyr saints and blesseds were ever recovered, but the monasteries where they lived and in some cases the places where they were imprisoned and martyred still stand. The London Charterhouse, which was home to sixteen martyrs, has survived largely intact and serves as a school. The fragmentary ruins of Beauvale Charterhouse, where Saint Robert Lawrence was prior, can be found at Beauvale, Nottinghamshire. The Axeholme Charterhouse in North Lincolnshire, where Saint Augustine Webster was prior, has been incorporated into a private home. A white marble stone inscribed with a cross marks the site of Tyburn, where seven of the Carthusians suffered, and is set in the pavement near the Marble Arch and Tyburn Convent in London. Six of the Carthusian martyrs were imprisoned in the Tower of London.

The first group of martyrs consisted of Saint John Houghton, prior of the London Charterhouse; Saint Robert Lawrence; Saint Augustine Webster; and Saint Richard Reynolds, a Bridgettine monk of Syon Abbey. They were hanged, disemboweled, and quartered for refusing to take an oath recognizing Henry VIII as Supreme Head of the Church in England. As they were led out of the Tower of London for execution, their fellow prisoner, Saint Thomas More, watched them from the window of his cell (by chance, his daughter Margaret Roper was visiting him at the time).

Three more monks of the London Charterhouse—the Blesseds Humphrey Middlemore, William Exmew, and Sebastian Newdigate—met the same barbarous martyrdom about six weeks later. Sebastian had been a courtier and close friend of Henry VIII before he entered the monastery. The king visited him twice in prison to persuade him to swear to the Act of Supremacy, promising to make him a wealthy man if he conformed. The saint refused.

Blessed John Rochester and Blessed James Walworth were separated from their community in London and exiled to York, where they were hung in chains from the city walls, left to die of dehydration, hunger, and exposure.

The Blesseds William Greenwood, John Davy, Robert Salt, Walter Pierson, Thomas Green, Thomas Scryven, Thomas Redyng, Richard Bere, and Thomas Johnson, all of the London Charterhouse, were incarcerated in Newgate Prison and were chained by the neck standing against wooden posts and left there to starve to death.

For reasons unknown a lay brother of the London Charterhouse, Blessed William Horne, was kept alive until 1540, when he was hanged, disemboweled, and quartered at Tyburn—the last of England's Carthusian martyrs.

Feast day: May 4.

**Saint Casimir (1460–1483).** The relics of Saint Casimir are enshrined in a silver casket over the altar in a side chapel of the Cathedral of St. Stanislaus in Vilna, Lithuania.

Bachelors were almost unheard of in the Middle Ages, particularly in royal families, which tended to regard each prince or princess born into a family as an opportunity to form either a political or an ecclesiastical alliance. But Casimir, the third child of the king and queen of Poland, had no interest in marriage and no vocation to the religious life. Instead, he became involved in improving the laws of the realm. As a prince he could speak candidly to his father, the king, about injustice and corruption in government—and he did so. He showed himself to be so insightful that when political trouble in Lithuania required the king's intervention, the king left Casimir as regent of Poland.

Justice tempered with mercy lay at the heart of Casimir's political reforms. At the same time he practiced the corporal works of mercy, ransoming captives and feeding and clothing the poor. He began every morning with Mass, and he visited the Blessed Sacrament in the castle chapel seven times a day.

In 1483 he was on his way to Lithuania to visit his father when he fell ill with tuberculosis and died.

Saint Casimir is the patron saint of bachelors and princes, and he is one of the patron saints of Lithuania and Poland. Feast day: March 4.

**Saint Catherine Labouré (1806–1876).** The body of Saint Catherine Labouré is displayed in a glass case beneath a side altar in the Chapel of Our Lady of the Miraculous Medal at 140 Rue du Bac in Paris—the place where she experienced visions of the Blessed Virgin Mary. When the saint's body was exhumed in 1933 it was found with its eyes open, and they remain open to this day. Pilgrims often comment on the intense shade of blue in Catherine's eyes.

Catherine came from a farm family of eleven children (she was the ninth). She never learned to read or write as a child—her father kept her busy with housework from age eight, when her mother died. As a young woman she moved to Paris, where she waited tables at her uncle's café. She had a vision of Saint Vincent de Paul, who instructed her to join the Daughters of Charity.

Catherine applied for admittance at the motherhouse on Rue du Bac in Paris and was accepted. On the night of July 18–19, 1830, a child woke Catherine in the convent dormitory and led her to the chapel, where Catherine found the Blessed Virgin sitting in a chair by the altar. "My child," Mary said, "I am going to give you a mission." In two more apparitions the mission became clear—to have a new holy medal struck and distributed throughout the world. On the front of the medal was an image of Mary and the inscription O MARY, CONCEIVED WITHOUT SIN, PRAY FOR US WHO HAVE RECOURSE TO THEE. On the reverse was a large *M* surmounted by a cross and the hearts of Jesus and Mary.

The first medals were distributed in Paris in 1823, and so many marvels were attributed to Our Lady's intercession—cures, conversions, even relief from financial troubles—that the medal became known as "the Miraculous Medal." In all this tumult Catherine appeared not at all. Only her confessor knew of her visions. She preferred to remain anonymous so she could continue her vocation as a Daughter of Charity without distraction. She was the porter of the motherhouse, and she tended the chickens and nursed the elderly in the convent's infirmary. Her superiors described her as "rather insignificant," and that is how Catherine preferred to be seen. Only in the last year of her life did she reveal her experience to her superior.

Word of Catherine's visions leaked to the public, and there was a crowd at her funeral. Soon thereafter a twelve-year-old child, crippled from birth, was healed at Catherine's grave.

Feast day: November 28.

**Saint Catherine of Alexandria (died c. 305).** In a monastery church built in the sixth century on the supposed site where God spoke to Moses out of a burning bush stands a golden sarcophagus that holds the relics of Saint Catherine of Alexandria. The bones of the saint had been discovered elsewhere on Mount Sinai, and in the eighth century they were brought to the monastery for safekeeping. Although the monastery had been dedicated to the Transfiguration of the Lord, because of the international popularity of the virgin martyr, it was renamed the Monastery of St. Catherine.

The legend of Saint Catherine tells us that she was the daughter of a king and that she was blessed with a brilliant intellect and great beauty. Once, while studying in the great Library of Alexandria, she nodded off. In a dream she saw a beautiful woman holding a handsome little boy on her lap. Pointing to Catherine the lady asked her son, "Would you like to marry her?" "No," the boy replied. "She is too ugly." Catherine awoke from the dream weeping.

An elderly man walked over to ask what was wrong, and she told him about her dream. "The lady you saw in your dream," the stranger said, "was the Blessed Virgin Mary, and the little boy was her Son, Jesus Christ. He found you ugly because you are unbaptized and your soul is stained with sin. If you became a Christian, He would find you beautiful. I am a priest. I can teach you the Christian faith." Eager to see the Lady and her Son again, Catherine begged the priest to instruct her.

After her baptism Catherine dreamed again. Once again Mary and Jesus appeared to her, and once again Mary asked the Child if He wanted to marry Catherine. "Oh, yes!" He said. "For now she is lovely!" Then the Christ Child placed a ring on Catherine's finger as a token that she belonged to Him. Many artists have depicted this mystical marriage of Saint Catherine, including Memling, Veronese, Poussin, and Van Dyck.

In 305 Catherine fell victim to the emperor Diocletian's empire-wide persecution of Christians. In Egypt the emperor's delegate Maximinus urged her to renounce her faith and save her life. Catherine countered by offering to defend Christianity in a public disputation. Maximinus agreed, pitting fifty pagan philosophers against Catherine. She not only confounded her opponents, she converted them. Enraged, Maximinus had the philosophers burned alive; then he sentenced Catherine to be torn apart on a spiked wheel. The moment she touched the wheel, it burst apart, so Maximinus had her beheaded. Angels carried her body to Mount Sinai for burial, where Christians discovered it centuries later.

Saint Joan of Arc testified that Saint Catherine was one of the three saints who spoke frequently to her.

Saint Catherine is the patron saint of libraries and librarians, philosophers, wheelwrights, yarn spinners, and unmarried women who want to find a husband. Feast day: November 25.

**Saint Catherine of Siena (1347–1380).** Saint Catherine's body lies buried under the high altar in the Church of St. Mary sopra

Minerva in Rome (the room where she died is also preserved as a chapel there); her head, dressed in the veil and wimple of a Dominican nun, is displayed behind a grille in the Church of St. Dominic in Siena; and one of her feet is enshrined in a crystal reliquary in the Church of Sts. John and Paul in Venice.

The twenty-fourth of the Benincasa family's twenty-five children, Catherine grew up in a large, comfortable house that is still standing in Siena. At age eighteen she joined a branch of the Dominican religious order known as the Mantellate, so called because they wore black mantels over their white religious garb. These women took the vows and wore the habit of a nun but lived separately in their own houses rather than together in a convent. In her own day Catherine became renowned for her mystical experiences, but she is most famous today for persuading Pope Gregory XI (r. 1370–1378) to leave the city of Avignon in France, where for seventy years the papacy had been under the thumb of the French kings, and return the papacy to Rome. In recognition of the great power of her mystical writings, in 1970 Pope Paul VI named Saint Catherine of Siena a Doctor of the Church, one of the first female saints so honored.

Saint Catherine of Siena is the patron saint of Siena and Italian nurses and with Saint Francis of Assisi is co-patron saint of Italy. Feast day: April 29.


**Saint Catherine of Sweden (c. 1331–1381).** During the Reformation the monks and nuns of Vadstena Abbey were dispersed and the church was used for Lutheran services. The Lutheran church has no cult of relics; nonetheless, the tombs of Saint Catherine and her mother, Saint Bridget of Sweden, were respected. In fact, the bones of the two saints were placed in a single casket, which is displayed at Vadstena Abbey to this day.

Catherine's father, Ulf Gudmarsson, was dying when he arranged a marriage for her with Edgard Kryn; Catherine was thirteen at the time. Kryn was as pious as Catherine, so when she suggested that they never consummate their marriage but live chastely as brother and sister, he agreed. They lived in the same house but slept in separate rooms.

Catherine was eighteen when her mother, Saint Bridget, left Sweden for Rome, where she would remain for the rest of her life. Mother and daughter were very close, and the separation caused Catherine a great deal of pain. After a year she could bear it no longer; with Kryn's consent she followed her mother to Italy.

Catherine was a great beauty, and Rome in 1350 was an unruly city, full of gangs of brigands who preyed on pilgrims. Bridget feared that Catherine might be attacked and raped, or perhaps abducted by some Italian lord who would force her daughter to marry him. For months Bridget kept Catherine at home, refusing to let her leave the house. In a letter to a friend Catherine complained, "I lead a wretched life here, caged like an animal."

Eventually Bridget and Catherine worked out an arrangement whereby both ladies would go out together to visit churches, call on friends, and assist the poor and the sick. When Bridget died in 1373, Catherine took her mother's body to Sweden for burial. Then she returned to Rome to initiate the process that would lead to Bridget's canonization. Once the process was well advanced, Catherine went home, arriving in Sweden in July 1380. She died eight months later.

Saint Catherine of Sweden is invoked against miscarriages. Feast day: March 24.

**Saint Cecilia (third century).** After Cecilia's martyrdom Christians carried her body to the Catacomb of St. Callixtus on the Appian Way, where they placed it within a niche outside the Crypt of the Popes where several of the early bishops of Rome were all buried together. In 817 Pope Paschal I built a basilica over Cecilia's house in Rome's Trastevere neighborhood; he had her body removed from the catacombs and enshrined beneath the high altar. In 1599, when the Basilica of St. Cecilia was undergoing a program of repairs and restoration, Cardinal Paolo Sfondrato ordered her sarcophagus to be opened. The body was found to be incorrupt, and the artist Stefano Maderno was summoned to sketch the saint so he could make a portrait sculpture of her. Cardinal Sfondrato had the body of Saint Cecilia buried in a crypt chapel directly beneath the sanctuary. Enshrined with Saint Cecilia in the crypt are the relics of three other Roman martyrs: Saints Valerian, Tiburtius, and Maximus. According to the legend of Saint Cecilia, Valerius was her husband and Tiburtius his brother. Maximus was the prison guard of the two men after they were arrested.

Very little is known about Cecilia. Judging from her house (which can be visited beneath the basilica), she belonged to a wealthy, noble family. During a period of anti-Christian persecution she was sentenced to be suffocated in her own bath; since she did not die quickly enough, the executioner hacked at her neck with a sword, mortally wounding her.

Another legend tells how during her wedding to Valerian (who was still a pagan at that date), as the musicians played bawdy songs, she sang in her heart a hymn to Christ, her spiritual Bridegroom.

Saint Cecilia is venerated as the patron saint of music, of professional musicians, and of students of music. Feast day: November 22.

**Saint Cessianus (died 303).** In the nineteenth century, American bishops who traveled to Rome were eager to acquire the relics of martyrs for their cathedrals back home. In 1838 the first bishop of Dubuque, Iowa, Matthias Loras, received from Pope Gregory XVI the bones of Saint Cessianus, an eight-year-old boy who was martyred during Emperor Diocletian's persecution of the Church. The relics are enshrined beneath of the main altar of Dubuque's Cathedral of St. Raphael. Aside from these few facts, nothing more is known of this child-saint.

The Dubuque diocese does not celebrate a feast day in honor of Saint Cessianus.

**Saint Charbel Maklhouf (1828–1898).** The body of Saint Charbel is enshrined in the Tomb Church of the Monastery of St. Maron in Annaya, Lebanon. His original grave is marked behind a large bronze sculpture of the saint. His hermitage, dedicated to Saints Peter and Paul, has been preserved, and many of the saint's personal belongings are displayed in the monastery's museum.

Even as a boy Joseph Maklhouf was drawn to a life of solitude and prayer. Near the pasture where he watched his family's sheep was a cave, and there he spent hours in darkness and solitude, praying and meditating. At age twenty-three he entered a Maronite Catholic monastery, taking the name Charbel, in honor of an ancient Syrian martyr.

Ultimately he settled at the Monastery of St. Maron in Annaya, where he was ordained a priest. The order was very austere, dividing the day into periods of intense prayer and onerous physical labor. After fifteen years with the monks, Charbel requested permission to withdraw to the monastery's Hermitage of Sts. Peter and Paul. He lived there for twenty-three years, giving himself up completely to celebrating the Divine Liturgy (as the Mass is known in the Maronite Rite) and meditating on its mysteries.

Charbel the hermit developed a reputation among Lebanese Christians for his wise advice. They brought their sick to him, and it is said he healed them with a touch of his hand. Since his death crowds have come to pray at his grave, and there are countless reports of miraculous healings through the intercession of Saint Charbel.

Feast day: December 24.

**Saint Charlemagne (742–814).** The original burial of Saint Charlemagne was unusual for a Christian: he was placed in a vault seated on a marble throne, wearing his crown, his scepter in his hand, and a book of the Gospels open on his lap. In 1165, the year of Charlemagne's canonization, German Holy Roman Emperor

Frederick Barbarossa opened the vault and moved the body to a marble sarcophagus. In 1215 Emperor Frederick II moved the relics into a magnificent golden shrine, studded with jewels and adorned with beautiful metal sculptures. Later, other reliquaries were made to hold Charlemagne's skull and other bones taken from the shrine; all of these lesser reliquaries are displayed, along with the main shrine, in the Treasury of Aachen Cathedral in Germany.

The name "Charlemagne" is French for Charles the Great, and there is no denying his greatness. It was the dream of his life to revive the Roman Empire, and although his empire fell short of the mark, his realm did include all of modern-day France, Germany, Belgium, the Netherlands, Luxembourg, Switzerland, Austria, the Czech Republic, and Italy down to Rome.

He was a zealous Catholic who sent missionary priests and bishops into lands, such as Saxony, where the Christian faith was unknown. He was also a staunch defender of the papacy, willing to use diplomacy or an army to ensure that the pope was secure and his authority respected. And he sponsored the construction of at least six hundred churches and monasteries throughout his realm.

One of Charlemagne's greatest accomplishments was initiating a cultural renaissance. He founded schools and invited the leading scholars of his day to come and teach the Greek and Roman classics to the students. He gave lavishly to monks who specialized in copying books. And he commissioned great works of art for his churches, particularly his chapel at Aachen.

Charlemagne's canonization is problematic as it was declared in 1165 by Pascal III, who was an antipope. In the eighteenth century Pope Benedict XIV gave his approval to the centuries-old veneration of Charlemagne.

Saint Charlemagne is one of the patron saints of the University of Paris. Feast day: January 28.

**Saint Charles Borromeo (1538–1584).** The body of Saint Charles Borromeo lies in a rock crystal casket in the cathedral of Milan. His heart is enshrined in a small side altar of the Church of Sts. Ambrose and Charles in Rome. Among his personal belongings, which are also considered relics, is his red cardinal's biretta, which is preserved in the museum of the Oratory of Sts. Fabian and Sebastian in Ascona, Switzerland.

Charles was a transitional figure in the Catholic Counter-Reformation. His uncle, Pope Pius IV, made Charles a cardinal—at the time, Charles was only twenty-two and not a priest. It was the type of abuse that gave ammunition to the Protestant reformers. But Charles took his rank seriously; he studied for the priesthood and was ordained in 1563. When he was appointed archbishop of Milan, he devoted himself to eradicating corruption among the clergy and religious and implementing the reforms of the Council of Trent.

He had inherited a fortune from his family, which he spent to found seminaries, schools, and hospitals. During a famine he fed three thousand hungry people every day. During an epidemic he led processions through the streets of Milan, imploring God's mercy, but he also worked in the hospitals, nursing the sick and comforting the dying.

He insisted that priests say Mass reverently and use the homily to teach the faith to their congregations. He commanded members of religious orders—men and women—to follow the rule of their congregations. Not surprisingly, he met opposition. One order, called the Humilati, hired an assassin to kill the archbishop. The man shot Charles in the back, but the wound was not fatal.

Charles died of a fever in 1584. He had been archbishop of Milan for twenty-one years.

Saint Charles Borromeo is the patron saint of bishops, spiritual directors, catechists, and seminarians. He is invoked against ulcers and other stomach ailments. He is one of the patron saints of Lombardy. Feast day: November 4.

**Saint Christina (died c. 250).** Saint Christina's relics are kept in Palermo, Sicily, and Torcelli. Her skull is preserved in the Cathedral of Milan.

Saint Christina's story is a bit confusing. It seems likely that she was a member of the Anicii, one of the noblest Roman families, and that she converted to Christianity while in her teens. A legend tells us that after her baptism she hurried home and smashed every image of a pagan god in her parents' house.

As the story goes, she was martyred at Lake Bolsena in Tuscany. Her father tried to drown her by tying a millstone to her neck and throwing her into the water, but Christina did not sink. The local magistrate had the girl tied to a tree or a stake and shot to death with arrows.

Saint Christina is the patron saint of archers, millers, and sailors. Feast day: July 24.

**Saint Christopher (died c. 250).** For centuries the skull of Saint Christopher was preserved in the Church of St. Mary in Rab, Croatia. Today, for safekeeping, it remains in its gilded reliquary box in Rab's municipal museum.

There is no doubt among hagiographers—scholars who study the saints—that there was a Christian named Christopher who died a martyr about the year 250. And contrary to a widespread misconception, the Catholic Church did not strip Christopher of his sainthood nor declare that he never existed.

The confusion is the result of Pope Paul VI's decision in 1969 to rework the liturgical calendar. Since July 25 is the feast of the apostle Saint James the Greater as well as Saint Christopher, Pope Paul declared that Mass on that day should be celebrated in honor of Saint James, since an apostle outranks virtually all other saints. But Mass may be offered in Christopher's honor on July 25 by priests named Christopher, in churches or chapels dedicated to Saint Christopher, and in places where there is great devotion to Saint Christopher.

Christopher has always been a popular saint, and popular saints tend to be the subjects of legends. The most famous of these tells us that Christopher was a giant of a man, very tall and immensely strong. After he converted to Christianity, Christopher, as penance for a lifetime of sins, built a hut beside a dangerous stretch of river and carried travelers across on his shoulders. One day a small boy asked to be taken across.

Christopher lifted the child easily onto his shoulders and waded into the water. The farther he went the stronger the current became and the heavier the child felt. Finally, exhausted, Christopher staggered up the riverbank and set the child down, "Boy, who are you?" he asked. "Today," the child said, "you carried the Creator of the world on your shoulders." Then the Christ Child vanished.

Saint Christopher is famously the patron saint of travelers. He is also the patron of Rab, Croatia, and of the Caribbean island of Saint Kitts, which is named for him. Feast day: July 25.

**Saints Chrysanthus and Daria (died c. 283).** The relics of this saintly couple are venerated in the Church of the Holy Apostles in Rome and the Church of Sts. Chrysanthus and Daria in Munstereifel, Germany.

All we know for certain regarding Saints Chrysanthus and Daria is that they were a husband and wife who were arrested during the reign of the Emperor Numerianus. They were thrown into a sand pit on Rome's Via Salaria and stoned to death.

Saints Chrysanthus and Daria are the patron saints of Munstereifel and are among the patron saints of Salzburg, Austria. Feast day: October 25.

**Saint Chrysogonus (died c. 304).** Perhaps as early as the eighth century the skull and an arm of the saint were enshrined in the Church of St. Chrysogonus in Rome's Trastevere neighborhood.

Aside from his name and his martyrdom we know very little

about Saint Chrysogonus. He was martyred in Aquileia in northern Italy; he may have been a Roman soldier. Nonetheless, devotion to Saint Chrysogonus is ancient, especially in Rome, and he is invoked in the Roman Canon of the Mass, also known as the First Eucharistic Prayer.

Feast day: November 24.


**Saint Clare of Assisi (1194–1253).** The body of Saint Clare is displayed in the crypt of Assisi's Basilica of St. Clare. A wax mask has been laid over the face. Also on exhibit in the crypt are Saint Clare's habit, the cord she used as a belt, and locks of her hair, shorn off by Saint Francis when she became the first Franciscan nun.

Clare was an aristocrat who ran away from her parents' palace on Palm Sunday 1212 to join the Franciscans. She made her vows to Saint Francis, who cut off her hair and clothed her in the Franciscan habit.

At San Damiano she founded the Order of the Poor Ladies (later known as the Poor Clares, in her honor). Like Saint Francis she was committed to absolute poverty. Other convents had sources of revenue such as farms, vineyards, or mills, but Clare and her nuns relied entirely on donations. A succession of popes felt that Clare's *Rule* for her order was too severe and refused to give it papal approval, but Clare would not compromise her commitment.

After forty-one years of negotiations, in 1253, as Clare lay on her deathbed, Pope Innocent IV traveled to Assisi to present to her personally the document that gave formal approval to her *Rule.*

Saint Clare of Assisi is the patron saint of goldsmiths, embroiderers, and television. She is one of the patron saints of Assisi. Feast day: August 11.


**Saint Clare of Montefalco (1268–1308).** The body of Saint Clare lies in a glass chest beneath the high altar of the Church of

The body of Saint Clare of Montefalco, dressed in the habit of an Augustinian nun, lies beneath the high altar of the Church of St. Clare in Montefalco, Italy. SCALA/ART RESOURCE, NY

St. Clare in Montefalco. Her heart, which was removed from her body immediately after her death, is preserved in a reliquary in the same church.

Clare's parents were a wealthy, pious couple who built a small convent for Franciscan nuns. Clare and her sister, Joan, joined this convent. In 1290, Joan, Clare, and several of the sisters founded a new convent; there Clare experience visions of Jesus Christ. During one of these visions Christ promised to plant his cross in Clare's heart. In 1303 Clare—now abbess of the community—had sufficient funds to build a large church for her nuns. She dedicated the church to the Holy Cross. After her canonization in 1881, the church was renamed St. Clare, or Santa Chiara in Italian.

Saint Clare is the patron saint of her hometown, Montefalco. Feast day: August 17.

**Saint Clement of Rome (died c. 101).** In the ninth century the missionary brothers, Saints Cyril and Methodius, found the grave of Saint Clement in the Crimea and carried the relics of the martyred pope—along with the anchor that he had been bound to his neck when he was drowned—back to Rome. In 867 the relics were placed in the Church of St. Clement, built over the site of what is very likely the saint's house. The saint lies before the high altar. Over his tomb is a stone slab bearing the inscription SANCTUS CLE-MENS MARTYR HIC FELICITER EST TUMULATUS, or "Saint Clement, martyr, is happily buried here."

Clement is believed to have been one of Christ's seventy disciples. He almost certainly knew Saint Peter, and we know from Philippians 4:3 that he worked with Saint Paul. About the year 88 he became the fourth pope. His Epistle to the Corinthians is an extremely valuable document as it shows that the bishop of Rome had authority to teach and correct other Christian communities. During Emperor Trajan's persecution of the Church, Clement was exiled to the Crimea, where an anchor was tied around his neck and he was drowned in the Black Sea.

Saint Clement is the patron saint of mariners and stonecutters. Feast day: November 23.

**Saint Colette of Corbie (1381–1447).** Saint Colette died in Ghent, Belgium, and there she was buried and eventually venerated as a saint. During the French Revolution the custodians of Colette's shrine, fearing that French radicals would destroy the relics, sent them to Poligny in the remote Jura region for safety. The relics are kept there still, in a casket of gilded bronze in the chapel of the Monastery of St. Colette.

Born near Corbie in Picardy, France, as a young woman Colette was convinced that she had a vocation to the religious life but did not seem to fit in any convent she joined. She was living as an anchoress, or recluse, in two small rooms attached to a church when she had a vision of Saint Francis of Assisi pleading with Christ to send Colette to reform the Franciscan order.

Initially she recoiled from the idea, but in time she accepted her vision as an authentic revelation of the will of God. She walked to Nice, where Pedro de Luna, the antipope known as Pope Benedict XIII, resided. Like virtually all the French, Colette regarded him as legitimate. De Luna received her in an audience, encouraged her mission of reform, and then accepted her vows as a Poor Clare nun.

Colette believed the Poor Clares, who already lived an austere life, should return to the even more austere *Rule* of their foundress, Saint Clare. She met opposition at almost every convent she visited. Since she could not reform the Poor Clares, she founded a new branch of the order that became known as the Colettines.

It is said that each time Colette received Holy Communion she went into an ecstasy that lasted for hours and that she had visions of Christ dying on the cross and of countless souls falling from grace. As a consequence of the vision of souls falling from grace, she began to pray with special fervor for the conversion of sinners. It is said that she was a wonder-worker who healed a nun of leprosy and raised many people from the dead, including a stillborn child.

Saint Colette is the patron saint of orphans. Feast day: March 6.

**Saint Columba of Iona (521–597).** Viking raids on the monasteries of Scotland from the eighth through the tenth centuries kept the relics of Saint Columba on the move. Monks carried them from Iona to various sites in mainland Scotland, including Dunkeld, and finally to Downpatrick in Northern Ireland, where they are believed to lie in the same grave with Saint Patrick and Saint Brigid, beneath a large stone outside the cathedral.

Columba is one of the few saints, possibly the only saint, who started a war. His colleague, Abbot Finnian, had a copy of the Psalms, made in Rome and so beautiful that Columba coveted it on sight. Secretly he made an exact copy of the book for himself. When Finnian discovered what Columba was doing he demanded that he hand over the unauthorized copy. Columba refused. The two monks went to court, where the judge ruled in Finnian's favor.

Angry and humiliated, Columba appealed to his clansmen to avenge the family's honor. Finnian rallied an army of his own and the two forces met near Ben Bulben in County Donegal. Columba's kinsmen crushed Finnian's army, killing three thousand men.

This private war over a book outraged the bishops and abbots of Ireland. At a specially called synod they agreed to banish Columba from Ireland for life, and they commanded him to convert three thousand pagans—one for each of the men who had died in his war.

Truly contrite, Columba, with a dozen or so disciples, sailed to the island of Iona off the western coast of Scotland, where he built a small monastery. From Iona he traveled to mainland Scotland, where his missionary activity brought into the Church many more souls than the three thousand the synod had demanded.

Saint Columba is the patron saint of bookbinders and poets. He is also one of the patron saints of Scotland and Ireland. Feast day: June 9.


**Saint Cornelius I (died 253).** The skull and arm bones of Saint Cornelius are preserved in the Kornelimünster, or Church of St. Cornelius, in Aachen, Germany.

When Cornelius was elected pope in 251 the Church was in disarray. After a ferocious persecution led by Emperor Decius, Christians were divided once again over the contentious issue of what should be done about the *lapsi,* those Christians who could not bear up to torture and death and so had capitulated and sacrificed to the Roman gods. Like his predecessor Pope Saint Callixtus, Cornelius insisted that repentant lapsed Christians should be allowed to come back to the Church after confessing their sin and doing penance.

In 252 Roman pagans blamed Roman Christians for an epidemic that was sweeping through the city. Pope Cornelius was arrested and exiled to Civitavecchia, where his guards mistreated him so severely that he died in 253. Rome's Christians claimed his body and buried it in a chapel with several other popes in the Catacomb of St. Callixtas.

Saint Cornelius is invoked against hearing ailments. Feast day: September 16.

**Saints Cosmas and Damian (died c. 287 or c. 303).** These martyred brothers were buried in the city of their execution, Cyrus, Syria. Pope Felix IV (r. 526–530) built a church in their honor in Rome, and their relics may have been translated to Rome at that time. They are still preserved in the crypt of the Church of Sts. Cosmas and Damian in the Roman Forum.

The brothers practiced medicine in what is now Iskendrun, Turkey. As they questioned their patients about their symptoms and prescribed treatments, they also urged them to adopt the Christian faith. They were denounced to the local governor for the crime of spreading Christianity.

Legend says the governor's executioners attempted to kill Cosmas and Damian by drowning, burning, arrows, and stoning, but miraculously they escaped all of these torments unharmed. In the end they were beheaded.

Saints Cosmas and Damian are the patron saints of physicians, surgeons, pharmacists, midwives, barbers, and individuals employed in the chemical industry. They are invoked against blindness and epidemics. Feast day: September 27.

**Saints Crispin and Crispinian (died c. 286).** These brothers were martyred together in Soissons, France. At a later date their relics were taken to Rome and enshrined in a side chapel of the Church St. Lawrence in Panisperna.

Crispin and Crispinian supported themselves as shoemakers in Soissons. Like Saints Cosmas and Damian they spoke of their faith with everyone who came into their shop. When a period of anti-Christian persecution broke out in Gaul, the brothers were arrested and tortured to force them to renounce Christianity. They held fast to their faith and ultimately were beheaded.

Saints Crispin and Crispinian are the patron saints of shoemakers and leatherworkers of all kinds. Feast day: October 25.

**Crown of Thorns (earliest reference 409).** Saint Paulinus of Nola tells us that in his day "the thorns with which Our Savior was crowned" were venerated in Jerusalem. The Crown of Thorns remained in Jerusalem for several centuries, although occasionally individual thorns were given away as relics to individuals or churches. About 1063 the relic was transferred to Constantinople. It appears that in 1204, when crusaders from Western Europe

In 2003 clergy of the Cathedral of Notre Dame in Paris displayed the reliquary that contains Christ's Crown of Thorns. The relic was brought to Paris in 1238 by the king of France, Saint Louis IX. © P Deliss/Godong/ corbis

sacked Constantinople, the Crown of Thorns was among the relics seized. In the 1230s the emperor of Constantinople, Baldwin II, pawned the Crown to the city of Venice. In 1238 Saint Louis IX, king of France, paid the debt and had the Crown of Thorns taken to Paris, where he built a glorious reliquary chapel for it, the renowned Sainte-Chapelle. During the French Revolution the government removed the relic from the chapel and put it on display as a museum piece in the Bibliothèque Nationale. Napoleon returned it to the Catholic Church in 1806. Since then it has been kept in the Treasury of the Cathedral of Notre-Dame de Paris. Only the crown portion of the relic remains—all the thorns were distributed long ago.

In Paris a feast day in honor of the Crown of Thorns was kept on the Friday after Ash Wednesday. In 1831 Pope Gregory XVI authorized moving the feast to August 11.

**Saint Cuthbert (634–687).** Saint Cuthbert was buried at the Monastery of Lindisfarne on an island off the eastern coast of Scotland. In 698 the monks of the abbey opened the grave to place the relics in a shrine in the monastery church. In 793 Viking raiders attacked the monastery, murdered many of the monks, stripped the church and shrine of its gold and silver, carried off young monks and students as slaves, and set fire to the monastery. The relics of Saint Cuthbert survived the attack, so the surviving monks, along with some of the local people, transported them to the mainland for safety. The monks and their relics wandered from place to place for many years, settling for a time at Chester-le-Street and finally in 995 at Durham. When the Cathedral of Durham was built in the eleventh century, Saint Cuthbert's body (his coffin was opened in 1104 and his body was found to be incorrupt) was placed in a shrine near the high altar. In 1538 Henry VIII ordered the demolition of the shrine; the relics were buried in an unmarked grave behind the high altar. The saint's bones still lie there, beneath a stone slab that now bears the inscription CUTHBERTUS. In the Durham Cathedral Treasury are a large portion of Saint Cuthbert's original wooden coffin, adorned with a carving of Christ and the symbols of the four evangelists; the pectoral cross with which the saint was buried; and the little portable altar he used to say Mass when he traveled.

Cuthbert was seventeen years old and watching his family's sheep when he saw legions of angels bearing the soul of Saint Aidan up to heaven. The vision inspired Cuthbert to become a monk.

He entered Melrose Abbey, where he became everyone's favorite novice. He learned Latin quickly; he had a fine voice and chanted the Divine Office beautifully; he was strong and enjoyed all types of outdoor work; he had a charming personality and made every guest to the monastery feel welcome.

He was appointed abbot of Lindisfarne at a time of transition in Britain. For more than two hundred years Catholics in Britain had followed a liturgical calendar and used liturgical practices that were unique to the British Isles. At a synod held in 664, the majority of the bishops, abbots, and abbesses of the British Isles voted to give up their rites and adopt the practices used in Rome and on the Continent. The monks of Lindisfarne Abbey adamantly refused to abandon their traditions. That is why Cuthbert was sent to be their abbot; through patience, kindness, and tact, he gradually convinced even the most obdurate monks to follow the Roman Rite.

For nearly a thousand years Cuthbert was one of the most beloved saints in England, which may explain why Henry VIII's commissioners did not destroy his relics but permitted them to be buried.

Saint Cuthbert is the patron saint of mariners and shepherds, and he is invoked against epidemics. He is one of the patron saints of England and of the city of Durham. Feast day: March 20.

**Saint Damien de Veuster (1840–1889).** At his death in 1889 Damien was buried in the graveyard beside his Church of St. Philomena on the Hawaiian island of Molokai. In 1936 the government of Belgium requested that Damien's body be exhumed for burial in his homeland. The U.S. government approved the request; today the saint's body lies beneath a black marble slab in the crypt of the church of his religious order, the Congregation of the Sacred Hearts of Jesus and Mary, in Leuven, or Louvain. When Pope John Paul II beatified Damien in 1995, he gave the right hand of Damien to the Catholic Church in Hawaii; it was buried in Damien's original grave. In 2009, after Damien was canonized, the superiors of his religious order presented the people of Hawaii with a bone from the saint's heel. It is displayed in a small wooden box in a shrine made of koa wood in the Cathedral of Our Lady of Peace in Honolulu.

Damien was the seventh of eight children born to a farm

family in Tremelo, Belgium. Two of his older sisters entered the Ursuline convent, and one of his older brothers, Augustine, joined the Congregation of the Sacred Hearts. When he was eighteen, Damien entered the seminary of the same congregation.

Augustine had been assigned to lead a band of priests and nuns to the Hawaiian Islands, but as the group was preparing for their voyage he fell gravely ill. Damien volunteered to take his brother's place. In May 1864, in Honolulu's Cathedral of Our Lady of Peace, Damien was ordained a priest. For ten years he served as an itinerant missionary on Hawaii's Big Island, establishing mission stations, building hospitals, and making hundreds of converts. In 1873 he received an assignment as chaplain to the island of Molokai, to Kalawao, a settlement where sufferers of leprosy, also known as Hansen's disease, were isolated and left to die.

Many of the sick were living in huts and lean-tos. Some, out of despair, were living degraded lives. One of Damien's first tasks was to help restore the patients' self-respect. With the assistance of some of the stronger members of the community he built houses.

There was no cure for leprosy at the time; nonetheless Damien made improvements to Kalawao's hospital so the sick and the dying would be more comfortable. He established an orphanage, and he built a church dedicated to Saint Philomena. He treated his congregation as he would have treated any other parishioners—visiting them in their homes and sharing meals with them, although physicians in the 1870s advocated isolating victims of leprosy and limiting their contact with healthy individuals.

Damien revived religious life on the island—not only daily Mass and recitation of the Rosary, but also perpetual adoration of the Blessed Sacrament. "Without the Blessed Sacrament," he wrote, "a position like mine would be intolerable."

In 1884 Damien realized that he had contracted leprosy. Five years later, at age 49, he died of the disease.

Saint Damien de Veuster is invoked against Hansen's disease, and he is the patron saint of those who suffer from it. Feast day: May 10.

**Saint Daniel of Padua (died 168).** The relics of Saint Daniel were discovered in Padua, Italy, in 1064. They are enshrined in the city's Cathedral of the Assumption.

Daniel was a deacon who served Prosdocimus, the first bishop of Padua. He was martyred and buried in Padua, but the location of his tomb was forgotten. It was found by chance almost nine hundred years later.

Saint Daniel is the patron saint of prisoners and of women whose husbands are at war. Like his fellow Paduan Saint Anthony, Saint Daniel is invoked to find lost objects. Feast day: January 3.

**Saint Demetrius (died c. 306).** The remains of Saint Demetrius are kept in a large silver chest in the Basilica of St. Demetrius in Thessaloniki, Greece. Beneath the church archaeologists discovered an ancient well that may be the one into which the saint's body was thrown by his executioners.

There are conflicting accounts of the life of Saint Demetrius. He is most often depicted as a soldier, but some sources say he was a deacon. Both Mitrovic, Serbia, and Thessaloniki, Greece, claim to be the place of his martyrdom. Most sources agree, however, that he was martyred by being run through with spears.

He is venerated as one of the warriors who protected the Christian faithful from their enemies. There are stories of Thessaloniki being miraculously saved from attackers through the intercession of Saint Demetrius. During the First Crusade, at the battle of Antioch in 1098, crusaders claimed that Saint Demetrius appeared with Saint Theodore and Saint George and helped them defeat the Turks.

Saint Demetrius is invoked against the devil. Crusaders took him as one of their patron saints. He is also the patron saint of Belgrade, Serbia; and Thessaloniki. Feast day: October 8.

**Saint Denis (died c. 250).** The government during the French Revolution shut down the Abbey of St. Denis and sent commissioners to empty the royal tombs, deface the church, and strip it of its treasures. Fortunately the relics of Saint Denis were spirited away to a nearby parish church where they were kept safe until 1819, when they were restored to the reopened abbey church, which by that time had been designated a national monument.

The church historian Saint Gregory of Tours tells us that in the third century Denis, or Dionysius, was one of five bishops sent by Pope Saint Fabian to serve the Christians of Gaul. Denis was sent to Paris and became the city's first bishop. About the year 250 Denis and two companions, Rusticus, a priest, and Eleutherius, a deacon, were arrested by the Roman authorities, tortured, then beheaded on the hill known as Montmartre, or Martyr's Mountain. A memorable legend says that after his execution Denis stood, picked up his head, and walked to the place where he wished to be buried—the present site of the Abbey of St. Denis.

Saint Denis is invoked against rabies, diabolical possession, and headaches. He is one of the patron saints of Paris and of France. Feast day: October 9.

**Saint Dismas (died c. 30).** The Romans would turn over the body of an executed criminal if his or her family requested it; otherwise the corpse was left to rot on the cross or was thrown into a garbage pit. That is probably what became of the body of Saint Dismas, the Good Thief. In Rome's Basilica of the Holy Cross in Jerusalem is displayed what is said to be the transverse beam from Dismas's cross, discovered by Saint Helen when she uncovered the True Cross in 326.

Saint Matthew and Saint Luke both mention the Good Thief, but in Saint Luke's Gospel we get a more complete story. As the three men hung dying on their crosses "the Bad Thief" mocked Jesus, saying, "Are you not the Christ? Save yourself and us!" At which point "the Good Thief" spoke up. "Do you not fear God?" he asks his companion. "We are receiving the due reward for our deeds; but this man has done nothing wrong." Then addressing Christ, he said, "Jesus, remember me when you come into your kingly power." "Truly I say to you," Jesus replied, "today you will be with me in Paradise."

By the year 400, Christians were venerating the Good Thief as a saint. About the year 600 an apocryphal Christian work gave the two thieves crucified with Christ names: the bad thief was Gestas, the Good Thief was Dismas.

Saint Dismas is the patron saint of thieves and all prisoners, especially prisoners on death row. Feast day: March 25.

**Saint Dominic (1170–1221).** On August 6, 1221, Dominic died in the Dominican priory of San Nicolo delle Vigne in Bologna, Italy; he was buried behind the high altar of the priory church. In 1228 San Nicolo was greatly expanded and rededicated as San Domenico. At that time the saint's relics were moved to a marble sarcophagus in the main body of the church where pilgrims would have access to it. In 1264 the Dominicans wanted a more impressive monument for their founder. Work on this shrine, known as the Arca di San Domenico, took nearly three centuries and involved some of the greatest artists of the Middle Ages and the Renaissance, including Nicola Pisano and Michelangelo. The saint's bones rest inside a marble sarcophagus carved by Pisano. Behind the tomb, in a golden octagonal reliquary, is the skull of the saint.

It was a crisis in the Catholic Church that set the direction of Dominic's life. In 1203 he accompanied his bishop on a journey from their home in Osma, Spain, to southern France. There he witnessed the animosity between Catholics and Cathars, who were confusing many of the Catholic faithful and tearing the Church apart.

The Cathars (the name comes from the Greek for "pure ones") believed in two gods: one good, the god of pure spirit, the other evil, the god of the material world. The Cathars regarded everything physical as wicked—this extended to food, sex, and their own bodies. They denied the Catholic tenet that the world created by God was good. They rejected the doctrine that Jesus Christ had taken on human flesh and was made man. They refused to admit that Christ's death on the cross—a physical event—could have any spiritual significance. Although the Cathars were concentrated in southern France, pockets of adherents could be found from Belgium to Italy and as far away as Bulgaria and Armenia.

Dominic responded to the crisis by traveling throughout the country, explaining the Catholic faith to uncertain Catholics and defending the faith against Cathar attacks. He gathered around him devout men who were well trained in doctrine and were skilled orators and debaters. They called themselves the Order of Preachers. In addition to preaching, Dominic called for more prayer, especially to the Blessed Virgin Mary. He and his Dominicans became particular advocates of frequent recitation of the Rosary.

Dominic's lifetime coincided with that of Saint Francis of Assisi, and on one occasion they met. Both men shared a similar ambition: to take the message of the Gospel out of the cloister and directly to the people in the streets and in the countryside.

Saint Dominic is the patron saint of astronomers, the Dominican Republic, and the city of Valletta, Malta. Feast day: August 8.

**Saint Dominic Savio (1842–1857).** This boy-saint is buried in the Basilica of Mary Help of Christians in Turin, Italy, near the tomb of his spiritual director, Saint John Bosco.

Dominic Savio was a spiritual prodigy. Saint John Bosco, who was headmaster of Dominic's school, said of him, "I marveled at the work of divine grace in one so young." Nonetheless Dominic was still a boy and as such was subject to boyish enthusiasms. He wanted to devote long hours to prayer and impose strict penances on himself, but Don Bosco forbade it. Instead, he gave Dominic a "penance" of befriending the tough street kids who had been sent to the school instead of a reformatory.

It wasn't easy. Dominic considered the street kids crude; the street kids wrote off Dominic as a prig. The turning point came during a schoolyard fight. Dominic got between two boys, each of whom had armed himself with rocks, and talked them out of beating each other senseless.

Shortly before his fifteenth birthday Dominic fell seriously ill with a lung infection. Don Bosco sent him home, but the family doctor could do nothing for him. Dominic died shortly after receiving Last Rites.

When Dominic was proposed for sainthood, some members of the Church hierarchy objected to the idea of canonizing a fourteen-year-old boy, but Pope Saint Pius X, who admired Dominic's innocence, dismissed such objections and let the investigation proceed. Pope Pius XII beatified Dominic Savio in 1950 and declared him a saint in 1954.

Saint Dominic Savio is the patron saint of boys, choirboys, and juvenile delinquents. Feast day: March 9.

**Saint Domitilla (died c. 95).** Before her martyrdom, Domitilla left her property outside Rome to the Church for use as a cemetery. She was buried there. In the thirteenth century her relics were moved from the Catacomb of Santa Domitilla along with the relics of two other martyrs, Saints Nereus and Achilleus. The bones of the saints were sealed inside the high altar of Rome's Church of Sts. Nereus and Achilleus.

This saint was a great-niece of the emperor Domitian and the niece of the martyr Saint Flavius Clemens. She was exiled to the Isle of Ponza, then returned to Terracina and executed there. A legend claims that Nereus and Achilleus were two of Domitilla's servants who were martyred with her, but this is unlikely.

Feast day: May 12.

**Saint Dorothy (died 311).** The relics of Saint Dorothy are preserved in a marble urn beneath the high altar of the Church of St. Dorothy in Rome.

The Martyrology of Jerome, a list of martyrs attributed to Saint

Jerome but probably compiled in the sixth century, mentions a Christian woman named Dorothy who was executed in what is present-day Cappadocia, Turkey, on February 6, 311. This is all we know for certain about this saint. A delightful legend supplies additional details.

At the time that Dorothy was arrested, her parents had already perished in Diocletian's persecution of the Church. The magistrate offered to spare the young woman's life if she agreed to marry a pagan; Dorothy replied that she had consecrated her virginity to Jesus Christ, who was her spiritual spouse. For her intransigence the magistrate condemned Dorothy to death.

As Dorothy was led to execution, a pagan lawyer named Theophilus called out from the crowd, "Bride of Christ! Send me some fruit and flowers from your bridegroom's garden!"

At the place of execution a little boy appeared beside Dorothy, bearing a basket full of roses and apples. "Take these to Theophilus," she instructed the boy. "Tell him I will meet him in the garden."

As the child delivered the message, the executioner cut off Dorothy's head. Immediately Theophilus confessed that he was a Christian, too. The magistrate sentenced him to execution, and the soul of the onetime scoffer flew to find Dorothy's spirit in the Bridegroom's garden.

Saint Dorothy is the patron saint of florists, greengrocers, gardeners, and brides. Feast day: February 6.


**Saint Dymphna (died seventh century).** In the ninth century two sarcophagi containing the remains of Saint Dymphna and Saint Gerebernus were discovered at the town of Gheel, Belgium. On the day the relics of Saint Dymphna were carried to a church built in her honor, a large crowd of the sick gathered, hoping to be cured as the relics passed. Many people suffering from mental illnesses were healed that day—a clear sign to the people of Gheel that Saint Dymphna was the patron saint of those suffering from mental and emotional disorders. Today Gheel has a renowned mental health hospital. The saint's relics, along with portions of her original sarcophagus, are preserved in Gheel's Church of St. Dymphna.

The earliest account of Dymphna's life was written in the thirteenth century, six hundred years after her death. According to the story, Dymphna's father, Damon, was a chieftain in Ireland. When his wife died he became unhinged—so much so that he tried to marry Dymphna, who bore a strong resemblance to her mother.

With her chaplain, Gerebernus, Dymphna escaped overseas to Belgium, but Damon followed. He caught up with the fugitives at Gheel. There he murdered his daughter while his guards murdered Gerebernus. The local inhabitants placed the bodies inside stone sarcophagi in a cave where they lay, forgotten, for two hundred years.

Saint Dymphna is the patron saint of psychiatrists, psychologists, and all mental health professionals. She is invoked against mental, emotional, and nervous disorders. Feast day: May 15.


**Saint Edmund Campion (1540–1581).** At the Shrine of Our Lady and the Martyrs in Ladyewell, England, is a sideboard that opens up as an altar. This secret altar was built in 1560, and Edmund Campion said Mass on it on Easter Sunday 1581. Stonyhurst College in England preserves several documents written by Campion, as well as a length of the rope with which he was hanged and a piece of linen stained with his blood. Stonyhurst also possesses an Agnus Dei that belonged to Saint Edmund. The wax medallion was presented to Campion by Pope Gregory XIII before he set out on his missionary journey to England. In 1959 electricians working in the attic of Lyford Grange, the manor house where Campion was arrested in July 1581, found a small wooden box concealed in the rafters. Inside, wrapped in vellum, was Campion's Agnus Dei.

As a young man Edmund Campion was considered one of the most promising young Anglican clergymen in England. In 1566, when Elizabeth I visited Oxford University, Campion was chosen to deliver an address of welcome, in Latin. His oration was so skillful that Robert Dudley, Earl of Leicester and the queen's most intimate male friend, became Campion's patron. Two years later Campion was ordained a deacon of the Church of England, and Elizabeth began considering an appropriate church office for him.

By that time Campion's reading of the Fathers of the Church led him to conclude that the Catholic Church was the church founded by Jesus Christ and the Church of England was in schism. In 1571 he sailed across the English Channel to Douai, France, where he entered the English seminary. After two years of study he moved on to Rome, where he joined the Jesuits. In 1580, when the Jesuit superior decided to send a mission to England, Campion was one of the men he chose for the dangerous assignment. Under English law, Catholic priests were forbidden to enter England—the penalty being imprisonment or death. English Catholics could not harbor a priest, nor could they hear him say Mass, make their confession to him, or ask him to baptize their children. In spite of the risks, Campion was eager to return home.

He arrived in England in 1580, in disguise and with false papers that identified him as a jewel merchant. For thirteen months he traveled from one Catholic house to the next in London, Berkshire, Norfolk, Lancashire, Oxfordshire, and Yorkshire. In July 1581, while at the home of the Yate family in Berkshire, Campion was betrayed by a renegade Catholic and arrested. Queen Elizabeth and the Earl of Leicester had him brought to them; they promised Campion a glorious career in the Church of England, perhaps even the archbishopric of Canterbury, if he abjured his Catholic faith. He declined the offer and was taken to the Tower of London where he was cruelly and repeatedly tortured on the rack.

Hoping to humiliate Campion, the Anglicans staged a debate. A panel of Protestant clergymen, armed with piles of notes and reference books and a small army of assistants, arrayed themselves against Campion, who was taken fresh from his cell. After four sessions Campion had scored so many points against the well-prepared ministers that they called off the debate before a winner could be declared.

On November 20, 1581, Campion and seven other priests were led into Westminster Hall for trial. There was no question what the verdict and sentence would be, and after the court pronounced them guilty of treason and condemned them to be hanged, drawn, and quartered, the priests left the Hall chanting the great hymn of praise, *Te Deum.*

On December 1 Campion, his fellow Jesuit Father Alexander Briant, and a diocesan priest Father Ralph Sherwin were dragged on hurdles through the filthy streets of London to the gallows at Tyburn. Campion was the first to die. He was hanged, cut down alive, disemboweled, his heart ripped out of his chest, and his body hacked into four quarters. English Catholics managed to secure a few fragments of the martyr's bones, but the rest of Campion's mutilated corpse was disposed of by the English government.

During his brief time in England Campion wrote a defense of the Catholic faith and of his mission to England. It became known as "Campion's Brag" and was read widely by English Catholics and Protestants; it remains one of the masterpieces of sixteenth-century English prose, as this brief excerpt reveals:

> Be it known to you that we have made a league—all the Jesuits in the world—cheerfully to carry the cross you shall lay upon us, and never to despair your recovery, while we have a man left to enjoy your Tyburn, or to be racked with your torments, or consumed with your prisons. The expense is reckoned, the enterprise is begun; it is of God, it cannot be withstood. So the faith was planted; so it must be restored.

Feast day: December 1.

## Saint Edmund Arrowsmith (1585–1628).

After Edmund Arrowsmith's execution his family managed to secure a major relic: his right hand. It was passed down through the generations until the Gerard family, relations of the Arrowsmiths (the martyr's mother's maiden name was Gerard), gave the relic to the Church of St. Oswald in Ashton-in-Makerfield, England. The church was subsequently rededicated to Saint Oswald and Saint Edmund Arrowsmith. Stonyhurst College preserves a small wooden trunk that contains a complete set of green Mass vestments, including alb, cincture, chalice veil, burse, and corporal, as well as a small pewter paten and chalice, which once belonged to Saint Edmund.

Edmund Arrowsmith's parents were Lancashire farmers who clung to the Catholic faith in spite of fines, harassment by priest-hunters, and imprisonment. After his ordination to the priesthood, Father Arrowsmith spent ten years ministering to Lancashire's large Catholic population. In 1623 he joined the Jesuits.

There was a young man of Father Arrowsmith's acquaintance named Holden who was living a dissolute life. When the priest chided him, Holden turned informer. Father Arrowsmith was condemned to death on a triple charge of being a Catholic priest, being a Jesuit, and having reconciled Anglicans to the Catholic Church. As he was led to execution he saw a fellow prisoner, Saint John Southworth, watching him from the window of his prison cell; from him the martyr received absolution.

While Father Arrowsmith was on the scaffold, government agents repeatedly offered to spare his life if he renounced Catholicism and joined the Anglican Church. "Tempt me no more," he said, "I will not do it, in no case, on no condition." Nonetheless the executioner showed mercy, letting the priest hang until he was dead before cutting him down and quartering his corpse.

Feast day: August 28.

**Blessed Edward Oldcorne (1561–1606).** Blessed Edward Oldcorne was sentenced to the ghastly death of being hanged, cut down while still alive, disemboweled, and having his head and limbs hacked off. The executioner used such force to behead him that one of Father Oldcorne's eyes popped out of his skull. It was recovered by a Catholic among the crowd of onlookers, and today it is among the sacred treasures of Stonyhurst College in England, preserved in a silver, eye-shaped reliquary. As was typical at the time, the quarters of Oldcorne's body were exhibited for a time in prominent public places and then disposed of.

Edward's father was Anglican, but his mother was a staunch Catholic who was imprisoned several times for refusing to attend Protestant church services. She raised Edward in her faith and prayed he would become a priest. He entered the English seminary in Rheims in 1581, completed his studies, was ordained in Rome in 1583, and joined the Jesuits in 1588. Several months later he was sent to England on a mission.

He made his headquarters at Hinlip Hall in Worcestershire, the home of the Habington family. There he made his first convert. The Hall's master, Thomas Habington, was a fervent Catholic, but his sister Dorothy was a fervent Protestant. She tolerated priests in the house and did not betray her brother, but she rebuffed all attempts to bring her into the Catholic Church. Oldcorne tried to persuade her, too, but with no success—until she learned that he had been fasting for days as an appeal to God to touch her heart. Oldcorne's act of penance convinced Dorothy more thoroughly than any of his sermons; she converted to Catholicism. For sixteen years Father Oldcorne used Hinlip Hall as his base of operations.

In 1605 a handful of radical Catholic gentlemen plotted to blow up King James I, the royal family, and Parliament. The plot was discovered at the last minute, and the government cast a wide net to draw in others suspected of complicity in the plot. Among those arrested was Father Oldcorne. For five hours a day, five days in succession, he was tortured on the rack, but still he insisted that he was innocent of any involvement in the Gunpowder Plot. With no other evidence against him, the government charged him with being a Jesuit who had entered England illegally and converted many English subjects to the Catholic faith.

Edward Oldcorne was executed in Worcester, where he had served for many years.

Feast day: April 7.

**Saint Edward the Confessor (1003–1066).** Saint Edward the Confessor, an Anglo-Saxon king of England, built a palace near the Benedictine Monastery of St. Peter in Westminster and erected a new church for the monks, which was dedicated on December 28, 1065. Days later, on January 5, 1066, Edward died and was buried in the new church. Following the king's canonization in 1161, his remains were lifted from their grave and placed in a shrine in the heart of Westminster Abbey (Saint Thomas Becket, archbishop of Canterbury, presided at the ceremony). In the thirteenth century King Henry III rebuilt the abbey church in the Gothic style, and Saint Edward's relics were placed in a new, elevated shrine. At the dissolution of Westminster's Benedictine monastery the shrine was stripped of its valuables, and Saint Edward's bones were buried. When Queen Mary I returned England to the practice of the Catholic faith, Saint Edward's relics were returned to their shrine, where they have remained to this day.

Edward had six older half brothers, so the chances of his becoming king of England were remote. As a result he cultivated his religious life, even persuading his wife, Edith, to live with him chastely, as brother and sister. Tragically, that decision would bring about the Norman Conquest and the destruction of Anglo-Saxon England.

In 1042, when the last of his elder brothers was dead, Edward was crowned king. He was a gentle, merciful king, beloved by his people, generous to the poor and to the Church. But because he had no child his succession was disputed. It is most likely that he left the crown to his cousin Harold Godwinson. But across the Channel another, more distant relative, William II of Normandy, insisted that the crown of England was rightfully his. In 1066 William invaded England, killed Harold II at the battle of Hastings, conquered the country, and was crowned in Westminster Abbey, just steps away from Edward's grave.

Saint Edward is the patron saint of England's royal family and is invoked by spouses suffering marriage difficulties. Feast day: October 13.


**Saint Elizabeth Ann Seton (1774–1821).** When Mother Seton died in 1821, the Sisters of Charity buried her in the nuns' cemetery in Emmitsburg, Maryland, beside her three daughters, Harriet, Anna Maria, and Rebecca, and her sister-in-law Cecilia Seton. With an initial donation of $250, her son William started a fund to construct a mortuary chapel for his mother's remains; the chapel was completed in 1846 and Mother Seton's body was exhumed and reburied below the chapel floor. In 1963, when Mother Seton was beatified, her tomb was opened and her relics placed in a small copper casket that was enshrined above the altar in the chapel of St. Joseph College, just a short walk from the cemetery. Five years later the relics were transferred to what is now the Basilica of St. Elizabeth Ann Seton on the convent grounds in Emmitsburg. In addition to the remains of the saint, the National Shrine of St. Elizabeth Ann Seton preserves many of Mother Seton's personal belongings, which are displayed in the shrine's museum and in the old convent and school known as the White House.

Mother Seton was the indispensable woman of Catholicism in the early days of the United States. In 1774, when she was born (the year before the start of the American Revolution), the practice of the Catholic faith was outlawed in every colony except Pennsylvania. There were about twenty priests in the colonies, all of them in Maryland or Pennsylvania. When they visited tiny Catholic communities in New York, New Jersey, Delaware, or Virginia, they traveled in disguise and used aliases. There were no parochial schools, no nuns, no Catholic bishops in British America. Mother Seton was instrumental in changing that.

Elizabeth Ann Bayley was brought up on Staten Island. Her parents were wealthy, well-connected Anglicans. In 1789, when George Washington was inaugurated as the first president of the United States, fifteen-year-old Elizabeth was among the guests at his inaugural ball. Four years later she married a successful merchant, William Seton. The couple had five children, three daughters and two sons. The Setons lived comfortably in Manhattan until William's business failed. Then he contracted tuberculosis. In 1803, hoping for a cure in a warmer climate, William, Elizabeth, and their eight-year-old daughter, Anna Maria, sailed to Italy, where William had a business associate, Antonio Filicchi.

William died in Italy, and Elizabeth and Anna Maria were taken in by the Filicchis. The family had a private chapel, and there Elizabeth had her first experience of Catholicism. While the furnishings of the chapel and the externals of the Mass were lovely, she was drawn by two essential facets of the Catholic faith: belief in the Real Presence of Christ in the Blessed Sacrament, and forgiveness of sins through the sacrament of confession.

In 1804 she returned to New York and began instruction in the Catholic faith. In 1805 she was baptized and made her First Holy Communion in St. Peter's Church on Barclay Street in lower Manhattan. She tried to support herself and her children by teaching, but entrenched anti-Catholicism in New York City made that impossible: parents would not send their children to a woman who had abandoned the Episcopal Church for the Church of Rome.

In 1808 she moved to Baltimore where there was a large Catholic population. There, in 1809, with the approval of America's first bishop, John Carroll, she founded a congregation of teaching nuns under the name Sisters of Charity. As their habit they adopted the black dress, cape, and bonnet worn by widows in Italy. A wealthy benefactor donated 269 acres near Emmitsburg, Maryland, to the sisters and there in 1810 they opened the first Catholic school in the United States; it was the beginning of the American parochial school system.

Between 1809 and her death in 1821 Mother Seton saw her

order grow from six to ninety-two sisters. In addition to schools, her sisters operated orphanages in Philadelphia and New York and ran the infirmary at Mount St. Mary's Seminary nearby. Mother Seton established a religious community that was American in its outlook rather than European, active rather than cloistered. And she laid the foundation of Catholic institutions that would increase one hundredfold thanks to the waves of Catholic immigrants who would arrive in America during the nineteenth century.

Saint Elizabeth Ann Seton is the patron saint of American Catholic schools, of widows, and of the Apostleship of the Sea. Feast day: January 4.

**Saint Elizabeth of Hungary (1207–1231).** Saint Elizabeth's body was first buried in the chapel of the hospital she founded in Marburg, Germany. After her canonization in 1235, her remains were transferred to a golden casket inside the grand Gothic church dedicated to her in the same city. In 1539 one of the saint's descendants, Philip I of Hesse, an ardent supporter of Martin Luther, opened the shrine, placed the saint's bones in a bag, and kept them in his palace. Emperor Charles V ordered Philip to restore the bones to their reliquary, after which they became dispersed. Some are still in the shrine in Marburg; Saint Elizabeth's skull and some other bones, as well as her crown, are preserved in the Convent of St. Elizabeth in Vienna, Austria.

Elizabeth was four years old when her parents, the king and queen of Hungary, forged an alliance with the neighboring German principality of Thurginia by betrothing their child to eleven-year-old Prince Ludwig. Elizabeth and Ludwig married ten years later. Unlike most politically expedient, arranged royal marriages, this one proved to be a love match. Elizabeth and Ludwig were devoted to each other, and in time they had three children, a son and two daughters.

Unfortunately there was a strong anti-Hungarian faction at the Thuringian court who opposed the alliance and the marriage;

among this faction's leaders were some of Elizabeth's in-laws. When Ludwig died while on crusade, his brother, Henry, who had always disliked Elizabeth, ordered her, her daughters, and her two ladies-in-waiting out of the royal castle. (Henry kept Elizabeth's son, Hermann, because he was the heir.)

Elizabeth settled in Marburg, where she opened a hospital and spent the last four years of her life nursing the sick and the dying.

Saint Elizabeth of Hungary is the patron saint of bakers, beggars, brides, widows, charitable institutions, hospitals, and nursing homes. She is also the patron saint of spouses who have difficulties with their in-laws. Feast day: November 17.

**Saint Elizabeth of Portugal (1271–1336).** Saint Elizabeth's body was entombed in a sarcophagus that bore a portrait sculpture of her in the habit of a Poor Clare but wearing a crown. In 1614 her relics were placed in a silver casket. Both the original sarcophagus and the silver reliquary are displayed at the Monastery of Santa Clara-a-Nova at Coimbra, Portugal.

Saint Elizabeth of Portugal was the great-niece of Saint Elizabeth of Hungary and queen of Portugal. Unlike her aunt's marriage, Elizabeth's marriage was wretched. Her husband the king, Dinis, fathered at least seven illegitimate children by various mistresses, then insisted that they be raised in the palace with the children he had had with Elizabeth. If she felt any bitterness toward Dinis, Elizabeth suppressed it and acted as a devoted foster mother.

Meanwhile, Dinis made a bad situation worse by showing distinct signs that he favored his illegitimate sons over his legitimate son and heir, Prince Afonso. The young man did not bear this insult patiently. Afraid that his father would try to disinherit him and pass the crown to one of his illegitimate half brothers, Afonso tried to depose his father and seize the crown. Four times he rebelled against Dinis; once he schemed to murder the half brother he regarded as his greatest threat. Each time Elizabeth intervened to restore peace between father and son. On one occasion Dinis and Afonso refused to be reconciled. Their armies were arrayed on the field, waiting for the order to charge, when Elizabeth rode between them and refused to leave until her husband and her son had made peace.

Dinis died in 1325 and his crown passed to Afonso. In his will Dinis named Elizabeth executor of his estate—a last-minute token of esteem for his long-suffering wife.

Saint Elizabeth of Portugal is the patron saint of peacemakers and victims of adultery. She is invoked against jealousy. She is the patron saint of Coimbra, Portugal. Feast day: July 4.

**Saint Emerentiana (died 304).** The relics of the saint are enshrined in the same silver casket as those of her foster sister, Saint Agnes, in Rome's Basilica of St. Agnes Outside the Walls.

A day or two after Saint Agnes had been martyred, Emerentiana went to the tomb of her foster sister to pray. A pagan mob discovered her there and stoned her to death.

Feast day: January 23.

**Saint Erasmus, or Ernest, or Elmo (died c. 303).** The relics of Saint Erasmus are kept in the Cathedral of the Assumption and St. Erasmus in Gaeta, Italy. They were moved there after Saracen raiders destroyed the city of Formiae in 842.

Erasmus was bishop of Formiae in southern Italy when Emperor Diocletian began his persecution of Christians. The local magistrate had Erasmus arrested and ordered him to sacrifice to Hercules; the bishop refused. According to legend, the executioners slit open Erasmus's stomach, nailed one end of his intestines to a windlass, or winch, then slowly turned the crank, winding his intestines on the cylinder.

Saint Erasmus is invoked against storms at sea and all pains and ailments of the stomach. He is the patron saint of mariners and of the city of Gaeta. Feast day: June 2.

**Saint Eric IX (1120–1160).** For nearly nine hundred years the Swedes have venerated Saint Eric as a royal martyr. His bones are enshrined in a gold and silver casket in Uppsala Cathedral.

Christianity came late to Sweden. In the twelfth century, although the royal family was devoutly Catholic, many Swedish nobles and a large percentage of the Swedish population, especially outside major cities and towns, still worshipped the Norse gods. About 1154, when he came to the throne, Eric issued new legislation that protected the Church, outlawed pagan worship, and required that all Swedes pay a tithe—10 percent of their annual income—to the Church, as was customary elsewhere in Christian Europe.

A group of anti-Christian Swedish nobles allied themselves with Eric's enemies in Denmark and ambushed the king as he came out of Uppsala's Holy Trinity Church after attending Mass on Ascension Day. They stabbed him repeatedly with their swords, mocking him as he writhed in pain on the ground. Finally one of the assassins—the sources do not agree on whether it was a Swede or a Dane—hacked at Eric's neck until he was dead.

Eric was never formally canonized, but devotion to him sprang up immediately after his death, and the Church recognizes him as a saint. Legend says that his banner, a gold cross upon a blue field, became Sweden's national flag.

Saint Eric is one of the patron saints of Sweden. Feast day: May 18.

**Saint Etheldreda, or Audrey (c. 636–679).** The shrine of Saint Etheldreda stood in Ely Cathedral from 694 until 1541, when Henry VIII's commissioners demolished the shrine and destroyed the saint's body. But one of the hands of Etheldreda survived and was kept by the Catholic dukes of Norfolk. The hand is preserved at the Catholic Church of St. Etheldreda in Ely; a portion of the relic is enshrined in a small chest in the sanctuary of the Catholic Church of St. Etheldreda in London.

Etheldreda was one of four royal sisters, all of whom became nuns and all of whom became saints (the other three are Saint Sexburga, Saint Ethelburga, and Saint Withburga). She was in her early teens when her father, King Anna of East Anglia, married her to an Anglo-Saxon prince named Tonbert. He died before the marriage was consummated, and Etheldreda went into retirement on the Isle of Ely, in preparation for life as a nun. Nonetheless, her family forced her to marry again, this time to a prince named Egfrid. Etheldreda agreed to another wedding if she and Egfrid could live chastely, as brother and sister; she insisted that she had no other option since she had consecrated her virginity to God.

Egfrid appealed to the archbishop of York, Saint Wilfrid, to order Etheldreda to live in the usual manner of husband and wife. To sweeten the appeal, Egfrid offered the holy archbishop a bribe. Wilfrid ruled in Etheldreda's favor.

She founded a convent at Ely and served as abbess. While her nuns wore linen habits, Etheldreda's was of coarse wool. Except on holy days she ate only once a day, and it was typical for her to spend her nights in prayer in the convent church. Her holiness and humility made her popular with the local people, and after her death Etheldreda was made a saint. Devotion to her remained strong in England throughout the Anglo-Saxon period and even after the Norman Conquest in 1066.

Saint Etheldreda is invoked against all ailments of the neck and throat. She is one of the patron saints of Cambridge University. Feast day: June 23.


**Saint Eulalia of Mérida (c. 292–c. 304).** For more than four hundred years the shrine of Saint Eulalia in Lusitania, modern-day Mérida, was one of the most popular in Spain. In the late eighth century King Silo translated the saint's relics to Oviedo, where they remain to this day, enshrined in the Chapel of St. Eulalia in the Oviedo Cathedral.

The story of Saint Eulalia comes to us from Prudentius, a fourth-century Spanish Christian poet who composed an ode in her honor. During Emperor Diocletian's persecution of the Church, Eulalia, about twelve years old, ran away from her parents' house to defend her fellow Christians. Marching into the courtroom of the magistrate of Lusitania, she denounced him for torturing and executing people who had done the emperor no harm. The judge tried to calm the child, but Eulalia couldn't be appeased by soothing words. Enraged by the injustice of the persecution, she toppled a small statue of a Roman god, dumped the propitiatory offerings on the floor, and stomped on them. The judge ordered the girl's execution.

Outside the court the executioners bound her to a stake, tore her sides with iron hooks, and scorched her breasts with torches. Then they burned Eulalia alive. The Christians of Lusitania collected the child-martyr's remains, and her tomb became a destination for pilgrims.

Saint Eulalia is the patron saint of runaways. She is one of the patron saints of Mérida and Oviedo. Feast day: December 10.

**Saint Faustina Kowalska (1905–1938).** Saint Faustina is buried in the chapel of the Sisters of Our Lady of Mercy on the grounds of the Basilica of Divine Mercy at Lagiewniki, Poland, outside Cracow.

Fasutina was one of ten children. Her parents' farm was too small to support such a large family, so when she was still a girl she left school and went to work as a housekeeper. In 1925 she joined the Sisters of Our Lady of Mercy in Warsaw. As she was poorly educated and had no special skills, she was assigned to humble tasks such as cooking and gardening.

On the evening of February 22, 1931, Sister Faustina had a vision of Christ, his right hand raised in blessing, his left hand pointing to two rays of light that emanated from his heart: the pale ray standing for the water and the red ray for the blood, both of which poured out of his side when it was pierced by the lance. The

Lord instructed Faustina to paint what she saw and inscribe below the image JESUS, I TRUST IN YOU.

Christ told Faustina that sinners should trust in his divine mercy and instructed her to petition the bishops of Poland to establish the Sunday after Easter as the Feast of Mercy. Sister Faustina reported her vision to her superior and to the priest who was her spiritual director. They instructed her to keep a journal of her revelations.

During World War II and then under Poland's Communist government, Faustina and her visions were all but forgotten. It was Pope John Paul II who in 1992 advanced Faustina's cause for sainthood and made devotion to the Divine Mercy of Christ known to the Catholic world.

Pope John Paul II declared Saint Faustina Kowalska "the Apostle of Divine Mercy." Feast day: October 5.


**Saint Felicitas of Rome (died c. 165).** Sometime between 800 and 816 Pope Saint Leo III moved the relics of Saint Felicitas from her tomb in the Catacomb of Maximus to the Church of St. Susanna.

We know that Felicitas was a Roman patrician who was beheaded during the reign of Marcus Aurelius. Pope Saint Damasus, who composed poems that he had carved above the tombs of popular Roman martyrs, tells us, "This woman feared not the sword, but perished with her sons." There is an ancient tradition that Saint Felicitas was forced to watch as her seven sons were all martyred before she herself was executed.

Saint Felicitas is the patron of parents praying for a male child, and she is invoked against infertility and the death of one's children. Feast day: November 23.


**Saint Florian (died 304).** In the fourth or fifth century Christians erected a simple memorial over the tomb of Saint Florian. A monastery was founded on the site in the year 800. The saint's relics are buried in the crypt of St. Florian's Abbey Church, located eleven miles from Linz, Austria. Part of the relics are enshrined at St. Florian's Church in Cracow, Poland.

Florian was a Roman officer stationed near present-day Lorch, Austria. One day he was crossing the bridge over the river Emms when he met a band of soldiers. "Where are you going, friends?" he asked.

"We are hunting for Christians," one of the soldiers replied.

"Brothers," Florian said, "I am a Christian."

Reluctantly, the soldiers arrested their officer and took him to the magistrate who threatened to burn Florian alive. "Then I will rise to Heaven in a burst of flames," Florian replied.

Instead of burning him, the magistrate sentenced Florian to be scourged, then drowned. After whipping him, the executioners dragged Florian to the Emms bridge, tied a millstone to his neck, and pushed him into the water. Some Christians recovered the martyr's body and gave it a decent burial outside the present-day city of Linz.

Saint Florian is the patron saint of firefighters and is invoked against fire and against drowning. He is one of the patron saints of Austria and Poland. Feast day: May 4.


**Forty Martyrs of Sebaste (died 320).** These forty martyrs were so popular in the early Church that many of their relics were quickly disseminated among a host of churches. Over the centuries many of these relics have been lost or destroyed. Some are preserved, however, in the Chapel of the Forty Martyrs in the Church of the Holy Sepulchre in Jerusalem and at Xeropotamou Monastery on Mount Athos, Greece.

The martyrs were all Roman soldiers serving in Armenia. The emperor Licinius sentenced them to an especially cruel death: they were all stripped naked and forced out onto the ice of a frozen lake. On shore the guards kindled large fires and prepared hot baths for any who apostasized. Only one lost his resolve, and he died shortly after immersing himself in the warm bathwater. His place was taken by one of the guards who was inspired by the courage of the martyrs.

When all appeared to be dead, the guards piled the corpses into a cart and took them away to be burned. They found that one man, the youngest of the forty, was still alive, and left him on the ice to die. But this young soldier's mother, who had witnessed the martyrdom, did not want her son to be parted from his thirty-nine companions. She lifted her dying son and placed him in the cart with the bodies of the others.

Feast day: March 10.

**Four Crowned Martyrs (died 305).** Saints Castorus, Claudius, Nicostratus, and Symphorian were stone carvers in what is now Mitrovic, Serbia. The emperor Diocletian, who had a palace at what is now Split, Croatia, commissioned the sculptors to carve a statue of the god Aesculapius for a temple. The four men, all Christians, refused to sculpt an idol to a false god. Diocletian ordered them sealed in lead chests and drowned in the Sava River.

Christians in the neighborhood recovered the martyrs' bodies and gave them a proper burial. Later they were moved to Rome and enshrined in the Church of the Four Holy Crowned Martyrs.

The Four Crowned Martyrs are the patron saints of sculptors and stonemasons. Feast day: November 8.

**Saint Foy, or Faith (died c. 285).** In 876 a monk from the Abbey of Conques stole the relics of Saint Foy from their shrine in the Abbey of Agen and brought them to his own community. The monks of Conques commissioned a wooden sculpture of the saint, placed the relics inside, then had the statue plated with gold. Today the golden statue is studded with gems—the gifts of many grateful pilgrims. For safekeeping the reliquary statue of Saint Foy is displayed in the abbey museum, although it is carried in solemn procession to the church on the saint's feast day.

All we know of Foy is that she was a young woman who was roasted on a grill in the town of Agen. This obscure martyr became famous after her relics were taken to Conques, a stop on the pilgrims' road to the shrine of Saint James at Compostela aka Santiago de Compostela. The shrine still attracts pilgrims, and devotion to Saint Foy is strong in Conques and the surrounding region.

Saint Foy is the patron saint of pilgrims and prisoners. Feast day: October 6.

**Saint Frances Xavier Cabrini (1850–1917).** In 1899 Mother Frances Xavier Cabrini founded Sacred Heart Villa, a residential high school for girls, in northern Manhattan. It was one of sixty-seven Catholic schools, hospitals, and charitable institutions she founded during her busy life serving the poor in the United States, especially Italian immigrants.

In Italy she established a new order of nuns, the Missionaries of the Sacred Heart of Jesus, with the expectation that she and her sisters would be missionaries in Asia. When she approached Pope Leo XIII for his blessing, he instructed her that her mission lay "not in the East but to the West." Hundreds of thousands of Italian immigrants were pouring into the United States, many of them desperately poor, but there were very few Italian priests and nuns in America to help them. With a handful of sisters, Mother Cabrini arrived in New York City in 1889. She rented a cockroach-infested apartment that became her first convent in the New World. By the next day she and her sisters were sheltering orphans, feeding the hungry, and nursing the sick.

She retired in Chicago, at Columbus Hospital (another of her foundations), where she died of malaria on December 22, 1917.

In 1933 the Missionaries of the Sacred Heart of Jesus moved Mother Cabrini's body to the school chapel of Sacred Heart Villa (now known as Mother Cabrini High School). Most of her bones are enshrined in an urn in the new chapel erected in 1957. The bones of her hands and her skull are enshrined in the Cabrini Basilica in her hometown, Sant'Angelo Lodigiano, in northern Italy. And the humerus bone of her right arm is enshrined in the Shrine Church of Our Lady of Pompeii in Chicago.

Mother Cabrini is the patron saint of immigrants. Feast day: November 13.

**Saint Frances of Rome (1384–1440).** Overlooking the Roman Forum is the church of St. Frances of Rome, formerly known as St. Mary the New. The skeleton of Saint Frances, wrapped in a shroud, lies in a glass case above the altar in the church's crypt.

Frances was twelve years old when her parents married her to Lorenzo Ponziani, the commander of the pope's troops in Rome. It proved to be a happy marriage that produced three children—two sons and a daughter. Unlike other aristocratic women of the time, Frances raised her children herself.

By nature generous and sympathetic, Frances devoted herself to helping the sick and the poor of Rome. During an epidemic she transformed her palace into a hospital. When famine came she fed the starving from her own storerooms, and when that food ran out she used her fortune to purchase more. During an especially harsh winter, when fuel was hard to come by and expensive, Frances collected wood on her estates outside the city and distributed it to the destitute.

It was said that she had a healing touch. Sixty witnesses came forward during Frances's canonization process to swear that she had cured them of all manner of diseases.

Frances said that at all times she could see her guardian angel at her side. When she was called out after dark, her angel walked before her shining a supernatural lamp. On her deathbed Frances said, "The angel has finished his work. He is beckoning me to follow."

Saint Frances of Rome is the patron saint of automobile drivers, taxi drivers, and Roman housewives. Feast day: March 9.

**Saint Francis de Sales (1567–1622).** The body of Saint Francis de Sales is enshrined in the Basilica of the Visitation in Annency, France. At the time of his death his heart was removed and sent to Lyon. During the French Revolution, when mobs of radicals often attacked churches and destroyed the relics of the saints, the saint's heart was sent to Venice for safekeeping. Today the heart is venerated at the Monastery of the Visitation in Treviso, Italy.

Francis de Sales was born in Savoy in southeastern France at a time when the Catholic faith was losing ground in the region as more and more of the Savoyards converted to Calvinism. The de Sales family, however, remained staunch Catholics, and both Francis and his cousin Louis de Sales entered the priesthood. After their ordination, with the approval of their bishop, they traveled throughout Savoy preaching and engaging in public debates with Calvinist ministers (at the time, religious debates were considered prime public entertainment).

To reach a wider audience, Francis wrote brief pamphlets that explained and defended Catholic doctrine, such as the Real Presence of Christ in the Eucharist, and Catholic devotional practices, such as praying the Rosary. Within five years Francis and Louis had brought approximately two-thirds of the population of Savoy back to the Catholic Church. The pope rewarded Francis's achievement by naming him bishop of Geneva.

In fact, he was bishop in name only. In 1533 John Calvin and his followers had driven out of Geneva the Catholic bishop, the clergy, and the monks and nuns. They destroyed all sacred statues, paintings, and even stained-glass windows, then passed legislation that outlawed the practice of the Catholic faith in the province. Consequently, Francis was barred from even setting foot inside Geneva let alone saying Mass in the cathedral there.

Nevertheless, as bishop he continued his campaign to bring Calvinists back to the Catholic faith. He also trained young men for the priesthood and reformed monasteries and convents where the religious had lost their original zeal. With Saint Jane Frances de Chantal he founded the Order of the Visitation of Holy Mary, an order of nuns who balanced the contemplative life with teaching children and caring for the elderly.

Francis's most enduring work is *Introduction to the Devout Life,* a practical handbook for laypeople on how to overcome their sins and grow in holiness while still fulfilling their obligations to their family and holding down a job. In four hundred years this book has never gone out of print.

Saint Francis de Sales is the patron saint of writers, educators, the deaf, and confessors. Feast day: January 24.

**Saint Francis of Assisi (1182–1226).** Relic theft was common in the Middle Ages. A church or monastery that possessed the relics of a popular saint could expect throngs of pilgrims who would leave donations and other offerings in honor of the saint. A town or religious house that had not been blessed with the relic of a well-known saint might "acquire" one by less than honest means. On May 25, 1230, when the body of Saint Francis was moved from its

The town of Gubbio, Italy, preserves the heavily patched tunic of Saint Francis of Assisi in an airtight glass case. © DANIELE LA MONACA/REUTERS/ CORBIS

original tomb in Assisi's Church of St. George to the new Basilica of St. Francis, Brother Elias, one of the saint's earliest disciples, ordered the coffin buried deep in the crypt and covered with stone slabs so no one would know where the relics lay. As a result, within a few generations the location of Francis's tomb was forgotten, and it was not rediscovered until 1818. When the Franciscans opened their founder's coffin, they found his complete skeleton. The tomb of Saint Francis is still in the crypt, but now it is accessible to pilgrims. In the Franciscans' chapter house is the Chapel of the Relics, which displays Saint Francis's gray habit, his hair shirt, the leather bandage that covered the stigmata wound on his side, a pair of sandals Saint Clare made for him, and other personal items. The Oratory of the Crucifix in Assisi's Basilica of St. Clare preserves the crucifix of San Damiano that spoke to Francis, thereby launching his mission.

No one who knew Francis as a young man would have predicted that the amateur troubadour, dilettante soldier, and playboy would become one of the most popular saints of all time, the saint said to be most like Jesus Christ.

Francis's parents were well-to-do middle-class cloth merchants who spoiled their son. As a teenager he ran the streets, spending his nights in the seedier neighborhoods of Assisi and squandering his parents' money. His conversion came during a petty war in which Francis was taken prisoner by the enemy and kept in a dungeon for a year. After his release he was a changed young man: quiet, pensive, prayerful. One day while praying in the dilapidated Church of San Damiano he heard the crucifix over the altar speak. "Francis," Christ said, "repair my Church which is falling into ruins." Francis assumed the Lord meant San Damiano, so he hurried home, gathered up his father's best merchandise, sold it in a neighboring market town, and gave the proceeds to the startled parish priest.

It was a grand gesture. Unfortunately Francis had made it with property that did not belong to him. Francis's father hauled his son before the bishop of Assisi, demanding restitution. Luckily, the priest of San Damiano had not spent a single coin, and he handed the entire sum to Francis's father. But in Francis's mind that was not enough. In the town square, with the bishop and a large crowd looking on, Francis renounced everything his father had ever given him, including his clothes, which he stripped off on the spot. The bishop scurried over and wrapped the naked young man in a cloak.

Francis began a new life, trying to imitate Christ and the apostles. He had no home, no money. He begged for food, slept indoors if someone offered him shelter for the night, slept outdoors if no such offer was forthcoming. He preached wherever he could draw a crowd. Soon other men joined him.

At a time when most clergy lived behind monastery walls, Francis imagined a community of men who would live and work among ordinary people, bringing them the sacraments, preaching the Gospel, teaching them the Catholic faith. Ideally Francis would have preferred his followers to live in huts and caves, but as the number of members of his community, who would be known as Franciscans, grew to the hundreds and then thousands such an arrangement was not practical.

In 1224, on the Feast of the Exaltation of the Holy Cross, Francis received the stigmata. The wounds Christ bore on the cross Francis received in his hands, feet, and side. They were painful, they oozed blood, and they embarrassed Francis. He wore shoes and sleeves to cover his feet and hands so the curious could not see the marks.

Francis is renowned for his love of the natural world. He is said to have tamed a wolf that was causing havoc around the town of Gubbio. In his hymn, the "Canticle of the Sun," he sang praise to God for the glory of His creation; there was a part of Francis that would always be a troubadour.

Saint Francis is the patron saint of animals and ecology, and he is one of the patron saints of Italy. Feast day: October 4. The feast of the Stigmata of Saint Francis is September 17.

**Blessed Francis Seelos (1819–1867).** The remains of Blessed Francis are kept in a large wooden church-shaped reliquary that is on permanent display in a shrine behind the Church of St. Mary of the Assumption in New Orleans. Attached to the shrine is a museum that exhibits many of Blessed Francis's personal belongings.

Father Seelos was a Redemptorist priest from Bavaria who emigrated to the United States to minister to German-speaking Catholics. He was assigned to the Church of St. Philomena in Pittsburgh, where he served as the assistant to the pastor, Saint John Neumann. Redemptorists are renowned for their preaching missions, and in addition to their responsibilities to the parish, Fathers Seelos and Neumann conducted missions in neighboring churches, too.

From Pittsburgh, Father Seelos was transferred to Maryland, where he served parishes in Baltimore, Cumberland, and Annapolis. In 1860 Blessed Pope Pius IX named him bishop of Pittsburgh, but Francis begged to be excused. Instead he lived as a permanent mission priest, traveling from New Jersey to Wisconsin, from Connecticut to Missouri. Finally he was sent as pastor to the Church of St. Mary of the Assumption in New Orleans.

He was still new to the parish when an epidemic of yellow fever broke out in the city. He exhausted himself visiting the sick and bringing the last sacraments to the dying. In September 1867 Father Seelos contracted yellow fever; he died on October 4, 1867.

Feast day: October 5.

**Saint Francis Xavier (1506–1552).** At age forty-six Saint Francis Xavier died of a fever on the island of Sancian off the coast of China. Xavier's two companions, a Chinese convert named Anthony, and a Portuguese sea captain who had stopped to help, buried his body on the island. Several months later a groups of Jesuits and laymen returned to Sancian to exhume Xavier's remains for a more dignified burial in the Portuguese colony of Malacca. When they lifted the body from the grave they found it to be incorrupt (although it is no longer in such pristine condition). Today Saint Francis

Xavier's body is housed in a glass and silver casket in Goa's Basilica of Bom Jesus, or Good Jesus. His right arm is enshrined in a chapel in the Jesuits' Church of Il Gesù in Rome, and other bones are preserved in other churches in Asia. One relic is in private hands: in 1554 when Saint Francis's body was exposed for veneration, a Portuguese woman, Dona Isabel Carom, bit off the little toe of the right foot and kept it for private devotion. The toe is still in the possession of Dona Isabel's descendants.

Xavier met Saint Ignatius of Loyola in Paris where they were both studying at the university. They had a great deal in common: both were from aristocratic families, both were Basques, and both were devout Catholics interested in deepening their spiritual life. With five friends they decided to form a religious order, the Society of Jesus, dedicated to missionary work, particularly in the Holy Land. The pope gave his formal approval to their order, but not to their plans to work in Palestine. Instead he instructed the Jesuits (as they were known) to focus their energies on bringing Protestants back to the church and strengthening the faith of Catholics. As for Xavier, he could go to the mission field in Asia.

Xavier traveled first to Goa, where he adopted an ambitious program: to protect the Indians from the cruelty and exploitation of the Portuguese; to teach the catechism to Indian children; to visit inmates in the prisons and the sick in hospitals; to bring comfort and the sacraments to lepers.

From Goa Francis moved to the Spice Islands in Indonesia. He was planning a mission to China when he fell ill and died on Sancian. It is said that during his career as a missionary Saint Francis Xavier baptized 100,000 souls.

Saint Francis Xavier is the patron saint of missionaries, and he is one of the patron saints of India, China, Japan, Borneo, the East Indies, Australia, and New Zealand. Feast day: December 3.

## Blessed Francois-Xavier de Montmorency-Laval (1623–1708).

At his death Bishop de Montmorency Laval was buried in the

Church of Notre Dame de Quebec, the first church erected in Canada. Today his remains lie beneath a modern tomb in Notre Dame's crypt.

As the first bishop of Quebec—and the only bishop in Canada—it fell to Laval to establish the institutional Church in what was still a wilderness. He insisted that all questions involving the clergy or nuns must be addressed to him. He opened a seminary to train native Canadian priests. He established new parishes and founded schools and charitable institutions. He refused to accept that the governor had any authority over the Church, and he fought a relentless campaign against traders who sold liquor to the Indians.

Many religious orders in France wished to send missionaries to Canada, but Bishop Laval turned them away. There were more than enough missionary priests and nuns in Quebec at the time; more religious men and women who relied on donations for their survival would be an unacceptable financial burden on the colonists.

In 1688 Bishop Laval retired and was replaced by Jean-Baptiste de La Croix de Chevrière de St.-Vallier, a man of great personal holiness but incapable of making friends. He alienated virtually everyone in Quebec, including the governor, the Jesuits, and even the priests of his cathedral. In 1704, while en route to France, Bishop Saint-Vallier's ship was captured by the British and he was imprisoned in England. Bishop Laval came out of retirement and administered the diocese until his death. Recognized at last as a pioneer of the Church in Canada and a defender of the Indians, the colonists, and the most helpless, he was mourned throughout New France.

Feast day: July 21; May 6 in Canada.

**Saint Frideswide (c. 650–735).** The shrine of Saint Frideswide stood in the church dedicated to her in Oxford (now Christ Church Cathedral). She was a popular saint among the students of Oxford University, who venerated her as their patron. After

Henry VIII broke with Rome, Frideswide's shrine was dismantled and her bones were buried in the church. In 1553 Catherine Cathie, an ex-nun married to Peter Martyr Vermigli, an ex-priest, died and was buried near the grave of Saint Frideswide. A few months later Mary I came to the throne and restored England to union with the Catholic Church. Cathie's body was removed from the church and plans were drawn up for a new shrine for Saint Frideswide. After Mary's death Elizabeth I returned England to the Anglican faith. A Protestant canon of Christ Church, James Calfhill, disinterred the bones of Catherine Cathie and the relics of Saint Frideswide, mixed them together, and dumped them in one grave behind the altar, where they remain to this day.

Frideswide was an Anglo-Saxon princess who refused to marry the king of Mercia and took vows as a nun at a convent in Oxford. Legend says that the jilted king stormed the convent and was physically carrying Frideswide out of the town when he was struck blind.

Saint Frideswide is one of the patron saints of the town of Oxford and of Oxford University. Feast day: October 19.

**Saint Genesius (died c. 300).** For many centuries the relics of Saint Genesius were enshrined in the Church of Saint John delle Pigni near the Pantheon in Rome. By 1591 the church had fallen into disrepair, and Princess Camilla Peretti, sister of Pope Sixtus V, had the relics moved to the Chapel of St. Lawrence, which she had built for her family in the Church of St. Susanna. Today Saint Susanna is the church for American Catholics in Rome; Saint Genesius's relics are still preserved in the princess's chapel.

Genesius was an actor who performed in Rome during the reign of Diocletian, the emperor who launched the first empire-wide persecution of Christians. The troupe to which Genesius belonged was commanded to perform at the palace for the emperor; in honor of the occasion they wrote a new play, a comedy that mocked Christians. Genesius was cast as a convert.

At the performance Genesius and the actor playing the priest walked downstage for their scene. As his fellow actor poured water over his head and recited the words of the baptismal rite, God's grace suddenly flowed through Genesius. When he rose, he was a convinced Christian. As he berated Diocletian for his cruelty to innocent men and women, the emperor laughed, thinking the audacious speech was part of the play. But as Genesius went on, Diocletian, the actors, and the audience realized Genesius was in earnest. The emperor had him arrested and sentenced on the spot to be tortured, then beheaded. As the executioners tore open his flesh with iron hooks and burned him with torches, Genesius said, "Were I to be killed a thousand times for my allegiance to Christ, I would still go on as I have begun."

Saint Genesius is the patron saint of actors, especially comedians. Feast day: August 25.


**Saint Genevieve (c. 422–c. 500).** In 1793 an anti-Catholic mob rampaged into Paris's Church of St. Genevieve, broke open the saint's shrine, and carried her bones to the Place de Greve, where they burned them. About a century later fragments of Genevieve's remains that had survived in other locations were collected and placed in a large casket in the Church of St. Stephen du Mont, on Montagne Ste-Genevieve in Paris.

Genevieve was born near Paris to a family of Gallo-Roman Christians. At age fifteen she took a nun's vows of poverty, chastity, and obedience, but she did not enter a convent; she preferred an active life.

The Roman Empire was collapsing as barbarian nations rampaged across Western Europe. When Genevieve was in her teens the Franks laid siege to Paris. By the time the city surrendered, the Parisians were on the brink of starvation. Genevieve traveled to Troyes, where she appealed for help. Days later she reappeared, leading up the Seine a flotilla of boats filled with food.

It was through Genevieve's prayers that Attila the Hun led his warriors away from Paris. When the Frankish kings Childeric and Clovis occupied Paris and seized its most distinguished citizens, Genevieve persuaded the kings to spare the lives of their prisoners.

After her death, Parisians venerated Genevieve as the patroness of their city. In 1129, during a severe epidemic of ergot poisoning, the saint's relics were carried in procession through the streets and the disease abated. Today many Paris churches hold an annual commemoration of the city's deliverance through the prayers of Saint Genevieve.

Saint Genevieve is invoked against disasters and plagues and is one of the patron saints of Paris. Feast day: January 3.

**Saint George (died c. 303).** Because he was one of the most popular saints of the Middle Ages, relics of Saint George were especially sought after, which has made it difficult, perhaps impossible, to determine which relics of the saint are authentic. There are at least five churches that claim or have claimed to possess the skull of Saint George: Saint George in Velabro in Rome; Saint George zu Oberzell in Reichenau, Germany; Marmoutier Abbey in France; Saint George's Chapel in Windsor Castle, England; and in 1971 the Benedictine monks at the Monastery of St. George Maggiore in Venice discovered a reliquary said to contain the saint's skull. Windsor Castle, by the way, also had part of an arm bone of Saint George and two of his fingers.

Saint George was martyred at what is now the city of Lod, Israel; he may have been a soldier. The legend of Saint George slaying a dragon came centuries later and added greatly to his popularity. Crusaders told stories of Saint George riding down from heaven to help them defeat the Saracens. And kings and knights adopted him as the patron saint of chivalry.

Saint George is the patron saint of soldiers, cavalrymen, knights, and the Boy Scouts. He is one of the patron saints of England, Greece, Palestine, Malta, Lithuania, Ethiopia, the Republic of Georgia, Germany, Portugal, and Canada, as well as the cities of Beirut, Venice, Constantinople, Genoa, Moscow, and many others. He is invoked against skin diseases. Feast day: April 23.

**Saint Gerard Majella (1725–1755).** The saint's relics are buried in the Basilica of San Gerardo Majella in Caposele, Italy, the town where he died.

Gerard Majella was a tailor who at age twenty-six gave up his profession to become a Redemptorist lay brother, joining a new religious order devoted to reviving religious life in parishes. Saint Alphonsus Liguori, founder of the Redemptorists, considered Gerard a prize: here was a man who followed the *Rule* faithfully, never committed a serious sin, and was so amiable that people of every social rank felt at ease with him.

And then there were the miracles. No less than twenty individuals came to Alphonsus to report supernatural events that they attributed to Gerard's prayers. A poor family's supply of wheat was miraculously replenished for months. A woman dying in childbirth delivered a robust child and was herself inexplicably restored to health. A child killed in a fall off a cliff was raised from the dead.

Saint Gerard Majella is the patron saint of expectant mothers, of women in labor, and of women who are having a difficult pregnancy or who are having trouble becoming pregnant. Feast day: October 16.

**Blessed Gérard Tonque (?–1120).** Blessed Gérard died in Jerusalem, in the arms of several of the brothers of the religious order he founded in the Holy City about the year 1099. He was buried in the Church of St. John the Baptist, but sometime between 1187 and 1283 his remains were exhumed and carried to the town of Manosque in the southern French province of Provence. Gérard's bones were laid inside a silver gilt chest, studded with jewels, and displayed to the faithful in the chapel of the hospital of the Knights of St. John. In 1749 Gérard's skull was transferred to Valletta on the island of Malta, the headquarters of the Knights of St. John. During the French Revolution anti-Christian extremists destroyed Gérard's bones, although a humerus and a vertebra were saved from the vandals. The vertebra and part of the humerus are preserved in Martigues, France. A portion of the humerus is venerated in the chapel of the Grand Magistry of the Order of Malta in Rome. Fragments of Gérard's bones are venerated in the Commandery of Malta in Ehreshoven, Germany; the Church of Blessed Gérard in Mandeni, South Africa; and the Grand Priory of England of the Order of Malta in London. His skull is displayed in a glass and silver case in the Convent of St. Ursula in Valletta.

Gérard was a Frenchman who traveled to the Holy Land late in the eleventh century; he made his home in Jerusalem. He opened a hospital for pilgrims beside the Church of St. John the Baptist. Soon other men joined him, forming a new nursing community. Veterans of the First Crusade joined Gérard's religious order and in time these men would give it a new character: the Brothers of St. John would live as monks, nurse the sick and the injured in their hospital, but also remain knights, patrolling the roads to keep pilgrims safe and doing battle against the Saracens to keep the Holy Land in Christain hands.

Over time Gérard's community became known as the Knights of St. John, the Knights of the Hospital (or Hospitallers), and then, after Emperor Charles V gave them the island of Malta as their headquarters, the Knights of Malta. The Knights survive to this day, caring for the sick and assisting refugees and victims of war and natural disasters.

Feast day: October 13.


**Saint Germaine Cousin (c. 1579–1601).** The body of Germaine Cousin was buried in her parish church at Pibrac, France. In 1644 her grave was opened and her body was found to be incorrupt. It was displayed in the church until 1793, when four men, supporters of the French Revolution, dumped Germaine's body in a grave and threw quicklime and water on it. After the revolution the bones of the saint were exhumed. Today the relics are encased inside a wax portrait sculpture lying within a glass and gold chest that resembles a Gothic church; the shrine is located in the Basilica of St. Germaine Cousin in Pibrac. Germaine Cousin's father's house still stands, as does the parish church of St. Mary Magdalene where she attended Mass every day.

Germaine Cousin was a tragic figure. She was born with a shriveled right arm and a hideous skin condition. Later she developed a form of tuberculosis that caused unsightly swellings on her neck. Soon after Germaine was born her mother died. Her father remarried, but his new wife had no compassion for her little stepdaughter. Germaine was forbidden to play with her stepbrothers and stepsisters and was banned from the family table; she ate where she slept, on a pallet under the stairs.

Germaine was still a young girl when her father put her to work minding the family's flock of sheep. Alone in the pasture she spent hours talking to God and praying the Rosary many times during the day. She began to attend daily Mass, entrusting the sheep to her guardian angel (none ever wandered off or was snatched away by a wolf).

Eventually Germaine's father's conscience got the better of him and he tried to make amends with his daughter; he offered her a proper bed and urged her to join the family at the table. Germaine declined.

One morning her father found Germaine dead on her pallet beneath the stairs. She was twenty-two years old. An intense devotion to Germaine sprang up in Pibrac and the surrounding area, which led to her beatification in 1864 and canonization in 1867.

Saint Germaine Cousin is the patron saint of the disabled, the physically unattractive, and victims of abuse. Feast day: June 15.

**Saints Gervasius and Protasius (second century).** In his auto-biography, *Confessions,* Saint Augustine tells us that his friend and spiritual mentor, Saint Ambrose, bishop of Milan, had a dream or vision in which he was told of the location of the graves of the two martyrs Saint Gervasius and Saint Protasius. On June 17, 386, Ambrose led his entourage as well as some workmen to the memo-rial chapel that held the relics of two other martyrs, Saint Felix and Saint Nabor. Inside the chapel, just outside the altar rail, he ordered the workmen to dig. To the surprise of everyone (except Ambrose), the workmen uncovered two skeletons. Ambrose ordered that the bones be left as they were until he had confirmation that they were the remains of the saints. He had some men and women who suf-fered from demonic possession brought into the chapel. As they approached the grave, the demons howled and left their victims. One possessed woman fell down on the floor and the demon within her cried out the names of the saints—Gervasius and Protasius.

This was all the confirmation Ambrose required. The next day the skeletons of Saint Gervasius and Saint Protasius were placed on litters and carried in solemn procession to Ambrose's cathedral. Crowds lined the streets; people who suffered a variety of ailments pushed forward to touch the litters, and many of them reported afterward that they had been cured.

Ambrose intended to enshrine the relics in his cathedral that day, but the congregation inside the church insisted upon a delay so more people could have access to the saints. Bishop Ambrose relented and delayed the burial for another twenty-four hours, dur-ing which time throngs of Christians, the sick and healthy, surged forward to venerate the relics.

Saint Gervasius and Saint Protasius were the first Christians martyred in Milan. Although the Milanese Christians remembered their names and their martyrdom, the details of their life and death, like the location of their grave, had been forgotten. The relics of Saint Gervasius and Saint Protasius lie enshrined in the Basilica of St. Ambrose in Milan. Feast day: June 19.

**Saint Gianna Beretta Molla (1922–1962).** The saint's tomb is in the mausoleum of Mesero cemetery in Magenta, Italy.

Gianna Beretta Molla was the mother of four children as well as a physician and surgeon who specialized in pediatric medicine. She was also a devout Catholic who was active in her parish's Society of St. Vincent de Paul, an organization that helps the poor.

During Gianna's fourth pregnancy a tumor was found growing on the wall of her uterus. The typical treatment in Italy at the time called for a hysterectomy, which would have taken the life of her unborn child. Gianna opted for surgery to remove the tumor—a delicate operation, but one that proved successful: the tumor was removed and the child was not harmed. Gianna went into labor on Good Friday 1962. The delivery proved so difficult that her attending physicians decided to perform a caesarean section. Tragically, septic peritonitis infected the wound and a week later Gianna died.

Gianna's family and friends regarded her as a Catholic who had fulfilled all the obligations of her life—wife, mother, physician, friend of the poor—to a heroic degree. They were especially moved by her willingness to risk her life to save the life of her unborn child. That the operation had been a success but that she had died after giving birth made her story particularly heartbreaking.

Saint Gianna Beretta Molla is the patron saint of pregnant women and of the right-to-life movement. Feast day: April 28.

**Saint Gregory Nazianzus (330–390).** Originally Saint Gregory was buried in Nazianzus, near the place where he had been born. In 950 his relics were moved to the Church of the Holy Apostles in Constantinople. During the sack of Constantinople in 1204, crusaders carried off most of the saint's bones. They were enshrined in St. Peter's Basilica in Rome until 2004, when Pope John Paul II returned all but a small portion of the relics to Ecumenical Patriarch Bartholomew I. Saint Gregory's relics are enshrined in the Patriarchal Cathedral of St. George in the Phanar neighborhood of Istanbul, Turkey.

Gregory's father, Gregory the Elder, his mother, Nonna, his brother Caesarius and his sister Gorgona are all venerated as saints. Gregory was a priest and a bishop during an especially contentious period, when the Arian heresy was tearing the Church apart. He was a brilliant writer and preacher, and he drew upon these gifts to explain and defend orthodox doctrine, particularly regarding the Holy Trinity.

After years of religious disputes Gregory grew weary of debate. In 384 he retired from his diocese, moved to a house in the countryside, and took up gardening. For his magnificent theological works, the Church in the East reveres Gregory as one of the Three Holy Hierarchs, while the Church in the West venerates him as one of the Four Greek Doctors of the Church.

Feast day: January 2.

**Saint Gregory the Great (c. 540–604).** Saint Gregory's remains were moved several times in the old Basilica of St. Peter. In 1606 the pope's bones were placed inside a white marble sarcophagus and enshrined behind a gilded bronze grille in the altar of St. Gregory the Great in the Basilica of St. Peter. Rome's Basilica of St. Stephen Rotondo displays the carved white marble chair that served as Saint Gregory's throne.

In every respect Gregory I was a remarkable pope. With the emperor in Constantinople, Rome had become a backwater, and it had fallen to the popes to administer the city and the surrounding region. Gregory made peace with pagan barbarian chieftains and made friends of Catholic kings and nobles. He encouraged Benedictine monks to open schools and continue to copy ancient Greek and Roman as well as Christian texts. When he learned that the pagan king of Kent had a Catholic queen, he seized the opportunity and sent missionaries to England to begin the conversion of the island.

Gregory loved the liturgy, and although it would be going too far to say that he invented what we know as Gregorian chant, he did foster it and even arranged some chant for Roman choirs. Under Gregory, chant in Rome became an art. Many distinguished visitors to Rome from far-off lands returned home with books of chant for their choirs. Sometimes kings and bishops returned home with Roman singers who trained Frankish or Saxon choirs how to chant in the Roman style.

Saint Gregory the Great is the patron saint of choirboys, musicians, and singers. He is one of the patron saints of England and the West Indies. Feast day: September 3.

**Saint Gregory the Illuminator (c. 240–332).** The relics of Saint Gregory are scattered between Armenia and Italy. His left hand is preserved in Etchmiadzin Cathedral in Armenia; his right hand is venerated in the Cathedral of Saint Gregory the Illuminator in Antelias, Lebanon; more of his bones are enshrined in the Church of Saint Gregory the Armenian in Naples, Italy.

Legends regarding Saint Gregory could fill volumes. He may have been an Armenian, or perhaps he was a Parthian, from the region that is now northern Iran. He was raised a Christian in Caesarea, modern-day Kayseri, Turkey. At some point he was ordained a priest. In 301 he baptized Tiridates the Great, king of Armenia, an event that triggered the conversion of the entire Armenian nation. Armenia became the world's first Christian nation. In 302 Gregory was consecrated first Patriarch of Armenia.

Saint Gregory the Illuminator is one of the patron saints of Armenia. Feast day: September 30.

**Saint Helen or Helena (c. 249–c. 329).** In the Pio Clementino Museum at the Vatican is a massive red porphyry sarcophagus adorned with sculptures of victorious Roman legionnaires and their barbarian prisoners. This grand work of art was intended as the tomb chest of Saint Helen, but it is not known if her body ever rested inside it. The relics of Saint Helen are to be found in Rome's Basilica of St. Mary in Ara Coeli, in a shrine that resembles a circular Roman temple.

Helen was born in what is now northern Turkey; her parents were innkeepers. In 270 she met and married Constantius Chlorus, a goat herder's son who was an officer in the Roman army. Two years later Helen gave birth to a boy whom they named Constantine.

Constantius did well in the military; eventually he was appointed governor of Dalmatia (modern-day Croatia). When the co-emperors Diocletian and Maximian were searching for likely men to help them administer a portion of the empire, Constantius was one of the two they chose. The emperors thought so highly of Constantius that Maximian offered his stepdaughter Flavia to Constantius to be his wife. Putting ambition above sentiment, Constantius accepted the offer, divorced Helen, and married Flavia. No surviving record tells us what became of Helen between 292 when her husband of twenty-two years divorced her, and 312, when her son Constantine became emperor of Rome. With one exception: we do know that in 309 she became a Christian.

In 313, very likely because of his mother's influence, Constantine issued the Edict of Milan, which put an end to anti-Christian persecution in the empire and recognized and even gave favored status to the Church.

In 326 Helen went on a two-year pilgrimage to the Holy Land, where she discovered the Holy Sepulcher and the True Cross, as well as other sacred sites such as the cave in Bethlehem where Christ was born.

Constantine honored his mother by minting coins bearing her image, granting her the titles Empress and Augusta, renaming her birthplace Helenopolis, and presenting her with the Sessorian Palace in Rome as her residence.

Saint Helen is the patron saint of archaeologists, of difficult marriages, and of those who are divorced or divorcing. Feast day: August 18.

**Saint Hermann Joseph (1150–1241).** Saint Herman Joseph is buried in the church of Steinfeld Abbey in Germany. His relics lie beneath a white marble sculpture of the saint with the Child Jesus in his arms.

It is said that while he was still a boy Hermann Joseph had mystical experiences: the Christ Child played with him, and one winter, when Hermann Joseph's parents could not afford to buy him shoes, the Blessed Virgin supplied the money.

Hermann Joseph joined the Norbertines and was ordained a priest. He received visions of Our Lady all his life. In his sermons and in private conversations he encouraged devotion to Mary; he also wrote prayers and hymns in her honor.

Feast day: April 7.

**Saint Hilary of Poitiers (c. 315–368).** In 1572 a mob of Huguenot vandals stormed the Church of St. Hilary in Poitiers, smashing works of art and destroying the relics of Saint Hilary. Some fragments survived and these are preserved in a shrine in the crypt. The Cathedral of Notre Dame at Le Puy also claims to possess some relics of Saint Hilary. The saint's portable altar stone, on which he celebrated Mass during journeys, is preserved in the Church of St. Hilary in Faye-l'Abbesse, France.

Hilary's family worshipped the Roman gods, but at school his studies in philosophy led him to the conclusion that there could be only one God. When he chanced upon the New Testament, the prologue to Saint John's Gospel, "In the beginning was the Word, and the Word was with God, and the Word was God," convinced him to become a Christian.

In 353 he was chosen to be bishop of Poitiers; the rest of his life would be consumed with the theological controversy between Catholics and Arians. When the emperor threw his support behind the Arians, many Catholic bishops joined the Arians or equivocated on the subject of the nature of Jesus Christ and the Holy Trinity. At one point Hilary was the only champion of orthodox

Catholicism in the West—even Pope Liberius had prevaricated to appease the emperor. Saint Jerome later wrote of this period, "The world groaned in amazement that it had become Arian."

Under Hilary and his disciple Saint Martin of Tours, Gaul (modern-day France and part of western Germany) became a bastion of Catholicism. At a synod the Gallic bishops repented their flirtation with Arianism and recommitted themselves to teaching the Nicene Creed—putting an end to the encroachment of the Arian heresy into Western Europe.

Saint Hilary is invoked against snakebite. Feast day: January 13.

**Saint Hildegarde of Bingen (1098–1179).** Since the seventeenth century the relics of Saint Hildegarde have been venerated in the parish church of Eibingen, Germany. In the 1929, to commemorate the 750th anniversary of Hildegarde's death, the remains were placed in a new gilded reliquary.

From the age of three Hildegarde received visions and private revelations from God, yet for most of her life she was confused, even embarrassed, by these signs of special grace. At age forty-two, when she was abbess of a convent in Disibodenberg, Germany, she spoke of her visions to her confessor and asked his advice. The monk instructed her to write down everything she had received from God; when Hildegarde protested that her Latin was not up to the task, the monk supplied her with secretaries to whom she could dictate her visions.

The result was a three-volume work known as *Scivias,* or *Know the Ways of the Lord.* The books are full of private revelations of God's love for humankind, as well as prophecies and apocalyptic visions. Hildegarde agreed to submit the *Scivias* to the archbishop of Mainz for review, and the archbishop passed the volumes on to Blessed Pope Eugenius III, who convened a commission to study the work and interview Hildegarde. One of the commissioners, Saint Bernard of Clairvaux, offered an enthusiastic endorsement of *Scivias.* Ultimately Eugenius sent a personal letter to Hildegarde, praising her work but cautioning her to be on guard against the sin of pride.

*Scivias* released a creative flood in Hildegarde. She wrote lengthy works on natural history and medicine. She wrote about saints' lives. She composed hymns for her nuns to sing in the choir. She even wrote morality plays.

Saint Hildegarde of Bingen is the patron saint of philologists. Feast day: September 17.

**Holy Bench (first century).** Across the street from Rome's Basilica of St. John Lateran stands a small building that contains the Scala Sancta, or Holy Stairs, and the Sancta Sanctorum, or Holy of Holies Chapel. Embedded in the chapel wall is a glass and gilded bronze case that contains a large piece of wood identified by the inscription as part of the bench upon which Jesus Christ sat during the Last Supper. It is not known when the relic came to Rome, nor who donated it to the pope.

**Holy Blood of Bruges (first mentioned in Bruges historical records in 1256).** This cloth is said to be a cloth with which Saint Joseph of Arimathea wiped the blood from the body of Christ before burial. According to the traditional account, during the Second Crusade the king of Jerusalem, Baldwin III, gave the relic to his cousin the Count of Flanders, Diederik van de Elzas. Count Diederik brought the relic to Bruges on April 7, 1150. Given the absence of twelfth-century texts that mention such a significant relic, some historians have speculated that the relic was looted during the sack of Constantinople in 1204 and eventually made its way to Bruges.

The reliquary is a crystal tube with golden angels at each end. Inside one may see clearly a stained cloth. The Holy Blood is enshrined in a silver baroque reliquary in the richly decorated

This gold, jasper, and enamel reliquary was made to hold a few drops of the Blood of Jesus Christ. During the sack of Constantinople in 1204, Venetians stole the relic and presented it to St. Mark's Basilica in Venice. TREASURY OF SAN MARCO, VENICE, ITALY/ THE BRIDGEMAN ART LIBRARY

Upper Chapel of the Little Basilica of the Holy Blood. Every Friday the relic is brought out for the veneration of the faithful.

Feast day: July 1, Feast of the Precious Blood. Every year on Ascension Thursday, forty days after Easter, the bishop of Bruges carries the relic in a grand procession through the streets of the old city.

## Holy Face of Lucca (earliest date of veneration, eleventh century?).

This much-revered crucifix is found in the Cathedral of St. Martin in Lucca, Italy.

Saint Nicodemus was a secret disciple of Christ (see John 3) who helped Saint Joseph of Arimathea remove the Lord's body from the cross. According to legend, he later carved a crucifix. Anxious that he would not be able to produce a perfect portrait of Jesus, he put off carving the face. One night as Nicodemus slept, an angel came down from heaven and carved the face of Christ for him.

The crucifix remained hidden in the Holy Land, where Bishop Gualfredo discovered it in 782 and brought it home to Lucca, installing it in the Cathedral of St. Martin.

The opportunity to gaze upon the actual face of Christ (the sacred image became known as "the Holy Face" not "the Holy Crucifix") drew pilgrims from across Europe. The figure is larger than life, fully dressed in regal robes. On major feast days the figure of Christ is dressed in black velvet and adorned with a golden crown, collar, and belt.

Feast days of the Holy Cross: September 13 and 14; May 3. Feast day of Saint Nicodemus: August 3.

**Holy Grail.** Typically the Holy Grail is thought to refer to the cup or chalice that Christ used at the Last Supper. In fact, the term "Grail" comes from pre-Christian Celtic legends about a cup or cauldron or even platter that provides a never-ending supply of good things to eat. It may have been the King Arthur legend, with its mystical tales of the Knights of the Round Table's quest for the Holy Grail, that acted as a transition, shifting the identity of the Grail from a thing out of pagan Celtic folklore to one of Christianity's most sacred relics. It is not much of a leap from a vessel that supplies an abundance of good things to the chalice of the Eucharist, the source of boundless graces.

The two most prominent claimants to the Holy Grail are Glastonbury Abbey in England and Valencia Cathedral in Spain.

A twelfth-century French poet, Robert de Boron, either invented the story of Joseph of Arimathea carrying the Grail to Britain, or wrote down an existing legend. In this story, which was set in about the year 63, Joseph travels to Britain with the Holy Grail as well as two cruets filled with Christ's blood, which he collected as Our Lord hung dying on the cross. At Glastonbury Joseph built a chapel and placed the Grail and the cruets within it. Over the centuries the relics were lost, although another version says that Joseph buried the Grail on a hill known as Glastonbury Tor. A spring, known as Chalice Well, marks the site.

The Cathedral of Valencia displays for veneration a small agate cup, about seven inches high, mounted on a gold base. This is the Holy Chalice said to have been used by Christ at the Last Supper. According to legend, it was brought from Jerusalem to Rome and was used by Saint Peter and many other early popes when they said Mass. Another legend claims that about the year 258, during Emperor Valerian's persecution of Christians, the Roman deacon Saint Lawrence sent the Holy Chalice with other treasures of the Church to Spain for safekeeping. Eventually the chalice found its way into the treasury of Valencia Cathedral.

Both Pope John Paul II and Pope Benedict XVI have used the Holy Chalice to say Mass during visits to Valencia, although using the Chalice at Mass is not equivalent to issuing a formal statement of its authenticity.

Feast day: The Feast of Holy Chalice is celebrated annually in Valencia on the last Thursday of October.


**The Holy House of Loreto (shrine established before 1472).** Loreto is a small city south of Ancona, Italy, not far from the Adriatic Sea. Inside Loreto's grand basilica is a small stone building measuring 31 by 13 feet, which tradition says is the house of Jesus, Mary, and Joseph.

How did the home of the Holy Family wind up in Italy? According to the story, in 1291, as Muslim armies reconquered the Holy Land from the crusaders, angels descended from heaven to Nazareth, lifted the Holy House from its foundations, and carried it to the town of Tersato in what is now Croatia. Three years later, as the Muslim forces moved into the Balkans, the angels returned and transported the Holy House to Italy, to a wooded hill near the town of Recanati, about ten miles west of Loreto. During the next year angels relocated the Holy House three more times before finally depositing it in Loreto, where it has remained ever since.

Over the centuries at least fifty popes have visited the shrine, or granted spiritual privileges to pilgrims who come to pray there. Blessed John XXIII made a pilgrimage to Loreto in October 1962 as the world's Catholic bishops were convening for the first session of the Second Vatican Council. John Paul II visited Loreto three times during his twenty-six-year pontificate. It may be splitting hairs, but papal visits and papal blessings do not necessarily mean papal endorsement of the legend of the Holy House. Pope Julius II, the warrior pope who bullied Michelangelo into painting the Sistine Chapel ceiling, was no religious sentimentalist. In 1507, as he was about to sign a document granting yet another privilege to the shrine, he read the description of the angelic transportation of the Holy House and inserted the phrase "as it is piously believed and reported."

There are problems with the tradition. Father Herbert Thurston, S.J., a respected scholar of the saints and the supernatural, was a man who could tell the difference between faith and credulity. In a lengthy article on the Holy House he wrote for the 1913 *Catholic Encyclopedia,* he threw the weight of his expertise on the side of the Church historian Canon Ulysses Chevalier, who in 1906 argued that the story of the Holy House has no historical basis. Canon Chevalier found that none of the early Christian and medieval descriptions of holy sites in the Holy Land tell of pilgrims to Nazareth visiting the house of the Holy Family (in fact, the site pointed out as the home of Jesus, Mary, and Joseph was a grotto or cave); Holy Land chronicles and other accounts for the year 1291 do not record that a house or shrine in Nazareth vanished; Italian documents of the fourteenth century mention a church and a wonder-working image of the Virgin and Child in Loreto but say nothing about the home of the Holy Family being there; finally, the earliest account of the miraculous transportation of the Holy House dates from 1472—178 years after angels are supposed to have set the house down in Loreto.

Purists will argue that the Loreto shrine should be closed or dismantled. The Catholic Church's policy is more tolerant. Although it is unlikely that the little stone house inside the basilica is authentically that of the Holy Family, the pilgrims' devotion to the Holy Family is genuine, and from the Church's standpoint sincere religious devotion is reason enough to keep the shrine open. The much-loved Litany of the Blessed Virgin, or Litany of Loreto, was composed at the shrine.

Our Lady of Loreto is the patron saint of aviators and air travel. Feast day: December 10.

**Holy Innocents (first century).** Bodies of the infant boys of Bethlehem and its vicinity murdered by the soldiers of King Herod are included among the relic collections of the Roman basilicas of St. Paul Outside the Walls and St. Mary Major, the Church of St. Justina in Padua, Italy, and the cathedrals of Lisbon and Milan.

Saint Matthew's Gospel (Matthew 2:16–18) is our only source for the story of the Holy Innocents, and it does not mention how many baby boys in Bethlehem were slaughtered by Herod's soldiers, but that has not stopped individuals from making estimates. The Greek liturgy gives the number as 14,000; the Syrians say 64,000; while in medieval Europe some took their inspiration from the Book of Revelation and asserted that Herod's men killed 144,000 children. Given that Bethlehem was a small town, it is likely that there were about a dozen boys two years or younger.

The Holy Innocents are the patron saints of babies and choirboys. Feast day: December 28.

**Holy Manger (first venerated in the fourth or seventh century).** Displayed in a tiny chapel below the high altar of Rome's Basilica of St. Mary Major is a large gold, silver, and crystal urn said to contain boards from the manger in which the Blessed Virgin

Mary placed the newborn Christ Child. The Romans often refer to the relic as the Sacra Cunambulum, the Sacred Crib.

Exactly when the relic arrived in Rome is uncertain: some claim that Saint Helen brought the pieces of the manger back from her pilgrimage to the Holy Land in 326–328; others say the relic arrived in Rome during the reign of Pope Theodore I, sometime between 642 and 649.

The relic consists of five boards of sycamore wood, which, sadly, are beginning to deteriorate. Traditionally the relic is put on view for the veneration of the faithful from Christmas Midnight Mass until January 6, the Feast of the Epiphany. In 2007 the administrators of St. Mary Major agreed that the relic was too fragile to be moved and so it remained in its chapel.

**Holy Nails.** According to the 1911 edition of the *Catholic Encyclopedia,* there are "thirty or more holy nails" in various collections across Europe. The most famous may be the one displayed in

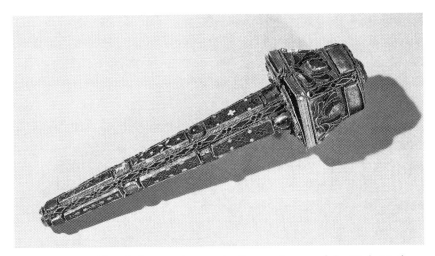

Encased in a gold and cloisonné enamel reliquary is one of the Holy Nails used at Christ's crucifixion. The relic has been in the possession of the Cathedral of Trier, Germany, since about 830. Bildarchiv Preussischer Kulturbesitz/Art Resource, NY

the Relic Chamber of the Basilica of the Holy Cross in Jerusalem in Rome. According to legend, when Saint Helen discovered the True Cross she also found the Holy Nails. Exactly how many she found—three or four—is open to dispute. One legend tells how, on her return voyage, she calmed a storm at sea by tossing one of the Nails overboard. Another story claims that Emperor Constantine used one or two of the Holy Nails as a bridle for his horse, which has struck many readers as odd if not sacrilegious.

**Holy Prepuce, or Foreskin, of Jesus Christ (first reference 800).** According to legend, in 800, as a token of his appreciation for having been crowned the first Holy Roman Emperor, Charlemagne presented to Pope Leo III the relic of the foreskin of Christ, which he had received as a gift from the Byzantine empress Irene. For centuries the relic was cherished in the Sancta Sanctorum, the Holy of Holies, the chapel in the Lateran Palace.

In 1527 an army of German Lutherans and Spanish Catholics under the command of Emperor Charles V captured Rome. Pope Clement VII escaped to the safety of Castel Sant'Angelo, but the inhabitants of Rome endured weeks of rape, torture, and murder, and every church and chapel in the city was looted. A German soldier who participated in the sack of the Lateran Palace stole the silver reliquary chest that contained the Holy Prepuce. Shortly thereafter he deserted and was making his way north, back home, when he was seized and imprisoned as a marauder in the village of Calcata, forty miles north of Rome.

What became of the German looter is unknown, but the villagers of Calcata claim he left behind the relic, which became their town's greatest treasure. Every year it was carried in procession on January 1, the Feast of the Circumcision of the Lord, then exposed in the village church for public veneration.

On January 1, 1983, Don Dario Magnoni, the parish priest, announced that the relic was gone, stolen from his house, where he had imagined it would be safe. The identity of the thieves remains a mystery and the relic has never been recovered.

During the Middle Ages other towns claimed to possess the Holy Foreskin, including Chartres, Metz, Conques, Antwerp, Hildesheim, and Santiago de Compostela.

Feast of the Circumcision of the Lord: January 1.

**Holy Robe (earliest surviving written reference, twelfth century).** The seamless robe of Christ, woven by the Blessed Virgin Mary, worn by Jesus to his crucifixion, the robe for which the soldiers threw dice at the foot of the cross, is enshrined in a baroque chapel behind the high altar of the Cathedral of St. Peter in Trier, Germany. The Russian Orthodox believe a portion of the Holy Robe is preserved at the Cathedral of the Dormition in Moscow.

According to legend, Saint Helen discovered the Holy Robe during her 324–328 pilgrimage to the Holy Land and presented it to St. Peter's in Trier (where she had once lived), the oldest church in Germany, built in 326 by Emperor Constantine, Helen's son.

The relic was venerated at least as early as the twelfth century, but apparently was forgotten until 1512, when the high altar was opened and the relic was found inside. Given its fragile condition, the Holy Robe is no longer exhibited to the public but is kept sealed in its reliquary.

**Holy Sepulcher.** Jerusalem's Church of the Holy Sepulcher stands over Christianity's two most sacred sites—the mount of Calvary where Jesus Christ was crucified and died, and the tomb, the Holy Sepulcher, in which he was buried and from which he rose from the dead.

On the first Good Friday these sites were outside the city walls in an abandoned quarry that was being used as a cemetery. History tells us that the Christians of Jerusalem revered the site and that the emperor Hadrian was aware of this: in 135 he had a temple dedicated to Venus built over the place. In 326, when Saint Helen came to Jerusalem to find Calvary and Our Lord's tomb, she tore down Hadrian's temple and dug beneath it—the first archaeological excavation of the site. Study continued in the twentieth century, leading Dan Bahat, former city archaeologist of Jerusalem, to state in *Biblical Archaeology Review,* "We may not be absolutely certain that the site of the Holy Sepulcher Church is the site of Jesus' burial, but we have no other site that can lay a claim nearly as weighty, and we really have no reason to reject the authenticity of the site."

Amid the labyrinth of chapels and shrines within the church are the two most important relics. Near the church's entrance a flight of stairs leads up to the Rock of Calvary. In the center of the church is the tomb itself.

**Holy Spear or Lance (earliest reference 570).** Saint John's Gospel records that after Jesus Christ died on the cross, "One of the soldiers pierced his side with a spear and at once there came out blood and water" (John 19:34). Saint Antoninus of Piacenza, an Italian pilgrim traveling in the late sixth century, is the first to record that the church on Mount Zion in Jerusalem preserved "the lance with which [Christ] was struck in the side." By the eighth century pilgrims to the Holy Land stop mentioning the Holy Spear; what became of the relic Antoninus saw is unknown. In 1492 Sultan Bayazid of Constantinople sent to Pope Innocent VIII a spear head that he said had been part of the relic collection of the Byzantine emperors. This relic is kept in St. Peter's Basilica.

There are other Holy Spears that are said to be the one that pierced Our Lord's side.

In 1098 during the First Crusade a French soldier named Peter Bartholomew had visions of Saint Andrew in which the apostle revealed to him that the Holy Spear was buried beneath the floor of the Church of St. Peter in Antioch. After the crusaders captured the city, one of the commanders, Count Raymond of St. Gilles, authorized an excavation in the church during which Bartholomew said he found the lance head. This Holy Spear is preserved in the Treasury of Etchmiadzin Cathedral in Armenia.

About the year 950 the Holy Roman Emperor Otto I acquired a relic said to be the Holy Spear, and it differs from other claimants: hammered into the blade of the spear is a spike said to be one of the nails used to crucify Christ. This relic is part of the collection of Vienna's Hofburg Palace. In 2003 a British metallurgist, Robert Feather, was permitted to run a series of tests on the Spear. He dated it to the seventh century and concluded that the iron spike is "consistent" in size and shape with other Roman nails of the first century AD.

**Holy Stairs, or Scala Sancta (first century?).** Tradition says that during her pilgrimage to the Holy Land in 326–328, Saint Helen discovered in Jerusalem the staircase from the palace of Pontius Pilate: Jesus Christ ascended and descended these stairs when he was tried before the Roman governor. The staircase is found today in the remnant of Rome's Lateran Palace, once the residence of the pope. The twenty-eight white marble steps are sheathed in wood. Pilgrims may ascend the Holy Stairs only on their knees; they are encouraged to pray an Our Father on each step. For those who are not equal to such effort, there are flights of stairs flanking the Scala Sancta.

**Saint Hubert (c. 656–727).** Initially Saint Hubert was buried in the Church of St. Peter in Liege, Belgium. In 825 his body was translated to an abbey in the forest of Ardennes, where he is said to have experienced the vision that converted him, and where he worked for many years as a missionary. During the Reformation the saint's relics disappeared, either destroyed by the Huguenots or hidden by the monks and their location forgotten. A few fragments of Saint Hubert's relics have been collected and are venerated in the church of St. Hubert's Abbey at Poix St. Hubert, Belgium.

Legend tells us that as a young man Hubert was indifferent to religion. One Good Friday, rather than go to church, he went hunting in the forest of Ardennes. He saw a magnificent stag and gave chase. Just as he was about to overtake the animal it turned toward him. Between the stag's antlers was a crucifix that spoke to him. "Hubert," said the figure of Christ, "unless you turn to the Lord you will fall into Hell."

Hubert become a priest and eventually was named bishop of Liege in what is now Belgium. He was especially active as a missionary in the Ardennes, a region where Christianity was unknown.

Saint Hubert is the patron saint of hunters, forest workers, and dogs. Feast day: November 3.


**Saint Hyacinth (1185–1257).** The saint's body is enshrined in the St. Hyacinth Chapel of the Church of the Holy Trinity in Cracow, Poland.

Hyacinth was one of the first Poles to join the Dominicans; in fact, he was received into the order by Saint Dominic. He became a zealous missionary, carrying the faith to pagans in Prussia, Lithuania, and Scandinavia, and establishing Dominican priories in the Ukraine in the hope of bringing Orthodox Christians back to the Catholic Church.

Legend says that in 1240 Hyacinth was at the Dominican priory in Kiev when the Mongols stormed the city. He took the ciborium containing the Blessed Sacrament from the tabernacle and prepared to flee the city when he heard the statue of the Blessed Mother speak to him: "Hyacinth, you have taken my Son, but you leave me behind?" Hyacinth returned, lifted the heavy marble sculpture from its altar, and found that it was weightless. With both the Blessed Sacrament and the statue of Our Lady he escaped safely to Poland.

Saint Hyacinth is one of the patron saints of Cracow, Poland, and Lithuania. Poles also venerate him as the patron saint of pierogi. Feast day: August 17.

**Saint Ignatius of Antioch (died c. 107).** A deacon named Philo carried the fragments of Saint Ignatius's relics back to Antioch, where they were buried in the Daphne suburb. In the fifth century Emperor Theodosius II moved the relics to a church he dedicated to the martyr inside the city walls. In 637 the relics were taken to Rome and placed in the Church of St. Clement before the high altar. A stone slab bears the inscription HIC REQUIESCUNT CORPORA SS. CLEMENTIS PAPÆ ET IGNATII, or "Here lie the bodies of Saint Clement the Pope and Saint Ignatius."

Ignatius was converted to Christianity by Saint John the Evangelist. About the year 70 he became bishop of Antioch. Ignatius was such a prominent leader of the Church that during Emperor Trajan's persecution of the Church the local governor had him sent to Rome for execution.

Along the way he wrote letters to various Christian communities in Asia Minor, the Christians of Rome, and to his friend and fellow martyr Saint Polycarp—all of these letters have survived.

He had been sentenced to be thrown to the lions. Writing to the Roman Christians, Ignatius said, "I am God's grain, and I am ground by the teeth of wild beasts, that I may be found the pure bread of Christ."

Feast day: October 17.

**Saint Ignatius of Loyola (1491–1556).** At his death Saint Ignatius of Loyola was buried in the little Church of Our Lady of the Way, the Jesuit's first church in Rome. When the church was torn down and the Church of Il Gesù, or Jesus, was built in its place, Saint Ignatius's relics were transferred to a magnificent tomb on the left side of the church. The life-size silver sculpture of Saint Ignatius that surmounts the tomb is a replica—the original was stolen by Napoleon in 1798 and melted down for bullion.

As the founder of the Jesuits, Saint Ignatius of Loyola is one of the most influential saints in Catholic history. He started his order in 1534, when corruption within the Church and the Protestant revolt were tearing Christendom apart. Ignatius and his Jesuits offered a new model of Catholic priesthood: men who were intensely trained in theology, in the art of debate and of preaching and in explaining and defending the faith. They went out as new missionaries to Europe, encouraging Catholics in their faith and reconciling Protestants to Rome. They founded schools that were recognized as the best in Europe; served as advisors to kings, noblemen, and popes; and traveled as missionaries to every corner of the globe.

As the son of a Basque nobleman, Ignatius had longed for a life of adventure and romance, of fighting heroically, selflessly, in some great cause. He had sought such glory as a knight until, at a petty battle at Navarre, a cannonball shattered one of his legs. During his long and painful recuperation at his family's castle, Ignatius read the only two books his parents possessed—a life of Christ and a collection of stories of the saints. By the time he could walk again he had changed the direction of his life: he would serve God and the Blessed Virgin, he would spend his life in defense of the faith, and he would make any sacrifice so that the message of the Gospel might be known throughout the world. He abandoned the selfish ideal of seeking glory for himself and lived instead "for the greater glory of God," which became the motto of the Society of Jesus.

Saint Ignatius of Loyola is the patron saint of the Jesuits, of retreatants, and of those who use the Spiritual Exercises. Feast day: July 31.


**Blessed Imelda Lambertini (1322–1333).** The body of Blessed Imelda is encased in a glass casket in the Church of San Sigismondo in Bologna, Italy.

Imelda was born in Bologna, Italy, the daughter of the count and countess Lambertini. At age nine she was sent to the local convent school operated by Dominican nuns. The religiously precocious girl told the nuns and their chaplain of her profound longing for the Blessed Sacrament, but in the fourteenth century First Holy Communion was delayed until a child was at least fourteen years old. The chaplain refused to make an exception for Imelda.

On Ascension Thursday 1333 Imelda attended Mass with her fellow students in the nuns' chapel, as usual. After Mass she stayed behind to pray before the tabernacle. As she prayed a Host was seen hovering above her. Many of the nuns witnessed the mystical event, as did the chaplain who hurried to the tabernacle, removed the ciborium, and gave Imelda her First Communion. Soon thereafter she died, it is said in an ecstasy of holy joy.

Blessed Imelda Lambertini is the patron saint of First Communicants. Feast day: May 12.


**Saint Irene (died c. 300).** The bones of Saint Irene were enshrined in a church dedicated to her in the fourth century in Constantinople. Part of her relics were taken from their shrine in 1204 when crusaders ransacked the city, and the rest of the relics were lost after the Turks conquered Constantinople in 1453. At some point during the nineteenth century the skull of Saint Irene was sent from Rome to the Sisters of St. Joseph in Carondolet, Missouri, a convent that had a large relic collection. In 1997 two Russian Orthodox priests, Very Reverend Martin Swanson and Father Joachim Parr, approached the sisters and asked them to return the skull of Saint Irene to the Orthodox, who greatly revere this martyr. After a period of discussion and consultation with canon lawyers, the sisters presented the relic to Father Martin, who enshrined it in St. Basil the Great Orthodox Church in St. Louis, Missouri.

Many legends about Saint Irene have sprung up in the East. All we know for certain regarding this martyr is that she was burned at the stake in Thessaloniki with two fellow Christians, Saint Irenaeus and Saint Peregrinus.

Saint Irene is the patron saint of peace. Feast day: May 5.


**Irish Martyrs (died 1579–1654).** Blessed Dermot O'Hurley (1530–1584) was buried in the Church of St. Kevin, Dublin. Blessed Maurice Kenraghty (died 1585) was buried behind the high altar of the Franciscan church in Clonmel. Catholics recovered the body of Blessed Dominic Collins (1566–1602) and buried it secretly in Youghal; the location has been forgotten. Presentation Convent on George's Hill, Dublin, marks the place of Blessed Conor O'Devaney's (c. 1532–1612) and Blessed Patrick O'Loughran's (c. 1577–1612) martyrdom; it is believed their bodies were buried in the church or churchyard of St. Kevin. Relatives of Blessed Francis Taylor (c. 1550–1621) buried him in the family tomb at St. Audoen's Church, Dublin. The body of Blessed Margaret Ball (c. 1515–1584) was given to her family, who buried it in the churchyard of St. Audoen in Dublin. Blessed Terence O'Brien (1601–1651) was buried on the grounds of the Dominican priory in Limerick; the site is occupied today by St. Mary's Convent of Mercy. Over the centuries the locations of the graves of Blessed Patrick O'Healy (c. 1543–1579), Blessed Conn O'Rourke (1549–1579), Blessed Peter Higgins (c. 1600–1642), Blessed John Kearney (1619–1653), Blessed William Tirry (1608–1654), Blessed Matthew Lambert (died 1581), Blessed Robert Tyler of Myler (died 1581), Blessed Edward Cheevers (died 1581), and Blessed Patrick Cavanagh (died 1581) have been forgotten.

Beginning in the nineteenth century the Irish hierarchy authorized investigations into the causes of almost three hundred Irish men and women—clergy, religious, and laity—who laid down their lives rather than renounce their Catholic faith. Assembling and assessing documentation for so many individuals proved unwieldy in the extreme, and so in the twentieth century the number was reduced to seventeen. In 1992 Pope John Paul II beatified this group. Among the most prominent are:

**Blessed Dermot O'Hurley.** While Father O'Hurley was studying law at the university of Louvain in Belgium the pope named him archbishop of Cashel. In 1583 the archbishop was betrayed by an informer. In Dublin Castle he was horribly tortured to force him to admit that he had returned to Ireland to overthrow the English government. Archbishop O'Hurley denied this charge and was hanged in Hoggen Green, Dublin.

**Blessed Margaret Ball.** She sheltered Catholic bishops and priests in her house in Dublin. In spite of his mother's example Margaret's son Walter joined the Protestant Church of Ireland. When he was elected mayor of Dublin he had his mother arrested. As she would not abandon her Catholic faith, Walter had Margaret imprisoned in a windowless cell. She died there three years later.

**Blessed Peter Higgins.** He was prior of the Dominicans at Naas. During the Uprising of 1641 he sheltered both Catholics and Protestants. In 1642 when the rebellion was put down, Father Higgins was arrested. The Protestant earl of Ormond, who knew of the prior's good works, tried to save him, but Father Higgins was condemned without trial. At the place of execution one of the men Father Higgins had sheltered tried to stop the proceedings. "This man is innocent," he cried, "this man is innocent! He saved my life." It did no good; Peter Higgins was hanged.

Feast day: June 20.

**Saint Isidore of Seville (c. 560–636).** The relics of Saint Isidore are preserved in the Cathedral of Murcia, Spain, along with the relics of his brother Saint Fulgentius and his sister Saint Florentina.

For many generations Isidore's family had served as administrators of the Roman Empire in Spain. By the sixth century, the empire had collapsed, the provinces were in the hands of barbarian tribes, and the entire infrastructure of Roman society was vanishing—its libraries, its roads, its aqueducts, its laws and literature. In a desperate effort to halt the decay, Isidore began to write a massive twenty-volume encyclopedia of all existing knowledge. He included all the arts and sciences; the engineering that made aqueducts and the arch possible; medicine, metallurgy, and agriculture; even how to build furniture. And he urged his people to learn to read. "When we pray," he said, "we talk to God; when we read, God talks to us."

Saint Isidore of Seville is the patron saint of the Internet. Feast day: April 4.

**Saint Isidore the Farmer (c. 1070–1130).** Saint Isidore and his wife, Saint Mary de la Cabeza (died c. 1175), were buried in their parish church, San Andres, in Madrid. In the seventeenth century a chapel was built on the site of their house. The saintly couple's relics now lie in the Church of San Isidro el Real in Madrid.

Isidore and Mary were tenant farmers on a nobleman's estate outside Madrid, which in the twelfth century was a small town. Every day Isidore rose early to attend Mass before going to work in the fields, and as he worked he prayed. Year after year, Isidore and Mary's tenant farm yielded three times the harvest of any other farm on the estate (their neighbors attributed the bounty to angels they said they had seen plowing Isidore's fields).

For five hundred years Isidore remained a local saint. Then, in 1615, King Philip III of Spain fell gravely ill. He invoked Saint Isidore and was healed. In thanksgiving for the cure Philip petitioned the pope to canonize Isidore formally; the king's request was granted in 1622, and Isidore was declared a saint in the same ceremony with Ignatius of Loyola, Francis Xavier, Teresa of Avila, and Philip Neri.

Saint Isidore is the patron saint of farmers and of the United

States National Rural Life Conference. He is also one of the patron saints of the cities of Madrid and Seville in Spain. Feast day: May 15.

**Saint Jadwiga, or Hedwig, the Queen (1374–1399).** The white marble sarcophagus of Saint Jadwiga is found in the upper church of Wawel Cathedral in Cracow. Displayed nearby are the wooden scepter and orb with which she was buried—the queen pawned all her jewels and regalia to refound the Jagiellonian University. Also nearby, hanging over a side altar, is the Black Christ of Cracow, a thirteen-foot-tall crucifix that belonged to Jadwiga and before which she prayed daily. It is said that on several occasions the crucifix spoke to her.

Jadwiga was eleven years old when she became queen of Poland (actually, she was addressed as "king"). At the time Poland and its neighbor Lithuania were under attack by the Teutonic Knights, a German military order that sought to carve out an empire for itself along the Baltic Sea. Poland was not strong enough to defeat the Knights alone, so Jadwiga made the Lithuanian leader, Jogaila, an offer: they would marry, become joint rulers of Poland and Lithuania, and combine their forces to drive out the Teutonic Knights. Jadwiga had one condition: Jogaila and the people of Lithuania—who still worshipped their pagan gods—would convert to Catholicism.

Jogaila agreed. He came to Poland, immersed himself in a three-day crash course in Catholicism, was baptized, then married Jadwiga. Since few Polish priests spoke Lithiuanian, Wladyslaw (Jogaila's new Christian name) assisted the missionaries, explaining to his people the basics of the faith and teaching them the Apostles' Creed and the Our Father.

Jadwaiga is revered in Poland as the queen who saved the country from the Teutonic Knights, brought Christianity to Lithuania, and revived Polish culture and intellectual life by refounding the Jagiellonian University.

Saint Jadwiga is the patron saint of queens. Feast day: February 28.

**Saint James the Greater (died 44).** According to legend, after Saint James's martyrdom in Jerusalem, angels placed his body in a rudderless ship, which sailed to Spain where, after several other miraculous events, it was translated to Compostela. In 814 a hermit named Pelayo followed a star out to an empty field where he found the grave of Saint James. The chapel built over the apostle's relics was the forerunner of the magnificent cathedral that preserves the relics today.

Saint James, his brother Saint John, and Saint Peter composed the inner circle of Christ's apostles. These three witnessed marvels the other apostles did not see, including the Transfiguration and the raising of Jairus's daughter from the dead.

After the first Pentecost, when the other apostles began to carry the Gospel to far-off lands, James remained in Jerusalem preaching to the Jews. In 44, during King Herod Agrippa's persecution of the Church, James was arrested and beheaded. He was the first of the apostles to suffer martyrdom.

Saint James the Greater is invoked against arthritis and rheumatism. He is the patron saint of pilgrims and knights; the Spanish conquistadors took him as their patron. He is one of the patron saints of Spain, Chile, Guatemala, and Nicaragua. Feast day: July 25.

**Saint James the Lesser (died c. 62).** The relics of Saint James the Lesser are enshrined in the crypt of the Church of the Holy Apostles in Rome.

Saint James the Lesser was the son of Alphaeus, the brother of Saint Jude Thaddeus, and a cousin of Jesus. He is the James who is referred to in the Acts of the Apostles as the leader of the Church in Jerusalem. It is likely that he wrote the Epistle of James found in the New Testament, which asserts the essential role of good works in salvation: "Faith apart from works is barren" (James 2:20).

Saint James was martyred in Jerusalem. He was thrown off the pinnacle of the Temple, stoned, then finally beaten to death with a club.

Saint James the Lesser is the patron saint of pharmacists and hatmakers. He is one of the patron saints of Uruguay. Feast day: May 3.

**Saints Jason and Sosipatros.** For many centuries the relics of the two saints who evangelized Corfu were venerated in the island's Catholic Church of St. Francis. In 1945 Corfu's Catholic bishop gave the saints' relics to the Greek Orthodox bishop, who enshrined them in the Church of Sts. Jason and Sosipatros.

The New Testament tells us that Jason was a friend and disciple of Saint Paul (Acts 17:5–9 and Romans 16:21) and that Sosipatros was related to Paul. Tradition claims that both Jason and Sosipatros preached the Gospel on the island of Corfu and died there.

Feast days: Saint Jason, July 12; Saint Sosipatros June 25.

**Saint Jane Frances de Chantal (1572–1641).** Saint Jane Frances de Chantal is buried in the Church of the Visitation in Annecy, France, near the tomb of her friend and spiritual director, Saint Francis de Sales.

At age twenty-nine Baroness Jane Frances de Chantal was a widow with three small children to raise and her elderly father and father-in-law to care for. Tragedy drew her to the religious life, but her spiritual director, Saint Francis de Sales, reminded her that her primary obligations were to her family. He helped her develop a reasonable life of prayer and works of charity in the neighborhood without neglecting her duties as a mother, daughter, and daughter-in-law.

In 1610, when her children were grown, Jane founded a new religious order for women, the Order of the Visitation of Holy Mary. She and Francis de Sales imagined an order of sisters active in the world, but most bishops in France were shocked by the idea of nuns who left their convents. Jane and Francis modified their vision so that the Visitation nuns could have attached to their convents a school for girls, a home for poor widows, or a hospital. By the end of her life there were sixty-five Visitation convents in Europe, most of them in France. In 1799 three Visitation nuns opened the first Catholic girls school in the United States in the Georgetown neighborhood of Washington, DC.

Saint Jane Frances de Chantal is the patron saint of widows. Feast day: December 12 (August 12 in the United States).

**Saint Januarius (died c. 305).** The southern Italian cities of Naples and Benevento both claim that Saint Januarius, popularly known as San Gennaro, was their bishop. The question has never been resolved. What is certain, however, is that Bishop Januarius was beheaded during the persecution of the Roman emperor Diocletian (245–313). Tradition says that Christian women collected some of Januarius's blood in two glass vials and placed it in his tomb. Today the vials of blood and the bones of the saint are enshrined in the Cathedral of Saint Januarius in Naples.

The relic of Saint Januarius's blood is said to liquefy miraculously on three feast days every year: September 19, believed to be the day Januarius was martyred; December 16, the anniversary of the day the intercession of the saint saved Naples from an eruption of Mount Vesuvius; and the commemoration of the translation, or removal, of Saint Januarius's relics from his tomb to a shrine, which is celebrated on the Saturday before the first Sunday in May.

On each of these occasions a silver portrait bust of Saint Januarius containing his skull is placed upon the altar and a glass vial containing Saint Januarius's blood is given to the presiding prelate, usually the archbishop of Naples. The vial, measuring about four inches high and two and a quarter inches in diameter, is set in a metal reliquary. Through the glass one can see that the vial is a little more than half full of a solid, dark red mass. The archbishop carries the reliquary of the blood to the altar, holding it next to the silver bust of the saint. The miracle in which the solid mass becomes liquid has been known to occur in anything from two minutes to an hour. At the moment of liquefaction the archbishop exclaims, "The miracle has happened!" at which point the congregation sings the hymn of thanksgiving, *Te Deum*. Then everyone in the cathedral surges forward to the altar rail to kiss the glass vial containing the liquefied blood.

The first recorded instance of the miracle dates from 1389. Since then the miracle of the liquefaction has been unpredictable. Sometimes it does not liquefy at all, which the faithful interpret as a sign of the saint's displeasure: a popular story insists that the year the voters of Naples elected a Communist mayor, the blood remained solid. There have also been instances of the blood liquefying spontaneously, most famously in 1978 when the late archbishop of New York, Cardinal Terence Cooke, visited the cathedral. Cardinal Cooke, by the way, is himself a candidate for sainthood, which may explain why the blood liquefied during his visit.

To date there is no scientific explanation for the liquefaction. Study of the phenomenon is difficult because church authorities refuse to break the seal on the vial to permit scientists to collect a sample of the substance inside. One theory claims that the blood has been mixed with wax, which gives it a solid appearance. According to this theory, as the body heat of the congregation raises the temperature in the cathedral, the wax melts. Yet records show that the blood has liquefied when the temperature in the cathedral was as low as 60 degrees Fahrenheit. On another occasion, when it was nearly 80 degrees Fahrenheit inside the cathedral, it took 45 minutes for the solid inside the vial to become liquid. Furthermore, the wax theory does not explain why the liquefied blood appears to increase in volume inside the glass vial, nor why in some years the liquid bubbles as if it were boiling, while in other years it has the consistency of thick mud.

In 1926 immigrants from Naples living in New York City's Little Italy neighborhood organized the first festival in honor of San Gennaro. Since then the tradition has continued every September.

Today the Feast of San Gennaro is New York City's biggest annual outdoor fair with more than one million visitors cramming themselves into the narrow streets of Little Italy during the eleven-day festival. A few tiny fragments of Saint Januarius's bones are venerated in the neighborhood's Church of the Most Precious Blood, also known as the National Shrine of San Gennaro.

Saint Januarius is the patron saint of Naples and Benevento, Italy; he is invoked against volcanic eruptions. Primary feast day: September 19.

**Saint Jerome (347–420).** It is not known when the relics of Saint Jerome were translated from their grave in Bethlehem to Rome. For many centuries they have been buried in the Basilica of St. Mary Major, in the crypt of the Chapel of the Blessed Sacrament.

About the year 366 Jerome, a priest from what is now Slovenia, became secretary to Pope Saint Damasus I. The pope noticed very quickly that Jerome had a way with words. At the time the available editions of the Bible in Latin were poor, clumsy, often inaccurate translations of the original Hebrew and Greek texts. Damasus dreamed of a new translation of the Bible that would faithfully render the ancient texts into beautiful Latin—and it seemed to the pope that Jerome was the man for the job.

Within three years Jerome produced new Latin translations of the Psalms, the four Gospels, all of the epistles of the New Testament, and the Book of Revelation. Pope Damasus was delighted.

After Damasus's death in 384, Jerome moved to the Holy Land, to Bethlehem, where he learned Hebrew from a Jewish rabbi. It took Jerome twenty-six years to complete his translation of the Bible, which the Church called the *versio vulgata,* the commonly used translation, or popularly known as the Vulgate. It is still the definitive Latin edition of the Bible.

Saint Jerome is the patron saint of biblical scholars, translators, librarians, and archivists. Feast day: September 30.

**Saint Joan of Arc (1412–1431).** The house where Joan was born in Domrémy-la-Pucelle still stands, as does the village's Church of St. Remy where she went to Mass and where she received her First Holy Communion. Nearby is the Chapel of Our Lady of Bermont, where Joan often went to pray before a statue of the Blessed Mother. The statue has also survived and is venerated in the Basilica of St. Joan about a mile outside the village of Domrémy. The Metropolitan Museum of Art in New York City has a helmet that is said to have been worn by Joan.

After Joan's execution her remains were swept up and dumped in the river Seine. In 1867 in a Paris apothecary's shop a glass bottle was discovered bearing a handwritten label that read "Remains found under the stake of Joan of Arc, virgin of Orleans." Inside the bottle were three bones, some charred wood, and about six inches of linen cloth. The "relics" were put on display at the Chinon Castle museum. In 2006 Philippe Charlier, a forensic scientist at Raymond Poincaré Hospital in Garches near Paris, received permission to open the bottle and examine its contents. He found that one of the bones was a human rib, another was a cat femur. Through carbon-14 dating Charlier determined that the bones and the wood dated from the third to sixth centuries B.C. Residue on the linen was consistent with the types of coatings brushed onto Egyptian mummy wrappings. Taken together, Charlier concluded the bottle's contents were actually fragments of a mummified human and cat, with a piece of wrapping linen and a chunk of the wooden mummy case.

We know more about Joan of Arc than we do about any other individual from the Middle Ages. At the beginning of her mission she was interviewed at length by a panel of churchmen, and the transcript of that examination has survived. So has the transcript of her trial. Furthermore, interviews with Joan's relatives, friends, and comrades recorded at the time when her case was being re-examined by the Church have also come down to us. What emerges from all these documents is a portrait of a forthright, devoutly religious young woman who believed absolutely in the veracity of her visions and the righteousness of her cause.

Joan is unusual in another sense as well: she is the only saint who was executed by men claiming to represent the Catholic Church. Five bishops, three abbots, seven physicians, forty-eight doctors of theology, forty-two doctors of canon and civil law; and fifty-five priests, lay brothers, and clerics were assembled to hear and judge Joan's case, but it was a show trial nonetheless. The presiding judge, Bishop Pierre Cauchon of Beauvais, along with all the other senior churchmen in the courtroom, were collaborators whose primary loyalty was to the king of England, not the pope in Rome. The court would not permit Joan to be represented by counsel, nor to call witnesses to testify in her defense, nor even to have one of the court's lawyers explain difficult questions of law and theology put to her during her trial.

The verdict was a foregone conclusion: Cauchon and his fellow judges found Joan guilty of heresy and witchcraft. On May 30, 1431, Cauchon turned Joan over to the secular authorities, who burned her at the stake in the marketplace of Rouen.

Saint Joan of Arc is the patron saint of the Women's Army Corps (WACs) and Women Appointed for Voluntary Emergency Service (WAVES). She is the patron saint of those who have been injured by the Church, and she is one of the patron saints of France. Feast day: May 30.

**Saint Joachim (first century).** In Jerusalem in the fourth century a church dedicated to either Saint Anne or Saint Mary the Blessed Mother was built over the site of the home of Saints Anne and Joachim. In the crypt were the tombs of the Blessed Virgin's parents. The relics of Saint Joachim disappeared about the year 890, when Muslim authorities converted the church into a madrassa, or school. Archaeologists uncovered the crypt and the remains of the tombs in 1889.

The Gospels do not mention the parents of the Blessed Virgin Mary, but an apocryphal work, *The Protoevangelium of James*, written about the year 150, tells us the story of Saint Joachim and Saint Anne.

They lived in Jerusalem and after many years of married life they still had no children. One day when Joachim took an offering to the Temple one of the worshippers mocked him for being child-less. Humiliated, Joachim left the city and went to the fields where his hired men were watching his flocks of sheep. There an angel appeared to him. "Joachim!" the angel said. "The Lord has heard your prayer. Go home, for your wife Anne shall conceive."

Meanwhile an angel had brought the same message to Saint Anne. Eager to share the wonderful news, Anne was on her way to the fields when she met Joachim at Jerusalem's Golden Gate. In their joy they forgot the customs of their time and kissed in the street. Nine months later Anne gave birth to a baby girl they named Mary.

Saint Joachim is the patron saint of grandfathers. Feast day: July 26.


**Saint John the Evangelist (died c. 100).** An ancient tradition identifies Ephesus in modern-day Turkey as the place where Saint John died. A chapel was built over his grave and then a great basilica, erected in the sixth century by Emperor Justinian. After the area was conquered by the Turks, the basilica was converted to a mosque, which in turn was destroyed by Tamerlane in 1402. The site of Saint John's grave has been identified, but no one knows what became of his body. Among the places associated with the evangelist is the House of Our Lady in Ephesus, where tradition says he cared for the Blessed Virgin, and the cave on the Aegean island of Patmos, where he is said to have received his visions of the Apocalypse.

John was the brother of the apostle Saint James the Greater. With Saint Peter, the brothers were Jesus's closest friends, but John was the Lord's favorite, known as "the Beloved Disciple."

After the arrest of Jesus, when all the other apostles ran away, John alone stayed close by, following Jesus as he suffered his Passion and then standing at the foot of the cross with the Blessed Mother. As he was dying, Christ entrusted Mary to John. Tradition says that after Christ ascended into heaven, John went to Ephesus to preach the Gospel and Mary went with him.

According to the Christian writer Tertullian (c. 160–c. 220), in 92 Emperor Domitian arrested John, by that time a very old man, and sentenced him to immersion in a giant cauldron of boiling oil. John emerged from the cauldron unharmed, so Domitian exiled him to Patmos. A tiny chapel, St. John in Oil, stands near the Latin Gate on what is said to be the exact spot where the oil vat had been heated.

After Domitian's death in 96, John returned to Ephesus and died there about the year 100.

Saint John is the patron saint of good friendships, theologians, and of anyone involved in the publishing industry. He is invoked against burns and poison. Feast days: December 27 and May 6.

**Saints John and Paul (died c. 362).** It is uncertain where the martyrs were first buried, but in 398 Pammachius, a Roman senator, converted the house of Saints John and Paul into a church and enshrined their relics within it. Visitors to the church can visit the saints' home, which has been excavated beneath the church.

It is believed that John and Paul were brothers who served as imperial bodyguards. They had protected Constantine and his daughter Constantia, but when Constantine's nephew, Julian the Apostate, inherited the throne, renounced his Christian faith, and tried to re-establish the cult of the Roman gods, John and Paul refused to serve him. Julian sent a detachment of troops to behead the brothers in their own home.

Feast day: June 26.

**Saint John Baptist de la Salle (1651–1719).** At his death Saint John was buried in the Church of St. Sever in Rouen. During the French Revolution the church was closed and the saint's tomb was desecrated, but his remains were not destroyed. In 1888, when John was beatified, his relics were buried beneath a side altar in the chapel of the College of Jean-Baptiste de La Salle in Rouen. In 1905 when the French government banished all religious orders from the country, the relics were moved to the Christian Brothers' Motherhouse in Rome. They are still there, although a major relic is venerated in the college chapel in Rouen.

John Baptist de la Salle was a wealthy priest assigned to the cathedral of Rheims in France. He used his fortune to found a school where he developed a teaching method that revolutionized education.

In John's day students read and wrote Latin first and learned their own language later; John began with literacy in the vernacular, then taught the children Latin. He introduced a question-and-answer method that encouraged students to think rather than simply memorize facts and repeat them back to their teachers. Since not all children learn in the same way, he encouraged his teachers to be creative in explaining lessons to pupils who needed individualized attention. To promote his methods John founded a community of men, the Brothers of the Christian Schools, popularly known as the Christian Brothers.

Saint John Baptist de la Salle is the patron saint of teachers and school principals. Feast day: April 7.

**Saint John Berchmans (1599–1621).** The relics of Saint John Berchmans are enshrined in the Jesuit Church of St. Ignatius of Loyola in Rome.

John Berchmans was the son of a Flemish shoemaker. During his brief life he worked no miracles, received no visions, experienced none of the dramatic events for which other saints are famous. His sanctity was grounded in the basics: a profound love for the Mass, at which he loved to serve as an acolyte; devotion to Our Lady, especially expressed through frequent recitation of the Rosary; and fidelity to the Rule of the Society of Jesus—he was a Jesuit novice at the time of his death. Saint John is a model of how ordinary people can become saints.

Saint John Berchmans is the patron saint of altar servers. Feast day: August 13.

**Saint John Bosco (1815–1888).** The body of Saint John Bosco lies inside a glass and silver casket in the Basilica of Our Lady Help of Christians in Turin, Italy.

As a peasant child growing up in northern Italy, John Bosco was a gregarious, athletic boy who performed circus acts—including acrobatics and walking a tightrope—for children in the neighborhood. After his ordination to the priesthood he was assigned to Turin, an industrial city plagued by poverty, ignorance, violence, and crime. Don Bosco ("Don" is the title used in Italy rather than "Father") opened a complex that was part orphanage, part vocational school, part preparatory seminary. He took in orphaned and abandoned boys, some of them juvenile delinquents, as well as boys from stable families. Other men joined him and they formed an order of priests and lay brothers known as the Salesians, in honor of their patron, Saint Francis de Sales.

Saint John Bosco is the patron saint of editors, acrobats, magicians, circus performers, and young people. Feast day: January 31.

**Saint John Chrysostom (c. 347–407).** During the sack of Constantinople in 1204, crusaders carried off the relics of Saint John Chrysostom. They were enshrined in St. Peter's Basilica until 2004, when Pope John Paul II returned all but a small portion of the relics of Saint John to the Bartholomew I, Ecumenical Patriarch of the Orthodox Church. The relics lie today in the Patriarchal Cathedral of St. George in the Phanar district of Istanbul.

The surname "Chrysostom" comes from the Greek for "golden-mouthed," a tribute to Saint John's extraordinary gifts as an orator. Many of his sermons have survived and they are masterpieces of the art of preaching. In 398 he was appointed patriarch of Constantinople, where he used the pulpit to defend orthodox doctrine and denounce the selfishness and sinfulness of the people of the city and particularly the imperial court. For his outspokenness John was exiled to Armenia, where he died.

Saint John Chrysostom is the patron saint of preachers and is invoked against epilepsy. He is one of the patron saints of Constantinople/Istanbul. Feast day: September 13.

**Saint John Fisher (1469–1535).** After his execution by order of Henry VIII, John Fisher's headless body was thrown into a shallow grave in the churchyard of All Hallows, Barking by the Tower. Later the body was exhumed and reburied in the crypt of the Chapel of St. Peter ad Vincula in the Tower of London. The saint's head was exposed on Tower Bridge for a time, then thrown into the river Thames because, it was said at the time, the face grew younger and fresher in appearance with each passing day. The bodies of so many prisoners were buried in St. Peter's crypt that it is impossible to distinguish the bones of Saint John.

The son of a Yorkshire cloth merchant, John Fisher was educated at Cambridge University where he studied for the priesthood. All his life he was deeply attached to his alma mater, and eventually served as chancellor of the university; he used his connections with the English royal family, the aristocracy, and the religious orders to increase Cambridge's endowment. Like his friend Saint Thomas More, Fisher's piety was deeply rooted in the Middle Ages, but his intellectual life was formed by "the New Learning," as humanism was referred to at the time.

In 1504 Fisher was appointed bishop of Rochester. Queen Catherine of Aragon asked Fisher to be her confessor, and so began his long involvement with Henry VIII, Catherine, and their daughter, Princess Mary. When Henry pressured the bishops of England to declare that his marriage to Catherine had been invalid from the beginning and to recognize him as Supreme Head of the Church in England, Bishop Fisher was the only member of the hierarchy to oppose him. For his fidelity to the Catholic faith John Fisher was imprisoned in the Tower of London and tried and condemned for treason. When Pope Paul III announced that, in recognition of Bishop Fisher's fidelity to the Catholic faith, he had made the good old man a cardinal and was sending him the great red tasseled cardinal's hat known as a galero, Henry declared he would see to it that Fisher would have no head on which to wear it.

It had been the government's intention to make an example of the bishop by having him hanged, disemboweled, and quartered, but Fisher was so elderly and so frail that it was feared he would die before the full horrors of the penalty could be inflicted upon him. Consequently the king commuted the sentence to beheading.

Feast day: June 22.

**Saint John Kemble (1599–1679).** Captain Richard Kemble, the martyr's nephew, collected the quartered remains and buried them in St. Mary's churchyard in Welsh Newton. One of the martyr's hands is venerated in the Church of St. Francis Xavier in Hereford.

At the time John was ordained to the priesthood, four of his Kemble relations were already priests, serving Welsh and English Catholics. His mission lasted for fifty-four years, until he was accused of being part of a vast Catholic conspiracy to assassinate King Charles II. The charge was false and absurd, but in the hysteria generated by a notorious perjurer named Titus Oates it was impossible for Father Kemble to receive a fair trial.

A large crowd gathered to witness the execution of the eighty-year-old priest. Either the executioner did not tie the noose properly, or he did not turn Father Kemble off the ladder quickly enough, for the old man dangled, slowly strangling, for half an hour before he died.

Feast day: August 22.


**Blessed John Henry Newman (1801–1890).** In 2008 the grave of John Henry Cardinal Newman was opened, but the excavators found that no trace of the cardinal body's remained. Blessed John's wooden coffin and his bones had simply deteriorated in the damp ground of Birmingham's Rednal Cemetery. All that remained were the brass plaque affixed to the coffin, bits of the clothing Newman's body had worn, and some wood of the coffin. These relics, along with a clipping of Newman's hair taken while he was alive, have been enshrined in a gilt and glass reliquary and placed in the Chapel of St. Charles Borromeo in the Birmingham Oratory. The Oratory preserves many of Cardinal Newman's personal possessions: his vestments and books, his writings, as well as his private chapel.

John Henry Newman's parents were churchgoing Anglicans but they were not particularly religious people. From age fifteen Newman began a spiritual quest that would lead him to ordination as an Anglican clergyman, an interest in the new High Church, or Anglo-Catholic movement in the Church of England, and ultimately to conversion to the Catholic faith and ordination as a priest of the Oratory. It was his study of the writings and history of the Early Church that proved especially instrumental in bringing about Newman's conversion. He said, "To be deep in history is to cease to be a Protestant."

Newman was a brilliant writer and a gifted speaker. He used those gifts to explain his conversion, defend Catholic doctrine, and encourage the fledgling Catholic revival that was just beginning in the British Isles in the mid-nineteenth century.

He founded the Oratory at Birmingham in a run-down neighborhood crowded with poor, barely educated Irish Catholic immigrants. Although he tried to be a good parish priest, he was always most at ease in a university setting, among accomplished, well-educated people.

In 1879 Pope Leo XIII created Newman a cardinal. In the traditional speech of thanks he declared that he had always been the enemy of "the doctrine that there is no truth in religion, but that one creed is as good as another [and that Christianity] is but a sentiment and taste, not an objective fact, not miraculous." In 2010, Pope Benedict XVI beatified John Henry Newman in a ceremony in Birmingham, England.

Feast day: October 9.

**Saint John Marie Vianney (1786–1859).** The saint's body is displayed in a glass and bronze reliquary casket in the Basilica of Ars in France. His heart is preserved in the nearby Shrine of the Curé's Heart. The original parish church where he served for forty-one years is open to pilgrims. The rectory where Saint John lived also survives and displays many of his personal belongings. Some of Saint John's belongings are enshrined at the London Oratory.

In the seminary John Marie Vianney was such a poor student that he required ten years of intense training and private tutoring before his bishop agreed to ordain him a priest. He was assigned as curate to the parish priest who helped him pass his examinations; then, after several years, he was assigned his own parish—Ars, a poor, out-of-the-way place that had not had a resident priest for many years. Father Vianney dedicated his life to converting his parishioners and, in spite of severe setbacks early on, he was enormously successful.

Father Vianney developed an international reputation as an inspired confessor who helped penitents to reveal and repent sins that they had long concealed. He spent eighteen hours a day in the confessional, and even as he lay on his deathbed, people who wanted to confess to him one last time formed a line outside his bedroom door.

Saint John Marie Vianney is the patron saint of parish priests and confessors. Feast day: August 4.

**Saint John Nepomucene (c. 1340–1393).** The body of Saint John is preserved in a silver monument in St. Vitus Cathedral in Prague, Czech Republic. A small bronze cross with five stars marks the spot on the Vltava Bridge where he was thrown into the river and drowned.

John Nepomucene was a canon of St. Vitus Cathedral and confessor to the queen of Bohemia. When King Wenceslaus IV tried to carve out a new diocese and install one of his cronies as bishop, John spoke on behalf of the Church, declaring that no king possessed such rights. Wenceslaus and John had clashed before: the king suspected his queen of infidelity and commanded John to reveal what she had said in confession. John refused.

Wenceslaus had John arrested and tortured to compel him to recognize the king's "rights" over the Church. But nothing the torturers did to him could make John submit. Wenceslaus had John dragged through the streets of Prague in chains and thrown off the Vltava Bridge into the Moldau River, where he drowned.

Saint John Nepomucene is the patron saint of confessors, silence, discretion, and bridges. He is invoked against flood and slander. He is one of the patron saints of the Czech Republic. Feast day: May 16.

**Saint John Nepomucene Neumann (1811–1860).** In 1860 the body of John Neumann was buried in the crypt of St. Peter's Church in Philadelphia. After Pope Paul VI beatified Bishop Neumann, his grave was opened. A wax face mask was placed over his skull, and his skeleton was dressed in new episcopal vestments.

John Nepomucene Neumann was one of those tireless missionary priests and bishops who established the Catholic Church in the United States. He was an immigrant from Bohemia and a member of the Redemptorist order. He brought the Mass and the sacraments to Catholics in the remote region around Niagara Falls and western Pennsylvania; he served parishes in Pittsburgh and Baltimore; and in 1852 he was consecrated bishop of Philadelphia. Some of his brother bishops felt Father Neumann was an unsuitable candidate: he was too self-effacing, had no sense of style, and lived too much like a pastor whose parish was not exactly thriving. But the immigrant Catholics of Philadelphia loved Bishop Neumann. German was his native language, and he had mastered English to work in America. Now he learned Gaelic and Italian so he could speak with Irish and Italian Catholics. He made his rounds on foot, the better to meet people. In his pockets he carried holy medals and holy cards, which he distributed to children.

Bishop Neumann opened new parishes and established new parochial schools. To assist him he founded an order of nuns, the Sisters of the Third Order of St. Francis. And he planned a magnificent new cathedral for Philadelphia, the Cathedral of Sts. Peter and Paul, which stands today at Logan Circle.

On a snowy day in January 1860, while running his own errands, on foot as usual, Bishop Neumann suffered a stroke and collapsed on the steps of a private home. He was carried inside but died before a priest arrived to give him Last Rites.

Feast day: January 5.


**Blessed Pope John Paul II (1920–2005).** In spring 2011, in preparation for the beatification of John Paul II, the pope's body was translated from its grave in the crypt of the Basilica of St. Peter in Rome to a white marble tomb beneath the altar of St. Sebastian in the basilica proper. A vial of his blood, which was drawn for medical tests during his life and preserved by the late pope's doctors, was given to John Paul II Institute in Cracow, Poland, where it will be enshrined in the altar of the institute's chapel. Many of Blessed John Paul's personal possessions, including his skis and a prayerbook, are displayed at his childhood home in Wadowice, Poland. Nearby is his family's parish church, the Presentation of the Blessed Virgin Mary, where Karol Wojtyla was baptized, received First Holy Communion, was confirmed, and served as an altar boy.

Karol Josef Wojtyla was born in Wadowice, a small town outside Cracow in southern Poland. His mother died when he was eight years old, his father when he was twenty-one.

During the Nazi occupation of Poland (1939–1945), Wojtyla worked in a stone quarry, but in 1942 he entered a clandestine underground seminary to study for the priesthood (the Nazis had shut down all the seminaries in Poland). On November 1, 1946—All Saints Day—Karol Wojtyla was ordained a priest; the next day, All Souls Day, he offered his first Mass in Cracow's historic Wawel Cathedral. Less than two weeks later he left Poland for advanced theological studies in Rome. After earning a doctorate in theology in 1948, Wojtyla taught ethics in Poland.

He rose quickly in the Polish hierarchy: auxiliary bishop in 1958, archbishop of Cracow in 1964, cardinal in 1967. In 1978, after the deaths of Paul VI and John Paul I, the cardinals elected Karol Wojtyla pope: he took the name John Paul II.

The new pope was a dynamic, charismatic, active man. During his entire adult life his freedom of action and expression had been severely curtailed, first under the Nazis, then under the Communists. Now, as pope, he could address the world, and he spoke often on the God-given rights of humankind, of freedom of conscience, and of the Christian roots of Europe, particularly Eastern Europe, where Catholic, Orthodox, and Protestants suffered persecution under Communist regimes.

On May 13, 1981, during a public audience in St. Peter's Square, Mehmet Ali Agca, a Turk, shot and severely wounded John Paul—suspicions persist that the government and secret service of the Soviet Union were behind the assassination attempt.

In the years after the conclusion of the Second Vatican Council, the Catholic Church, particularly in the West, was torn apart by confusion, dissention, and liturgical abuses. John Paul asserted that the council was not a break with the past but must be seen in continuity with the Church's sacred traditions. He encouraged the revival of traditional devotions such as praying the Rosary and the Stations of the Cross and holding elaborate Corpus Christi processions in honor of the Blessed Sacrament. He called upon Catholic colleges to reclaim their identities and give their students an authentic Catholic education. To encourage devotion to the saints he created 1,338 new blesseds and 432 new saints. He authorized the first universal catechism for the Catholic Church since the Council of Trent in 1556 and a new Code of Canon Law, the first major revision since 1917. He granted an indult so that Catholics who were attached to the pre–Vatican II Latin liturgy could attend that Mass (with the permission of their bishop); he authorized new religious orders that served the Latin Mass community; and he welcomed back into full communion with the Church traditionalist groups that had gone into schism. He encouraged new organizations such as Opus Dei and Communion and Liberation, which sought to help all Catholics grow in personal holiness. As a result, John Paul sparked a spiritual revival in the Church.

John Paul's visits to 129 countries around the globe were heavily covered by the media, so he used those occasions to act as catechism teacher to the world, reinforcing the Catholic Church's doctrinal and moral teachings.

During his final years, when he suffered from Parkinson's disease, John Paul II set an example for faith, courage, and patience. At his death in 2005, hundreds of thousands of mourners traveled to Rome to see him lie in state inside St. Peter's Basilica. At his funeral mass, members of the throng in St. Peter's Square unfurled a banner that read SANTO SUBITO!—"Sainthood Now!"

**Saint John of God (1495–1550).** The saint's tomb lies in the church adjacent to the Hospital of St. John of God in Granada, Spain.

John was one of those individuals who had a difficult time finding his way in life. He was a shepherd, worked at odd jobs, and served in the army of Spain. In Granada he opened a little shop where he sold religious books and holy pictures.

One day he closed his shop to hear a renowned preacher, Saint John of Avila. Saint John preached on repentance and the mercy of God. As he listened John was overwhelmed by a sense of his own wickedness. Running out of the church, he raced through the streets howling with grief over his sins. The city authorities apprehended him and locked him up as a madman. In his cell John was visited by John of Avila who talked sense to him, heard his confession, then instructed him to do something useful for God and his fellow man.

With his mental equilibrium restored, John was released. He opened a small hospital for the poor where he did all the nursing, cooking, and cleaning himself—until volunteers came to assist him. Once the people of Granada considered John deranged; now they regard him as a saint.

Saint John of God is the patron saint of booksellers, hospitals, hospital workers, the sick, and firefighters. Feast day: March 8.

**Saint John the Baptist (died c. 30).** The head of Saint John the Baptist was one of the most coveted relics of the Middle Ages, and as a result many places claimed to possess the holy skull, including the Church of St. Sylvester in Capite in Rome; the Cathedral of Amiens in France; the Treasury of the Residenz Museum in Munich, Germany; the Gandzasar Monastery in Armenia; and the Umayyad Mosque in Damascus. Portions of the skull are claimed to be in the possession of the Treasury of the Topkapi Palace in Istanbul and the Monastery of St. Macarius the Great in Scetes, Egypt. The Skete of the Forerunner on Mount Athos in Greece and the Cetinje Monastery in Montenegro both claim to have the right hand of Saint John, with which he baptized Our Lord.

In August 2010 a team of archaeologists working in Bulgaria

announced that they had found an ancient reliquary said to contain bones of Saint John the Baptist—including portions of his skull, his arm, and a tooth. According to Professor Kazimir Popkonstantinov, leader of the excavation, the relics were found within an altar in the ruins of the fourth- or fifth-century Church of St. John the Forerunner on the island of St. Ivan. A portion of the bones were sent to a laboratory for forensic tests while the majority were transferred to the Bulgarian Orthodox Church. They were enshrined in the Church of St. George in Sozopol until the renovation of the larger Church of Sts. Cyril and Methodius was completed.

John the Baptist was the cousin of Jesus Christ, the last of the biblical prophets, and the man who prepared the way for the coming of the Messiah. As a young man he left the home of his parents, Saint Elizabeth and Saint Zachary, to live a life of penance in the desert. He dressed in an old camel hide and he lived on locusts and wild honey.

This two-piece gold-and-jewel-encrusted reliquary preserves a portion of the skull of John the Baptist. The relic once belonged to the Byzantine emperors. WERNER FORMAN/ART RESOURCE, NY

He preached, "Repent! For the kingdom of God is at hand!" Crowds came out from Jerusalem and elsewhere in Israel to hear him, and those who were moved to repent their sins John baptized in the Jordan River. Jesus began his public ministry by presenting himself to John to be baptized.

Later John traveled to Jerusalem where he denounced the illicit marriage of King Herod to his brother's wife, Herodias. Enraged at being reviled in the streets, Herodias demanded that Herod have John executed, but the king was afraid to harm a man he revered as a prophet. Instead he kept John locked in prison.

On Herod's birthday, when he was half drunk, Herodias sent her daughter Salome to the king. Before all his guests Herod begged Salome to dance for him, promising her anything she liked, even if she demanded half the kingdom. Coached by her mother, Salome asked for the head of John the Baptist. Dismayed by the request but unable to back down without shaming himself, Herod agreed and sent an executioner to the prison. A short time later the executioner returned with Saint John's head on a platter; he presented it to Salome, who in turn gave it to her mother.

When Jesus learned that John was dead he declared, "Truly, I say to you, among those born of women there has arisen no one greater than John the Baptist" (Matthew 11:11).

Saint John the Baptist is the patron saint of baptism, highway workers, lambs, and French Canadians. He is one of the patron saints of Puerto Rico, Jordan, and the Knights of Malta. Feast days: June 24 (nativity) and August 29 (beheading).

**Saint John of the Cross (1542–1591).** The relics of Saint John are encased in a magnificent shrine of gold, silver, and marble in the church of the Carmelite monastery in Segovia, Spain.

John was a born contemplative who would have been content to spend his life in a cloister, but he met Saint Teresa of Avila, one of the spiritual dynamos of the Counter-Reformation and a woman who would not take no for an answer. She dragooned John into assisting her ambitious campaign to restore the Carmelite order to its austere ideal. Teresa would reform the nuns; John would reform the friars.

Some Carmelites resented John's interference, especially a community in Toledo who kidnapped him and locked him a cell where they starved him and flogged him. Close to despair in what John described as "the dark night of the soul," he took refuge in hours of mental prayer and contemplation. He also found a way to disassemble the lock on his cell door and escape.

Once he was free, secular and religious authorities stepped forward to protect him from his fellow Carmelites. But like Teresa, they would not permit John to retire to a cloister. He directed a college and a Carmelite priory and eventually was made one of the superiors of his order in Spain.

Saint John of the Cross is the patron saint of mystics, contemplatives, and Spanish poets. Feast day: December 14.

**Saint John Southworth (1592–1654).** Spain's ambassador to England attended the execution of Father John Southworth and purchased the dismembered remains from the executioner. Initially the relics were buried on the estate of the duke of Norfolk, England's most prominent Catholic peer. Later the relics were carried to the English seminary in Douai, France, where they drew pilgrims. During the French Revolution the faculty at Douai hid the relics. Agents of the revolution shut down the seminary, and for more than a century the location of the hiding place was forgotten. The relics were rediscovered by chance in 1927 by a construction crew that was working on the site of the old seminary grounds. Upon opening the chest the body was found to be cut into four quarters. The hands were missing—perhaps removed as relics and now lost—but the head was present. In 1930 the relics were enshrined in a side chapel in Westminster Cathedral, the Catholic cathedral in London. The relics lie in a glass chest, dressed in the vestments of a priest, with silver hands and a silver mask over the face.

John Southworth was born in Lancashire, a Catholic stronghold in Anglican England. To become a priest he was obliged to travel to a seminary in Douai, France. In 1619 he joined the English mission and returned home to minister secretly to Catholics and to try to bring Protestants back to the faith of their ancestors. He was arrested in 1627 and imprisoned in London's notorious Clink Prison. He spent three years in that ghastly place awaiting trial and execution, but in 1630 the king issued a pardon to a dozen Catholic priests—and Father Southworth's name was on the list.

He remained in London for the next twenty-four years, spending much of his time in the run-down Westminster district. By then England had endured a civil war, and the Puritan rebels had beheaded King Charles I and installed a government that was virulently intolerant of Catholics. Father Southworth was arrested, tried, and condemned to be hanged, drawn, and quartered. On the scaffold Father Southworth said, "Catholics, being free-born subjects should enjoy that liberty [of conscience] as others do as long as they live obedient subjects to the Lord Protector and the laws of the nation."

Feast day: June 28.


**Blessed Pope John XXIII (1881–1963).** Originally Pope John XXIII was buried in the Vatican Grottoes beneath St. Peter's Basilica. After his beatification his body was moved to a glass casket beneath the altar of Saint Jerome in the main body of the church.

Pope John XXIII is a contentious figure—something rare among the saints, and unexpected in his case since during his papacy he was regarded as a warm, personable, grandfatherly figure.

Angelo Roncalli came from a family of peasants, yet he grew up to be a Vatican diplomat. As the papal representative in Turkey during World War II, Roncalli helped Jewish refugees escape the Nazis by distributing among them forged baptismal certificates. After the war, in 1953, Pope Pius XII named him patriarch of Venice.

On October 28, 1958, Cardinal Angelo Roncalli was elected pope. In sermons and encyclicals he called on bishops especially to remember that they were shepherds of souls, not just administrators of dioceses. He tried to establish at least cordial relations with leaders of the Orthodox and Protestant churches. Building upon the principles established by his predecessors such as Leo XIII, Pope John called for justice for workers and deplored the industrialized West's exploitation of developing nations. And he took a hard line against Communism, forbidding Catholics to vote for Communist political candidates.

On January 25, 1959, Pope John called for a council of the world's bishops to be held at the Vatican to discuss the role of the Catholic Church in twentieth-century society. This decision would be the most controversial act of his papacy. Typically councils were called to address a doctrinal or temporal crisis confronting the Church, but that was not the case in 1959. What Pope John had in mind, what he hoped the fruits of the council would be, are difficult to pin down. He is said to have been the architect of the dramatic changes to the life and worship of the Church that followed the Vatican Council, yet one of his final acts was to publish a document that condemned those in the Catholic Church who wanted to abolish the use of Latin in the liturgy or even as the language of the seminary classroom: "In the exercise of their paternal care [bishops and superiors-general of religious orders] shall be on their guard lest anyone under their jurisdiction, eager for revolutionary changes, writes against the use of Latin in the teaching of the higher sacred studies or in the liturgy, or through prejudice makes light of the Holy See's will in this regard or interprets it falsely" (*Veterum Sapientia,* February 22, 1962).

Sorting out Pope John's intentions and how or if they were enacted falls to Church historians. To the majority of Catholics he is remembered as a genial, lovable pope.

Blessed Pope John XXIII is the patron saint of papal diplomats. Feast day: October 11.

**Saint Josaphat Kunsevich (1584–1623).** The saint's murderers threw his body into the Dvina River, but it was recovered and buried in Biala, Poland. Today the body of Saint Josaphat may be seen in a glass casket beneath the altar of Saint Basil in St. Peter's Basilica in Rome.

Josaphat Kunsevich was raised in the Ruthenian Orthodox Church but became a Catholic when his church reunited with the Roman Catholic Church in 1595. He became a monk of the Byzantine Rite and eventually was appointed bishop of Vitebsk. He made it his mission to bring Orthodox Christians into the Catholic Church and assure them that Rome would respect their liturgy and their traditions (alarmists were spreading rumors that Rome would insist that all the Uniates, as those reconciled with the Catholic Church were called, would be forced to accept the Latin Mass).

In 1623 a mob of Orthodox extremists attacked Josaphat's residence. He got his servants to safety but was captured before he could escape. The mob beat and hacked him to death.

Saint Josaphat is one of the patron saints of the Ukraine. Feast day: November 12.

**Saint Joseph (first century).** The body of Saint Joseph has never been found, but the Church of St. Anastasia claims to possess the saint's cloak. The Holy House of Loreto, said to be the home of the Holy Family, would also qualify as a relic of Saint Joseph's.

In the Gospels, Joseph does not utter a single word, yet he was essential in the plan of salvation as the guardian and husband of the Virgin Mary and the protector and foster father of Jesus Christ. He is a model of obedience to God's will, even when its workings are a mystery, and of selfless love for his family.

Saint Joseph was a casualty of the early Church's often violent controversies regarding the nature of Christ, whether he was truly God, or a specially selected man, or was both God and man simultaneously. The debate that raged around the issue precluded the development of devotion to Saint Joseph—it would only be asking for more trouble. And so as love for the Blessed Virgin and her parents Saint Anne and Saint Joachim flourished, Joseph remained a bit player who attracted very little notice. As a result, no place claimed to possess his tomb or his remains.

Interest in Saint Joseph increased in the fifteenth century, and in the sixteenth century the Jesuits and the Carmelites encouraged devotion to him, setting off a religious revival. Since then Saint Joseph has become one of the most beloved figures in the Catholic world, second among the saints only to Our Lady.

Saint Joseph is the patron saint of fathers, husbands, families, virgins, carpenters, and working people. He is invoked for a successful real estate transaction and for a good death; he is also invoked against doubt and against Communism. He is the patron and protector of the Catholic Church. Saint Joseph is also one of the patron saints of the Americas, Austria, Belgium, Canada, China, the Czech Republic, Korea, Mexico, Peru, Sicily, and Vietnam. Feast days: March 19 and May 1 (Saint Joseph the Worker).

**Saint Joseph of Cupertino (1603–1663).** The body of Joseph of Cupertino lies beneath the altar of the Church of St. Joseph of Cupetino, in Osimo, Italy.

Joseph of Cupertino was a Franciscan priest who was renowned in his day for floating through the air. Typically the sight of an image of Our Lady or of the Blessed Sacrament would cause him to levitate and move through the air to the statue or the tabernacle where he would remain suspended above the floor for a period of time. Seventy of these episodes were recorded during the last seventeen years of Joseph's life. In 1638 the Inquisition summoned Joseph to a tribunal of investigators, and as the panel questioned him, he levitated. Pope Urban VIII commanded Joseph's superior to bring him to Rome, where Joseph levitated before the pope.

Saint Joseph of Cupertino is the patron saint of astronauts, aviators, paratroopers, and students taking tests. He is also the patron saint of Cupertino, Italy. Feast day: September 18.

**Saint Joseph of Arimathea (first century).** According to legend, Joseph of Arimathea died and was buried at Glastonbury, England. The location of his grave is unknown; however, the Glastonbury Thorn may be regarded as a relic of the saint. It is said that upon arriving at Glastonbury Joseph stuck his walking staff into the ground and it flowered. Today's flowering Glastonbury Thorn bush is said to be a descendant of the original that sprouted from Joseph's staff.

All four Gospels tell us that Joseph of Arimathea was a wealthy resident of Jerusalem and a secret disciple of Christ. When Christ hung dead on the cross, Joseph called upon Pontius Pilate and requested the body. With another secret disciple, Nicodemus, Joseph took Jesus down from the cross, wrapped the body in a linen shroud, and placed it nearby in a rock-cut tomb he had prepared for his own burial.

The New Testament never mentions Joseph again, but a host of legends sprang up around him. One of the most popular claims that he was a merchant and an uncle of the Blessed Virgin Mary. When Jesus was a boy, Joseph took him on a business trip to the island of Britain. Another story tells of Joseph standing at the foot of the cross, collecting Christ's blood in the chalice the Lord had used at the Last Supper. The relics of the Precious Blood and the cup, or Holy Grail, Joseph took to Britain, placing them in a chapel he built on the site of Glastonbury.

Saint Joseph of Arimathea is the patron saint of funeral directors, pallbearers, and tin miners. Feast day: March 17.

**Saint Josephine Bakhita (1869–1947).** The relics of Saint Josephine Bakhita lie beneath the high altar of the Church of the Canossian Daughters of Charity in Schio, Italy.

At the age of seven this Sudanese child (her original name is not known) was kidnapped by slave traders. Between 1876 and 1883 she was sold several times, until at the slave market in Khartoum she was purchased by the Italian consul, Callisto Legnani, who emancipated her. Bakhita (the name the slavers gave her—it means "fortunate") joined the consul's household staff. Two years later when Legnani returned to Italy, Bakhita came along. She found work as a nanny in Venice. One of her responsibilities was to take the little girl in her care to the convent of the Canossian Sisters for catechism classes.

At the convent Bakhita had her first in-depth exposure to Catholicism. She asked the nuns to instruct her. In 1890 she was baptized and took the name Josephine. Three years later she joined the Canossian Sisters as a novice.

In 1902 Sister Josephine was assigned to the convent at Schio near Verona. She worked as a cook, a seamstress, and a portress, welcoming and screening visitors to the convent. Sister Josephine's kindness and gentleness drew adults and children. "Be good," she said, "love the Lord, pray for those who do not know Him. What a great grace it is to know God!"

In her final years she was often ill, but no one ever heard her complain. When asked how she was feeling she replied, "As the Master desires." On her deathbed she became delirious and thought she was a slave again; she cried, "Please loosen the chains! They are heavy!"

Saint Josephine Bakhita is the patron saint of the Sudan. Feast day: February 8.


**Saint Juan Diego Cuauhtlatoatzin (1474–1548).** It is believed that Juan Diego was buried in the Church of Santiago Tlateloloco, the parish church of the Indians near the shrine of Our Lady of Guadalupe, but the location of his grave has been forgotten. The sole relic of the saint is his tilma, which is at the Basilica of Our Lady of Guadalupe and bears her miraculous image.

A member of the Chichimeca people, Cuauhtlatoatzin (the name means "talking eagle") was born in Cuautitlán, which is now part of sprawling Mexico City. In 1524 at age fifty he was baptized a Catholic and received the name Juan Diego.

On December 9, 1531, while on his way to Mass, Juan Diego heard unearthly music on Tepeyac Hill. He followed the sound and found the Blessed Mother waiting for him. "I am your merciful mother," she said, "to you and to all the inhabitants of this land and to all the rest who love me, invoke and confide in me." Then Mary instructed Juan Diego to call upon the bishop, Juan de Zumárraga, and say that she wished a chapel built on this spot. Twice Juan Diego brought Our Lady's message to Bishop de Zumárraga, who treated him kindly but made it plain that he did not believe the story of an apparition of the Blessed Virgin at Tepeyac.

Finally, Mary directed Juan Diego to climb to the summit of the hill and gather the flowers he found there. Inexplicably, he found Castillian roses growing wild on Tepeyac—out of place and out of season. After filling his tilma, or cloak, with the roses he returned to the bishop's residence.

"You asked for a sign," Juan Diego said. "Look." As he unfolded his tilma the roses cascaded onto the floor. More marvelous than the roses was the image of Our Lady imprinted on the tilma.

Bishop de Zumárraga built a church on the site of the apparition and enshrined the image of Our Lady within it. Juan Diego moved into a small room attached to the church and lived there until his death on May 30, 1548.

Feast day: December 9.

**Saint Jude (first century).** The relics of Saint Jude lie under the altar of Saint Joseph in St. Peter's Basilica in Rome. A large piece of bone from the relics of Saint Jude is venerated at the National Shrine of St. Jude in Chicago.

In addition to being one of the twelve apostles, Jude was also related to Jesus Christ. He is believed to have written the New

Testament Epistle of Jude, which warns Christians to shun novel doctrines promulgated by false preachers and cling to the teachings they received from Christ's apostles.

According to tradition Jude and his fellow apostle Simon brought the Gospel to Persia and were martyred there: Simon was sawn in half; Jude was beaten to death with a club.

Saint Jude is invoked in cases that appear impossible or desperate. Feast day: October 28.

**Saint Julia (died c. 620).** Saint Julia's body was moved from her grave on Corsica to the Benedictine Monastery of San Salvatore, or Holy Savior, also known as St. Julia, in Brescia, Italy.

There are two versions of Saint Julia's story. The simplest says she was a Corsican Christian who was killed by Saracen invaders. The more elaborate version claims that she was a Christian from North Africa who was kidnapped and sold into slavery. En route back to his home in Syria, Julia's master stopped at the island of Corsica. A festival in honor of a pagan god was being celebrated, and Julia's master joined the merrymaking, but Julia remained on the ship.

The governor of the island was offended that a slave should keep herself aloof. After Julia's master passed out from heavy drinking, the governor tried to persuade Julia to sacrifice to the god whose holiday they were celebrating. Julia's persistent refusals enraged the governor, who ordered his guards to crucify her.

Saint Julia is one of the patron saints of Corsica. Feast day: May 22.

**Blessed Junípero Serra (1713–1784).** Father Serra died at the Mission of San Carlos Borromeo in California and was buried beneath the sanctuary floor before the high altar. The museum at the mission preserves many of Father Serra's personal belongings.

As a boy Junípero Serra's parents sent him to a school run by the

Franciscans near their home on the island of Majorca. His teachers were delighted to find that Junípero was intellectually precocious as well as religiously devout. At age sixteen he joined the Franciscans. At age twenty-four he was already a priest and a professor of theology. But when he was thirty-six years old Father Junípero left the comforts of his university to serve as a missionary in Mexico.

The Franciscan authorities in Mexico were reluctant to permit a man of Father Junípero's gifts to work exclusively as a missionary; they compelled him to teach theology in their college but permitted him to minister to Catholic Indians in the vicinity.

It was not until 1767, when he was fifty-four years old, that Father Junípero was permitted at last to become a full-time missionary. The Spanish government had resolved to settle what is now the state of California, and Father Junípero was sent as superior of the Franciscans who would establish missions in the territory. Between 1767 and his death in 1784 he founded nine flourishing missions in California and converted approximately five thousand Indians. His missions were the beginnings of the Californian cities of San Diego, Los Angeles, San Francisco, and Carmel.

Although he fought for—and won—government recognition that the Franciscans' authority over the Indians and the missions superceded that of the military, in many respects the mission system was not a success. The Franciscans moved their converts onto the mission grounds to teach them European skills and create European-style communities, but European diseases, to which the Indians had no immunity, took the lives of thousands.

Nonetheless Father Junípero was dedicated to his task and to his Indians. He was a crucial factor in the settlement of California and the establishment of the Catholic Church in what would become the American West.

Feast day: July 1.

**Saint Justin Martyr (c. 100–165).** Relics of Saint Justin lie buried with the remains of Saint Lawrence in the Basilica of St. Lawrence

Outside the Walls in Rome and are venerated in the Church of St. John the Baptist in Sacrofano, Italy.

At age thirty Justin, an avid student of the philosophers of Greece and Rome, encountered an elderly Christian from whom he learned about Christianity. "I discovered," he wrote, "that his was the only sure and useful philosophy."

After his baptism Justin opened the world's first Christian school of philosophy in Ephesus, where debates with pagans, Gnostics, and Jews were a regular feature of the curriculum. In 150 he moved his school to Rome, where he continued to teach, debate, and write in defense of the Christian faith.

During Emperor Marcus Aurelius's persecution of the Church, Justin, along with six of his students, was arrested. When the prefect urged them to sacrifice to the Roman gods and save their lives, Justin, speaking for them all, replied, "No one in his right mind gives up piety for impiety." Teacher and students were led out, flogged, then beheaded.

Saint Justin Martyr is the patron saint of philosophers, orators, and those who defend the Catholic faith. Feast day: June 1.

**Saint Justina of Padua (died 304).** The Basilica of St. Justina in Padua began as a small oratory over the martyr's grave. The saint's relics are preserved inside the church.

A medieval legend claims that Justina was converted by Saint Prosdocimus, whom Saint Peter sent to Padua as its first bishop. All we know for certain is that Justina was a Christian who lived in Padua in the early fourth century and was martyred there.

Saint Justina is one of the patron saints of Padua. Feast day: October 7.

**Saint Katharine Drexel (1858–1955).** The body of Saint Katharine lies beneath the main altar in the Chapel of St. Elizabeth at the National Shrine of St. Katharine Drexel in Bensalem,

Pennsylvania. Many of Mother Drexel's personal belongings are on display in the shrine's museum.

Katharine Drexel was the daughter of a wealthy Philadelphia banker and investment broker. Katharine's father and stepmother (her mother died shortly after she was born) raised her to be conscious of the needs of the less fortunate. In 1885, after the death of her father and stepmother, Katharine inherited an immense, multimillion-dollar estate. With her two sisters she traveled to the American West, where they saw firsthand the deprivations of the Indians on reservations. Immediately Katharine purchased food, clothing, and medicine for the Indians. She built schools and furnished them, as well as hired the teachers and paid their salaries. And she recruited Catholic priests to establish missions on the reservations.

Encouraged by her friends and spiritual directors, Bishop James O'Connor and Archbishop Patrick Ryan of Philadelphia, Katharine trained for the religious life and founded a new congregation of nuns, the Sisters of the Blessed Sacrament, who would dedicate their lives to serving Indian and black children.

Mother Mary Katharine, as she was known in the religious life, founded schools for Indian children in New Mexico, and schools for black children in Virginia. In Louisiana she establish Xavier College (now Xavier University), the first Catholic college for African Americans. By the end of her life she had founded sixty schools and missions and spent $20 million of her fortune on their support.

Feast day: March 3.

**Blessed Kateri Tekakwitha (1656–1680).** The relics of Blessed Kateri are enshrined in a marble tomb in St. Francis Xavier Church, Kahnawake, Quebec.

Tekakwitha was born in the Mohawk village of Ossernenon (near present-day Auriesville, New York), where several years earlier three Jesuits—Saint René Goupil, Saint Isaac Jogues, and Saint

John de Lalande—had been martyred. When she was four years old a smallpox epidemic took the lives of her parents and her baby brother; Tekakwitha survived the disease, but her face was badly scarred and her eyesight was weakened. An uncle and several aunts adopted the orphan.

In 1675 a Jesuit missionary, Father Jacques de Lamberville, came to Tekakwitha's village; she became his one and only convert. At her baptism she took the name Kateri, Mohawk for "Catherine."

Kateri's conversion incensed her family and her fellow tribesmen. Her aunts beat her on the slightest pretext. When she walked through the village children stoned her. On at least one occasion a Mohawk warrior threatened to kill her. Seeing life had become unbearable for Kateri, Father de Lamberville convinced her to leave her village and travel to Kahnawake, Quebec, a village of Christian Indians two hundred miles away. It was a journey of three months, and she walked the entire distance alone.

Kateri was taken in by Anastasia Tegonhatsihonga, an Algonquin who had known her mother. At Kahnawake, Kateri was among fellow Catholics and for the first time since her conversion she felt at ease. She attended two Masses every morning and vespers in the afternoon. She asked the mission's priests for further instruction in the faith.

After four happy years at Kahnawake, Kateri fell ill and died during Holy Week, 1680. The Jesuits of the mission, convinced that Kateri was a saint, began collecting documentation. Among the papers sent to Rome shortly after Kateri's death was a deer hide signed by Algonquin men and women who had known Kateri, petitioning the pope to declare her a saint.

Blessed Kateri Tekakwitha is the patron saint of Native Americans and of people mocked for their piety. Feast day: July 14.

**Saint Kevin (died c. 618).** Saint Kevin was buried at Glendalough, his monastery in the Wicklow Hills south of Dublin, but the location of the grave has been forgotten. Saint Kevin's Cell, Saint

Kevin's Bed, and the chapel known as Temple-na-Skellig are associated with Saint Kevin.

The son of a noble Irish family, Kevin entered a monastery at age twelve. When he reached adulthood he was ordained a priest; then he traveled into the Wicklow Mountains to live as a hermit in a beautiful mountain valley called Glendalough. Other would-be hermits assembled near Kevin's hut, so he built a monastery and agreed to serve as abbot.

As tends to be the case with Irish saints, Kevin's story has been embellished with legends. One such story tells of a monk who suffered from epilepsy; he was told in a vision that he would be cured if he ate apples. Since there was no apple tree in Glendalough, Kevin commanded a willow tree to produce the fruit.

Saint Kevin is the patron saint of blackbirds. He is also one of the patron saints of Ireland and the archdiocese of Dublin. Feast day: June 3.

**Saint Knud, or Canute, Lavard. (c. 1090–1131).** As Lutheranism took hold in Denmark, the Benedictine monks of St. Bendt's Church in Ringsted took the bones of Saint Knud Lavard from their shrine and carried them to safety in Catholic France. Since then the relics have been lost, but a few fragments of the saint's relics remain in his original tomb in St. Bendt.

Knud Lavard was a member of Denmark's royal family and a zealous Christian at a time when the kingdom was still overwhelmingly pagan.

As a young man Knud had traveled in Germany and France, where he was dazzled by the grand architecture, lovely works of art, enchanting music, and the new code of chivalry. He wanted those things for his countrymen, and he also wanted Denmark to be allied with the powerful kingdoms of Christian Europe—and there was a better chance of such alliances if Denmark was a Christian land. As duke of Jutland, Knud tried to implement these innovations among his people, and he tried to convince them to become Christians.

Especially galling to Knud's pagan relatives was his determination to eradicate piracy along the coast of Jutland. The men he called pirates most Danes called Vikings, and in the traditional Danish worldview Vikings were an honorable class of warriors.

Knud's Christianity, his interest in foreign cultures, and his opposition to the Viking code antagonized his uncle King Nils and his cousin Prince Magnus. To make matters worse, Knud was popular among the people of Jutland, while Magnus, the heir to the Danish throne, had no such grassroots support. To ensure that the crown passed to his son, Nils plotted with Magnus to murder Knud.

In 1131, as Knud rode through the Haraldsted Forest, henchmen of the king and the prince ambushed and murdered him. The killing set off a civil war, which Magnus lost—the crown passed to Knud's son, Valdemar, who erected the Church of St. Bendt in Ringsted and buried his father there.

Saint Knud Lavard is the patron saint of the Danish province of Zeeland. Feast day: January 7.

**Korean Martyrs (died 1839, 1846, 1866).** More than ten thousand Korean Catholics were executed for their faith in the nineteenth century by the Korean government; 106 of these martyrs have been canonized. In many cases the bodies of the martyrs were destroyed or taken away by their executioners, but some of the relics have survived and are preserved in the Saenamtemo Memorial Church and the Chŏltusan Shrine, both in Seoul, South Korea. The grave of Saint Andrew Kim Dae-gon is found at the Mirinae Shrine at Anseong City.

Among the martyrs canonized by Pope John Paul II in 1984 were forty-seven laywomen, forty-five laymen, eight priests or seminarians, four French missionary priests, and two French missionary bishops. The youngest was thirteen-year-old Peter Yu-Tae-choi; the oldest was seventy-two-year-old Mark Chong.

Prominent among the martyrs is Saint Andrew Kim Dae-gon, the first Korean ordained to the priesthood. His father, Saint Ignatius Kim (1796–1839), had been martyred during an earlier persecution. Andrew was arrested, cruelly tortured, then beheaded at the site of the present-day Saenamtemo Memorial Church. Among the other martyrs are:

**Saint Barbara Choe Yong-i (1819–1840).** Twenty-two years old when she was arrested, Barbara was imprisoned with her infant son. In the filthy cell, where there was scarcely any fresh air and insufficient food and water, Barbara feared her child would die. The prison authorities permitted her to give the baby to relatives. Shortly thereafter Barbara was beheaded.

**Saint Charles Hyon Song-mun (1799–1846)** had served as a guide through Korea for the French missionaries and martyrs Saint Laurent-Marie-Joseph Imbert (1796–1839) and Saint Jacques-Honore Chastan (1803–1839). Saint Charles's father had been martyred in 1801. Charles, his wife, and his children were all arrested together. Charles was beheaded; his family died in prison. Later his sister Benedicta Hyon was executed.

**Saints Catharine Yi (1782–1839) and Magdalene Cho (1806–1839)** were mother and daughter, two poor women who supported themselves by working as servants, taking in sewing, and serving as private nurses. They were arrested together and so severely beaten that they died in prison before they could be executed.

The Korean Martyrs are among the patron saints of Korea. Saint Andrew Kim Dae-gon is the patron saint of Korea's Catholic clergy. Feast day: September 20.

**Blessed Laura Vicuña (1891–1904).** This saintly girl's body is enshrined in the National Sanctuary of Laura Vicuña in Santiago, Chile. The Church of Our Lady of the Snows and Blessed Laura Vincuña in Junin de los Andes, Argentina, preserves one of her vertebrae.

Laura Vicuña was born in Chile. When she was three months old civil war broke out in the country; with her husband in the army, Laura's mother, Mercedes Pino Vicuña, felt vulnerable and unprotected, so she took her infant daughter to Argentina. Soon thereafter Laura's mother received word that her husband had been killed in battle.

Mercedes had no way to support herself and Laura, so when an acquaintance, Manuel Mora, invited her to move into his home as his mistress, she accepted. When Laura reached school age Mora paid for her to attend a boarding school operated by the Salesian Sisters. Laura was a devout young girl who dreamed of becoming a Salesian nun. She wrote in her journal, "Oh my God, I want to love you and serve you all my life, give you my soul, my heart, my whole self."

At Christmas 1901 Mora tried repeatedly to seduce ten-year-old Laura. Back at school she begged to be allowed to enter the convent, but her confessor reminded her that she was too young. She could, however, join the sodality of the Children of Mary.

Late in 1903 Laura fell gravely ill; the sisters sent her home to recuperate. During her convalescence she endured Mora's violent temper and sexual advances. After months of these assaults she ran away from the house, but Mora pursued her and when he found her he beat her unconscious. She died eight days later.

Laura's death gave Mercedes the courage to leave Mora, make her confession, and return to the Church.

Blessed Laura Vicuña is the patron saint of victims of incest and abuse; she is also one of the patron saints of Argentina. Feast day: January 22.

**Saint Lawrence (died 258).** The body of Saint Lawrence was buried in the Cemetery of Cyriaca outside the walls of Rome. Sometime before 335, Emperor Constantine commissioned a basilica to be built over the martyr's grave. The builders dug away the hillside catacomb of Cyriaca to expose the tomb; it can be seen today, protected by an iron grille, in the crypt beneath the high altar of the Basilica of St. Lawrence Outside the Walls. The grille on which the saint was martyred is preserved beneath the high altar in Rome's Church of St. Lawrence in Lucina.

Lawrence was a deacon in the household of Pope Saint Sixtus II. On August 6, 258, after Mass, as Sixtus was seated teaching the congregation, Roman soldiers burst in and dragged away the pope and six of his deacons—but they did not arrest Lawrence. In tears, Lawrence clutched at Sixtus's robes and said, "Where are you going, priest, without your deacon? Where are you going, father, without your son?" Sixtus comforted Lawrence, saying that in a few days they would be reunited.

Saint Ambrose tells us that shortly after Sixtus and his deacons were beheaded, Lawrence was arraigned before the prefect of Rome, who demanded that he surrender the treasures of the Church. Lawrence asked for three days' time to gather them, then went away and distributed all the Church's valuables to the sick, the hungry, and the poor. Three days later he returned to the prefect with a crowd of cripples, the blind, and the poor, and declared to the prefect, "These are the treasures of the Church."

The prefect sentenced Lawrence to be bound to an iron grille and roasted over a slow fire. According to tradition, before he died he told his executioners, "Turn me over. I'm done on this side."

Saint Lawrence is the patron saint of cooks, deacons, and seminarians. He is invoked against fire. Saint Lawrence is one of the patron saints of Sri Lanka and Rome. Feast day: August 10.

**Saint Lawrence O'Toole (c. 1128–1180).** Lawrence O'Toole died at the Abbey of Eu in Normandy. He was buried in the abbey church, but his heart was sent for interment in his cathedral, Christ Church in Dublin. The saint's relics were destroyed during the French Revolution, but his heart is still entombed in Christ Church.

At age twenty-five Lawrence O'Toole was elected abbot of the Augustinian monastery of Glendalough. Although extremely young for such a post, Lawrence had the necessary qualities: he was devout, dedicated to enforcing the rule of his order, and a capable problem solver who during the first years of his abbacy was confronted with a famine in the countryside, bandits in the hills, and lax, surly monks who resented his authority. Based on his success at Glendalough, in 1161 he was chosen archbishop of Dublin.

Once again Lawrence set about reforming the clergy. He set the example by living in the style of a monk rather than of an archbishop. He let it be known that any person of any rank could call on him for help.

During this period the English launched their first invasion of Ireland. Lawrence often acted as the mediator between the Irish kings and chiefs and the English king, Henry II. During a diplomatic visit to England, Lawrence made a pilgrimage to Canterbury to pray at the tomb of Saint Thomas Becket. Later, while vesting for Mass, he was attacked by an assassin. Lawrence survived unharmed and persuaded King Henry to pardon the man rather than hang him.

From England he traveled to Rome, where Pope Alexander III created Lawrence papal legate to Ireland, with authority to reform clerical life there and settle any disputes related to the Church, its liberties, and its property. Henry II regarded Lawrence's legatine powers as a challenge to royal authority and no longer made himself available to the Irish archbishop. It was while traveling through France in the hope of gaining an audience with the king that Lawrence fell ill and died.

Saint Lawrence O'Toole is one of the patron saints of Dublin, Ireland. Feast day: November 14.

**Saint Lazarus (first century).** There are claims that three locations possess, or have possessed, the relics of Saint Lazarus: the Church of St. Lazarus in Larnaca, Cyprus, built over the site where they were found in 890 (in 898 the relics were transferred to Constantinople; they were lost during the sack of the city in 1204); the Cathedral of St. Lazarus in Autun, France, where the relics were destroyed during the French Revolution; and the Abbey Church of St. Victor in Marseilles, where some of the saint's relics are venerated. The tomb from which Christ raised Lazarus from the dead is shown to Holy Land pilgrims in Bethany.

Lazarus with his sisters Mary and Martha lived in the village of Bethany, modern-day al-Eizariya, less than two miles from Jerusalem. The Gospels of Luke and John describe the family as close friends of Jesus's.

Shortly before Jesus's arrest, Mary and Martha sent him word that Lazarus was seriously ill. By the time Jesus arrived, Lazarus was dead and had lain in the tomb for four days. Nonetheless, Christ insisted that the stone be rolled away. Then he called in a loud voice, "Lazarus, come forth!" And Lazarus, restored to life, stepped out of the tomb.

The New Testament never mentions Lazarus again. The French claim that after Christ's Ascension into heaven Lazarus, his sisters, and other disciples of the Lord sailed to the South of France where they established the Church. The Greeks claim that Lazarus sailed to Cyprus and preached the Gospel there.

Feast day: July 21.

**Pope Saint Leo the Great (c. 400–461).** The relics of Pope Leo the Great are enshrined within the altar dedicated to him in St. Peter's Basilica in Rome.

In 452 Attila the Hun led his army on Rome. As they approached the city the gates swung open and out rode Pope Leo I accompanied by a small entourage of clergy. No record of the conversation between the pope and the king of the Huns survives, but at the end of the conference Attila and his army rode away, leaving Rome in peace. Given the near invincibility of the Huns, Attila's decision struck many Christian writers of the Middle Ages as inexplicable, and so a legend sprang up that during the conference Attila saw the figures of Saint Peter and Saint Paul, each brandishing a sword, standing behind Pope Leo.

Three years later the king of the Vandals, Gaiseric, marched on Rome, and once again Pope Leo went out to appeal for mercy. Although Gaiseric was an Arian Christian, nothing the pope said could dissuade him from sacking Rome. But he did agree to leave the people unharmed and not to burn the city. The Vandals stripped Rome of all its valuables and carried off members of the imperial family and many aristocrats (Gaiseric couldn't resist these opportunities for ransom), but left Rome's buildings and monuments intact.

Saint Leo is best remembered for these two dramatic moments in his life, but he was also a gifted preacher and theologian and a tireless defender of the Catholic faith at a time when heresies were sweeping across the Mediterranean world.

Feast day: November 10.

**Saint Louis IX of France (1214–1270).** Relics of Saint Louis survive in the Cathedral of Monreale, Sicily, and the Church of St. Dominic in Bologna. His shrine in the Basilica of St. Denis outside Paris was melted down during the French Revolution and his bones destroyed. Only a single finger bone was recovered, and this is venerated today at St. Denis. Some of the saint's personal possessions have survived, including a tunic and the cilice, or haircloth, which he wore around his waist; these are preserved in the Treasury of the Cathedral of Notre Dame in Paris.

Louis IX, king of France, strove to be the ideal Christian monarch. He worked to root out corruption and favoritism in his court system, appointing judges who he believed would be impartial and temper justice with mercy. He also made himself available to settle disputes.

Louis gave generously to the University of Paris and encouraged the arts; his most significant contribution being Sainte Chapelle, the exquisite Gothic shrine he built for the Crown of Thorns.

Unlike most of his brother kings, Louis genuinely loved his wife, Margaret, and never betrayed her. During forty-two years of marriage they had eleven children.

Louis is especially famous for trying to revive the spirit of the Crusades at a time when the crusader kingdoms in the Holy Land were on the brink of destruction. His crusades failed, and he died of disease in Tunis.

Saint Louis's dynasty ruled France for more than five hundred years, until his descendant Louis XVI was guillotined during the French Revolution. At the moment the blade fell King Louis's chaplain exclaimed, "Son of Saint Louis, ascend to heaven!"

Saint Louis is the patron saint of bridegrooms, crusaders, the kings of France, and prisoners. He is the patron saint of the cities of Versailles, France; New Orleans, Louisiana; and St. Louis, Missouri. Feast day: August 25.

**Saint Louis Marie Grignon de Montfort (1673–1716).** Saint Louis de Montfort's relics are encased within a sarcophagus in the basilica dedicated to him in the town of Saint-Laurent-sur-Sevre, France.

Even as a boy Louis Grignon de Montfort knew he wanted to be a priest. He began and ended his school day with visits to the Blessed Sacrament. He and several classmates formed a group that visited and nursed the sick in charity hospitals.

After his ordination Louis served first as a hospital chaplain, then as a roving preacher. He attempted to live a life of constant prayer and to subsist entirely on what food or coins strangers felt moved to give him.

Louis was devoted to the Blessed Virgin Mary, wrote and preached about her often, and encouraged Catholics to recite the Rosary daily. His work, *True Devotion to Mary,* has been one of the most influential Marian texts of the last three hundred years. It calls for "total consecration to Jesus Christ through Mary" and has influenced millions of Catholics as well as many popes, including John Paul II, whose papal motto, *Totus tuus,* "entirely yours," was taken from de Montfort's work.

Feast day: April 28.

**Saint Louise de Marillac (1591–1660).** The bones of Saint Louise de Marillac are encased in a wax portrait sculpture and displayed in the Chapel of Our Lady of the Miraculous Medal at 140 Rue du Bac in Paris.

Louise de Marillac was a widow living in Paris when she met Saint Vincent de Paul, a priest who was trying, with mixed success, to manage several ambitious charitable organizations. Madame de Marillac possessed financial resources, good sense, management skills, and a deep desire to serve God. She volunteered to assist Father de Paul.

She recruited strong young women who worked in Paris as servants or had grown up on farms, forming them into a community of sisters who would go into the streets, the slums, the charity hospitals, wherever they were needed to feed the hungry, nurse the sick, comfort the dying, and shelter orphans, the elderly, and the homeless. These women became the Daughters of Charity.

Louise and her sisters tried to meet every need they encountered: they taught school to poor children whose parents could not afford tuition; they opened a shelter for the mentally ill; they nursed in battlefield hospitals; and they brought food, clothes, medicine, and their faith to convicts. Saint Louise's Daughters of Charity was the first Catholic religious organization to tend the poor and needy at every stage of life, from cradle to grave.

Saint Louise de Marillac is the patron saint of orphans, widows, and parents troubled by disappointing children. In 1960 Pope John XXIII declared her the patron saint of social workers.

Feast day: March 15.

**Saint Lucy (c. 283–c. 304).** For four hundred years the body of Saint Lucy lay in a grave in her native Sicily. Early in the eighth century Faroald II, duke of Spoleto, conquered the island and took the relics to Abruzzo in Italy. Exactly what became of the saint's remains is uncertain thanks to conflicting, often legendary accounts that place various bones in Bourges, Metz, and Constantinople. Venice claims to have the entire body of the saint, which is enshrined in a large side chapel in the Church of San Geremia. In 1981 thieves stole the relics of Saint Lucy, but the police recovered them on December 13—the saint's feast day.

Lucy was a Christian who lived in Syracuse, Sicily. During Emperor Diocletian's persecution of the Church she was martyred when a dagger was plunged into her throat.

Almost invariably artists depict Saint Lucy holding a plate or cup containing two eyes. This grisly symbol refers to a legend concerning a pagan suitor who tried to convince Lucy to renounce her faith and marry him. He began with flattery, complimenting her on the beauty of her eyes. According this story, Lucy plucked out her eyes and gave them to the man.

Saint Lucy is invoked against eye ailments. She is the patron saint of the city of Syracuse in Sicily. Feast day: December 13.

**Saint Ludmilla (860–921).** The body of Saint Ludmilla lies in a stone sarcophagus in the Basilica of St. George in Prague, Czech Republic.

Ludmilla and her husband, Boriwoi, were the first Christian duke and duchess of Bohemia (modern-day Czech Republic). They tried to establish the Catholic faith in their country but met strong resistance from the people as well as an influential anti-Christian faction among the nobility, including their son and daughter-in-law, Spitignev and Drahomíra.

After Borowoi's death Ludmilla became the guardian of her grandson, Wenceslaus. She raised him as a Catholic, which enraged Drahomíra and the anti-Christian party. Drahomíra hired assassins to get rid of the elderly duchess. They ambushed her and strangled her with her own scarf.

Saint Ludmilla is the patron saint of widows and is invoked against troubles with in-laws. She is one of the patron saints of the Czech Republic. Feast day: September 16.

**Saint Luke the Evangelist (first century).** About the year 357 the relics of Saint Luke were moved from their tomb in Thebes, Greece, to Constantinople. During the sack of Constantinople in 1204 crusaders stole the relics and gave them to the city of Padua. The bones of the saint have been enshrined in the Basilica of St. Justina ever since. In 1998 a team of forensic scientists opened the tomb and examined the bones. They found the skeleton of a man of Syrian descent, approximately seventy to eight-five years of age

Sancia of Mallorca (1309–1343), queen of Naples, commissioned this elaborate reliquary for the right arm of Saint Luke the Evangelist. Saint Luke wrote the Gospel that bears his name—note the quill pen in his hand. Réunion des Musées Nationaux/Art Resource, NY

at the time of death. The bones were dated from between 100 and 400 AD. The bishop of Padua gave the rib bone that would have been over the saint's heart to the Greek Orthodox metropolitan of Thebes, who enshrined it in Saint Luke's original sarcophagus.

Luke was a Greek physician from Antioch in Syria who became a Christian and a disciple of Saint Paul. When Paul was sent to Rome for trial Luke accompanied him and remained there until Paul was martyred.

Luke wrote the Gospel that bears his name and the Acts of the Apostles. Because his gospel contains so much material about the Blessed Virgin Mary, there is an ancient tradition that Our Lady was one of his sources.

Saint Luke is the patron saint of artists and physicians. Feast day: October 18.


**Saint Lydwina (1380–1433).** Initially Lydwina was buried inside her parish church in Schiedam, Netherlands. In the sixteenth century, after a mob of Calvinists ransacked the church, the saint's relics were moved to the Cathedral of St. Michael and St. Gudula in Brussels, Belgium.

While skating with friends on the frozen Schie River, fifteen-year-old Lydwina fell and struck her head on the ice. The injury left her a permanent invalid. Confined to her bed and frequently in pain, the girl fell into a deep depression. Her parish priest, Father John Pot, visited her and reminded Lydwina that once she had told him of her desire to be a nun; now Father John suggested that she look upon her sick room as her convent and offer up to God her physical ailments, as a nun offers up her penances and sacrifices. He also taught her how to deepen her prayer life and meditate for long periods.

As Lydwina's spiritual life matured, her depression lifted. Neighbors came to ask for her prayers and advice. The local bishop was so impressed by Lydwina that he permitted her parish priest to bring her Holy Communion twice each week—a rare privilege in the fifteenth century, when most Catholics received the Eucharist only once or twice a year.

Saint Lydwina is the patron saint of skaters and invalids. Feast day: April 14.


**Saint Madeline Sophie Barat (1779–1865).** The body of Saint Madeline Sophie Barat is enshrined in a gilt reliquary in the Church of St. Francis Xavier of the Foreign Missions in Paris.

Madeline Sophie Barat's older brother was a seminary professor who taught her Latin, Greek, science, and history. Such an education was rare for a girl in late-eighteeth-century France, and Madeline took such delight in the privilege that she vowed to share what she had learned with other young girls.

In 1800 with three companions she founded the Society of the Sacred Heart, a new community of nuns dedicated to female education.

In spite of the aftereffects of the French Revolution and the upheavals caused by the Napoleonic Wars, Mother Madeline Sophie founded convents and schools across France, Italy, and Switzerland. Her sisters opened free schools for poor girls as well as boarding schools for girls whose families could afford to pay tuition. By the end of her life the Sacred Heart nuns were operating more than one hundred schools in Europe and the Americas.

Feast day: May 25.


**Saint Magnus (c. 1076–1115).** The bones of Saint Magnus were interred in the stone pier at the southern end of the choir in the Cathedral of St. Magnus at Kirkwall in Scotland's Orkney Islands. The relics were rediscovered in 1919. His original coffin is on display at the Orkney Museum.

In an age when Norsemen were still expected to go on Viking raids, Magnus, son of the earl of Orkney, refused to participate. It is said that when he was compelled to accompany one such raid in Wales, he stayed on the Viking ship chanting psalms while his fellow Vikings indulged themselves in pillage, rape, and slaughter.

When his cousin Haakon seized control of Orkney, Magnus took refuge in Scotland. The king of Norway arbitrated a settlement between the two cousins, who agreed to rule the island jointly. In 1114 Haakon attempted to drive Magnus from power. Caught unawares, Magnus had only two ships of supporters to Haakon's eight. He tried to negotiate a truce, but Haakon would not accept any terms. Instead, he gave his cook an axe and ordered him to kill Magnus. As he knelt for the deathblow Magnus prayed aloud for his murderers.

Saint Magnus is the patron saint of Orkney. Feast day: April 16.

**Saint Malachy (1094–1148).** In 1148 Saint Malachy, archbishop of Armagh in Ireland, was on his way to Rome when he stopped at Clairvaux Abbey in France to call on his closest friend, Saint Bernard of Clairvaux. During his visit Malachy fell ill; he died on November 2, All Souls Day, and was buried in the abbey church. Five years later Saint Bernard died and was buried beside his friend. When partisans of the French Revolution shut down the abbey in 1790, the relics of Saint Malachy and Saint Bernard were transferred to Troyes Cathedral, where they are preserved to this day in the same reliquary casket.

As archbishop of Armagh, Malachy was primate, or chief bishop, of Ireland. He used his authority to enforce church discipline among the clergy and persuade parishes and monastic communities that followed the ancient Celtic liturgy to adopt the liturgy used in Rome and elsewhere in the Latin world.

He was a friend of Saint Bernard and often visited him at Clairvaux Abbey. Malachy petitioned the pope to relieve him of the burden of being archbishop and permit him to become a monk at Clairvaux. The pope declined Malachy's request; Malachy was too effective as primate.

There is a legend that Malachy was a prophet who predicted

every pope from his own day until the end of the world. If that is true, then Benedict XVI is the next to last pope. In fact, the "Prophecies of Saint Malachy" are a forgery invented about the year 1590.

Saint Malachy is one of the patron saints of the archdiocese of Armagh in Ireland. Feast day: November 3.

**Saint Margaret of Antioch (c. 304).** Saint Margaret was a popular saint in the East and the West throughout the Middle Ages; as a result many churches, monasteries, and convents claimed to possess her relics, including the Church of St. Peter della Valle near Lake Bolsena and the Cathedral of Montefalcone, both in Italy. A portion of her bones are venerated in the Church of St. Marina in Athens, Greece, and one of her hands is preserved in the Vatopedi Monastery on Mount Athos, Greece.

There probably was a Christian named Margaret or Marina (her name in the Greek Church) who was martyred in Antioch during Diocletian's persecution of the Church. But that is all we know for certain about her.

Legend says that she was swallowed by a dragon, but when she made the sign of the cross in the dragon's belly its body split open and she emerged unscathed.

Saint Joan of Arc said that one of the three saints who spoke to her was Saint Margaret of Antioch; she is among the Fourteen Holy Helpers.

Saint Margaret is the patron saint of women in childbirth, and she is invoked against the devil. Feast day: July 20.

**Blessed Margaret of Castello (1287–1320).** When Margaret of Castello died, her parish priest planned to bury her in the churchyard, but the mourners who filled the church for her Requiem Mass insisted that she be buried inside the church with all the other distinguished dead of the parish. The priest and the congregation were still arguing the point when a girl whose legs were crippled dragged herself to Margaret's coffin. She touched the casket, then stood up and began to walk. The miracle convinced the priest to give Margaret a tomb inside the church. Today her remains lie beneath the high altar of Castello's Church of St. Dominic.

Margaret was born blind and with severe curvature of the spine, and her right leg was an inch and a half shorter than her left. When she was six years old her mother and father took her to a shrine in the town of Castello, hoping for a miracle. When Margaret was not healed, her parents abandoned her.

Some kind women rescued the frightened child and found a home for her with a childless couple named Venfarino and Grigia. Perhaps for the first time in her life Margaret was surrounded by people who loved her: her adoptive parents, the good ladies who rushed to her aid the day she was abandoned, as well as a convent of nuns next door who treated her like a beloved niece.

At age fifteen Margaret joined the Third Order of Saint Dominic; she took the vows of a nun and wore the Dominican habit but lived at home. She made the care of the sick and the sorrowing her particular mission. She even talked her way into the local prison, where she consoled the convicts.

When Margaret died at age thirty-three, virtually every inhabitant of Castello crowded into the church for her Requiem Mass.

Blessed Margaret of Castello is the patron saint of the disabled. Feast day: April 13.


**Saint Margaret Clitheroe or Clitherow (c. 1553–1586).** The sergeants of York had been ordered by the sheriff to bury the body of Saint Margaret "in an obscure and filthy corner of the city." But her spiritual director, Father John Mush, with other Catholics of York, exhumed it and buried it far outside the city in an unknown location. Tradition holds that these Catholics removed the martyr's right hand and kept it as a relic; it is preserved today at St. Mary's Convent, also known as Bar Convent, in York, England.

Margaret's house still stands in the York neighborhood known as the Shambles.

Margaret Middleton, the daughter of successful candle makers in York, England, married John Clitheroe, a wealthy butcher, when she was eighteen years old. Margaret and John were Anglicans, but one of John's brothers, William, had remained Catholic; it appears that he was instrumental in bringing Margaret back to the Catholic faith.

In 1574 a Catholic priest reconciled Margaret to the Church. From that day onward she wanted to attend Mass daily and provide her children with a Catholic education. She brought in carpenters to build a secret room and cupboards; then she opened her home to a priest and a Catholic tutor. For twelve years the Clitheroe house was a Mass center for the Catholics of York and the surrounding region.

But Margaret could not elude the priest-hunters forever. In March 1586 government agents burst into her house. The priest and the tutor escaped, but an eleven-year-old, who was living with the Clitheroes, was arrested and threatened with a beating if he didn't reveal everything he knew. The terrified child confessed that a priest said Mass daily in the house; then he led the authorities to the priest's secret room and to the secret cupboards that held the vestments, books, and sacred vessels used for Mass. Margaret was arrested for harboring a Catholic priest and attending Mass.

At her arraignment Margaret refused to plead guilty or innocent. This legal strategy frustrated the government's plan to prosecute her and spared her family and friends the agony of being forced to testify against her. But there was a terrible penalty for a suspect who refused to enter a plea.

On March 25 Margaret was led from prison, stripped down to her shift, then staked out on the ground. A heavy wooden door was laid over her body, and large stones were piled on the door, one by one. It took the executioners fifteen minutes to crush Margaret Clitheroe to death.

Saint Margaret Clitheroe is the patron saint of businesswomen. Feast day: March 25.

**Saint Margaret Mary Alacoque (1647–1690).** The saint's bones are encased in a wax portrait sculpture dressed in the habit of a Vistation nun in the chapel of the Visitation Monastery at Paray-le-Monial, France.

Margaret Mary Alacoque was a Visitation nun who received visions of Jesus Christ in which he called upon all Christians to venerate his Sacred Heart, the emblem of his love for all human-kind. Active in France at this time was a puritanical Catholic move-ment known as the Jansenists; they rejected Margaret's revelations, arguing that devotion to the Sacred Heart of Jesus was too physical and corporeal and not sufficiently spiritual. The Jesuits, however, embraced Margaret's revelations and promoted the Sacred Heart widely throughout their parishes and schools and in their foreign missions.

Devotion to the Sacred Heart was a mainstay of Catholic devo-tional life for almost three hundred years until, in the wake of the upheavals that followed the Second Vatican Council, it was dismissed in many quarters of the Church as sentimental. In the twenty-first century the devotion has seen a revival, led by Pope John Paul II and Pope Benedict XVI, who urge Catholics to see in the Sacred Heart the image of the Lord's boundless love and mercy.

Saint Margaret Mary Alacoque is invoked against polio. She is the patron saint of all those devoted to the Sacred Heart of Jesus. Feast day: October 16.

**Saint Margaret of Cortona (1247–1297).** Saint Margaret's relics are encased in a silver reliquary in the Sanctuary of St. Margaret in Cortona, Italy.

Margaret was about thirteen years old when she came to the

attention of Arsenio, the sixteen-year-old son of the local baron. She was attractive, bold, and unhappy at home (Margaret and her stepmother had been squabbling almost from the moment the woman set foot in the house). Arsenio invited Margaret to live at the castle as his mistress, and she accepted. Arsenio told her candidly that he would never marry her; the idea of making a peasant girl his wife was out of the question. Margaret, however, convinced herself that she could persuade Arsenio otherwise.

For nine years the couple lived together. They had a son. But still Arsenio had not made Margaret his wife.

One day he left home to attend to family business at a far-off estate. When the day of Arsenio's return had passed Margaret began to worry. Then Arsenio's dog arrived at the castle alone. Agitated, the animal kept circling Margaret, walking to the door, then returning to her, until finally she followed the animal. The dog led her into the woods, to a pile of dry brush. When Margaret cleared it away she found in a shallow pit Arsenio's decomposing body.

The shock was the first step of her conversion. For nine years she and Arsenio had put their religion out of their minds. Now Margaret wondered about the state of Arsenio's soul: Had he had time to repent before his murderers killed him? She also feared for her own soul. She went to confession, left the baron's castle with her son, and walked to Cortona, where the Franciscan friars had a reputation for helping penitents.

The Franciscans enrolled Margaret's son in one of their schools and found her a home with two unmarried sisters. Perhaps because she always feared what had become of Arsenio, Margaret prayed with special fervor for the Poor Souls in Purgatory. On her deathbed she said that she saw a great crowd coming from heaven to greet her; they were the souls she had ransomed by her prayers.

Saint Margaret of Cortona is the patron saint of single mothers. Feast day: February 22.

**Saint Margaret of Scotland (c. 1045–1093).** Saint Margaret was buried at Dunfermline with her husband, King Malcolm. At the Reformation the relics of Saint Margaret and the body of Malcolm were taken to safety in Douai, Belgium, then to Spain, where King Philip II and Queen Isabella enshrined them in the church of the Escorial Palace. In 1863 Bishop James Gillis of Edinburgh traveled to Spain and petitioned the king for a major relic of Saint Margaret to bring back to Scotland. That relic, part of the saint's shoulder bone, was subsequently presented to the Ursuline nuns in Edinburgh. In 2008 the nuns presented the relic to the National Shrine of St. Margaret of Scotland in Dunfermline.

Margaret was born in Hungary, the daughter of a Hungarian princess and an Anglo-Saxon prince. She received an excellent education, and all her life she loved books and encouraged learning. In 1070 she married Malcolm III, king of Scotland. It was a love match that produced four sons and two daughters.

Scotland was a backward place in the eleventh century; Queen Margaret brought a new level of culture to Scots society, promoted religious practices followed by the Catholics in Rome and elsewhere on the Continent, rebuilt the Abbey of Iona, built a hostel for pilgrims to the shrine of Saint Andrew, and founded Dunfermline Abbey. She raised her children herself and cared for the poor personally. Her leisure hours she filled with either praying or reading.

Saint Margaret of Scotland is the patron saint of learning and is one of the patron saints of Scotland. Feast day: November 16.

**Blessed Margaret Pole (1473–1541).** As was the case with other distinguished offenders against the English Crown, the body of Margaret Pole was buried in the crypt of the Chapel of St. Peter ad Vincula in the Tower of London.

Because she was one of the last of England's Plantagenet dynasty, Margaret's life was full of sorrow. Her father, her brother, and her two first cousins—the famous "Little Princes in the Tower"—were all judicially murdered, victims of the bloody struggle for the English Crown known as the War of the Roses.

At age eighteen Margaret married Richard Pole, a gentleman who enjoyed the favor of the first Tudor king, Henry VII. The next king, young Henry VIII, was kind to Margaret, whom he addressed as "aunt": he restored to her the estates that had been confiscated when her brother, Edward, was executed, asked her to serve as god-mother to Princess Mary, and named her governess of the princess's household—a position she held until Henry annulled his marriage to Queen Catherine and married Anne Boleyn.

With the Boleyn marriage Henry severed England's ties with Rome and declared himself Supreme Head of the Church in England. At that point Margaret faced a dual crisis: how to remain true to her faith and loyal to Catherine and Mary. Further com-plicating her life was her son Reginald, who was pursuing a career in the Church on the Continent; he published a book denouncing Henry's claim to supremacy over the Church.

Since Reginald Pole was out of reach, Henry turned against the entire Pole family. In 1538 Margaret and more than a dozen mem-bers of her family, including her eleven-year-old grandson, were arrested. Most were executed within weeks of their arrest. Margaret was imprisoned for three years before she was led out to a summary execution, without trial. As she knelt before the headsman's block she declared, "Blessed are they who suffer persecution for justice's sake, for theirs is the Kingdom of Heaven."

Feast day: May 28.

**Saint Marguerite Bourgeoys (1620–1700).** In 2005 the relics of Marguerite Bourgeoys were entombed in the side altar of the cha-pel of Notre-Dame-de-Bon-Secours, below the little wooden statue of Our Lady that she carried to Montreal from France exactly 350 years earlier. In the chapel's museum are artifacts associated with Saint Marguerite.

During a procession in honor of Our Lady of the Rosary, Marguerite Bourgeoys, then nineteen years old, felt called to enter the convent. In 1652 she met Monsieur de Maisonneuve, founder of Montreal and governor of the colony of New France; he told her that he needed nuns to teach the French and Indian children of the colony. Drawn by the challenge of missionary work, longing to serve God in the New World, but uncertain if she was up to the hardships of life in Canada, Marguerite prayed to Our Lady for guidance. She had a vision in which the Blessed Mother said, "Go! I will not forsake you."

She arrived in Montreal in November 1653. It was not a city but an outpost in the wilderness, surrounded by hostile Indian tribes. Marguerite set to work, opening a school in a disused stable, constructing a chapel dedicated to Our Lady of Good Help (Notre-Dame-de-Bon-Secours), and teaching the young women of the colony how to cook, sew, and run a household. She founded a community of nuns who performed any task or service the people of Montreal needed. The colonists referred to Marguerite as "the Mother of the Colony."

Saint Marguerite Bourgeoys is invoked against poverty. Feast day: January 12.

**Saint Marguerite d'Youville (1701–1771).** The relics of Marguerite d'Youville are enshrined in the Basilica of St. Anne in Varenne, Quebec, her birthplace.

Marguerite d'Youville is the first native-born Canadian to be proclaimed a saint. She was twenty-one when she married François d'Youville; the couple lived with François's mother. Marguerite and her mother-in-law did not get along well. Meanwhile, François and Marguerite's marriage began to unravel thanks to his adultery and bootlegging. Nevertheless she gave birth to six children, four of whom died in infancy. In 1730 François died. To pay off her husband's debts and support herself and her two surviving children, Marguerite opened a small store in Montreal. Out of her meager income she put aside a few coins for those who were even poorer than she. And she took in a blind woman who had no place else to live.

In 1737 Marguerite and three companions formed a community that became known as the Sisters of Charity of Montreal. They devoted themselves to the service of the poor, the sick, and the abandoned. At a time when social rank meant everything, Marguerite and her sisters were tireless champions of the rights of the lower classes, and this commitment attracted the mockery and hostility of Montreal's middle and upper classes.

The sisters' life was very hard. They were often short of funds. They lost their home to one fire, and then their hospital to another. Yet Marguerite and her nuns persevered. Their order spread across the province of Quebec, and then into the United States.

Saint Marguerite d'Youville is the patron saint of spouses in a difficult marriage. Feast day: October 16.


**Saint Maria Goretti (1890–1902).** Originally the body of Maria Goretti was buried in the cemetery of Nettuno, Italy. In 1929 Maria's remains were exhumed and entombed in Nettuno's Basilica of Our Lady of Grace. After her beatification in 1947 the bones of the saint were encased in a wax portrait sculpture, which lies in a glass casket beneath the altar of the basilica's crypt chapel of Saint Maria Goretti.

The Goretti family were tenant farmers on an estate near Ancona in southern Italy. They shared a large loft over a barn with another family of tenant farmers, the Serenellis. While the adults and older children worked in the fields, Maria stayed at the loft, cooking, cleaning, and watching her younger sisters.

At age eleven she looked forward to making her First Holy Communion, but her mother said she must postpone it as she had not attended any catechism classes. Maria solved the problem by approaching a local priest and asking him to prepare her. She made her Communion in May 1902. A few weeks afterward nineteen-year-old Alessandro Serenelli made sexual advances toward Maria. She rebuffed him.

On July 5 Maria was alone outside the barn with her baby sister when Alessandro appeared. He dragged her into the loft and tried to rape her. Maria fought back. Alessandro drew a knife and stabbed her fourteen times. As Maria fell to the floor, Alessandro fled.

Maria was still alive and conscious when her family and the Serenellis returned from the fields. She was taken to a hospital, but her wounds were too severe. Before she died, she said that she forgave Alessandro.

Saint Maria Goretti is the patron saint of victims of rape, of young girls, and of the Solidarity of the Children of Mary. Feast day: July 6.

**Saint Mariana de Jesus de Paredes (1618–1645).** The remains of Mariana de Jesus de Paredes are enclosed in a sarcophagus beneath the high altar of the Church of the Society of Jesus in Quito, Ecuador. The church's museum displays several items that belonged to Saint Mariana.

The daughter of Spanish aristocrats who had settled in Quito, Ecuador, Mariana was a religious prodigy who vowed herself to a life of poverty, chastity, and obedience when she was only ten years old. She tried to live as a cloistered nun in her parents' house, but her fame spread throughout the city. It is said that she survived on nothing but the Holy Eucharist and that she experienced ecstasies, could foretell the future, and could cure the sick by sprinkling them with holy water or making the sign of the cross over them. There are stories of Mariana raising people from the dead.

Saint Mariana de Jesus de Paredes is the patron saint of the sick, and she is one of the patron saints of the Americas. Feast day: May 26.

**Blessed Marianne Cope (1838–1918).** Following her Requiem Mass, Mother Marianne Cope was buried in the cemetery of St. Francis Church in Kalaupapa, Hawaii. In 2009 her remains were transferred to a beautifully carved wooden reliquary chest located in the Chapel of the Sisters of St. Francis motherhouse in Syracuse, New York. A museum at the motherhouse displays many items that belonged to Mother Marianne.

Barbara Cope (Marianne was the name she took upon entering the convent) was a year old when her family emigrated from Germany to Utica, New York. She completed eighth grade, then took a job in a factory to help support her family (she was the eldest of ten children). At age twenty-four she entered the convent of the Sisters of St. Francis in Syracuse. She studied medicine and worked as a nurse-administrator of St. Joseph's Hospital in Syracuse.

In 1883, when Mother Marianne was superior general of her order, she received a letter from the bishop of the Sandwich Islands (as Hawaii was known at that time), asking for nursing sisters, particularly nuns who were willing to care for leprosy patients. Thirty-five sisters volunteered; Mother Marianne chose six and appointed herself as their leader, saying, "I am not afraid of any disease."

The nuns arrived in Honolulu on November 8, 1883. They opened a hospital on the island of Maui, reorganized a substandard hospital on Oahu, and opened a home for orphaned girls whose parents had died of leprosy. In 1884 Mother Marianne met Father Damien de Veuster; two years later she was treating him for leprosy. In 1888 Mother Marianne and two sisters volunteered to operate the leprosy hospital on Molokai, where victims of the disease were exiled. By this time Father Damien was dying; the nuns nursed him during the final months of his life. After Father Damien's death Mother Marianne took over the care of the leprosy patients, remaining among them for the rest of her life.

Blessed Marianne Cope is invoked against leprosy. Feast day: January 23.

**Maria Stein Center—Shrine of the Holy Relics (founded 1875).**
In the second half of the nineteenth century two relic collections
were united at Maria Stein, Ohio, in the convent of the Sisters of
the Precious Blood. In 1845 Sister Lucy Joos and Sister Johanna
Gruenfelder brought from Europe six hundred relics representing every saint on the liturgical calendar at the time and presented
the collection to Father Francis de Sales Brunner, an avid collector of sacred relics. The complete remains of five early Christian
martyrs, Saints Concordia, Victoria, Innocent, Cruser, and Roga-
tus, were the centerpiece of Father Brunner's collection, which
passed to the Precious Blood Sisters after the priest's death in
1859. Then, in 1872, Father J. M. Gartner traveled to Rome where
he acquired 175 relics. In 1875 he presented this collection to the
sisters.

With more than eleven hundred relics, Maria Stein possesses
the second-largest relic collection in the United States. The relics
are displayed in the Sacred Heart Relic Chapel at Maria Stein.

**Blessed Marie of the Incarnation Guyart (1599–1672).** The
remains of Marie of the Incarnation are enclosed within a black
marble sarcophagus in the Chapel of the Ursulines in Quebec City.
The adjacent museum displays several objects that belonged to
Blessed Marie, including her rosary.

At age twenty-one Marie Guyart began receiving visions and
private revelations. After the death of her husband and when her
son was fifteen, Marie entrusted the boy to her sister and entered
the Ursuline convent at Tours, her hometown. She taught school
for six years, but her visions instructed her to go to Canada as a
missionary. In 1639 Mother Marie and two Ursuline nuns, along
with their patron, Madame Marie-Madeleine de Gruel de la Peltrie,
arrived in Quebec, where they established the first Ursuline convent and school in Canada. Mother Marie and Blessed François
Laval, bishop of Quebec, quarreled often over the subject of the
independence of the Ursulines. The bishop argued that he had

authority over the nuns; Mother Marie insisted that the Ursulines were independent of diocesan control.

Mother Marie taught French and Indian girls. She compiled Iroquois and Algonquin dictionaries, and she wrote a catechism in Iroquois.

Feast day: April 30.

**Saint Mark the Evangelist (first century).** According to an ancient tradition among the Christians of Egypt, Saint Mark was buried in Alexandria. In 828 two Venetian merchants, Buono of Malamocco and Rustico of Torcello, were in Alexandria on business when they met several priests assigned to the church where the relics of Saint Mark were enshrined. Since the armies of Islam had conquered Egypt in 647, there had been incidents of mobs attacking Christians and ransacking churches and monasteries. The priests lived in dread of rioters breaking into their church and destroying the relics of Saint Mark. According to this story, Buono and Rustico offered to carry the body of the saint to Venice, where it would be safe and greatly venerated. The priests agreed and helped the merchants transfer the relics from their sarcophagus into a wooden chest. To deter Muslim custom officials, the Christians covered the saint's bones with a thick layer of raw pork, which Muslims regard as unclean. The pork did the trick: when customs officers opened the chest they recoiled from the meat and did not probe further. The opulent Basilica of St. Mark in Venice was built for the relics, which lie in a stone chest beneath the high altar. In 1968 Pope Paul VI gave some of the relics to a visiting delegation of Coptic clergy; the rest of the saint's bones remain in Venice.

It is likely that Mark the evangelist is John Mark, the young cousin of Saint Barnabas, mentioned in the Acts of the Apostles. Saint Paul found the boy unreliable and insufferable; ultimately John Mark was the cause of a falling-out between Barnabas and Paul. Saint Peter on the other hand was very fond of John Mark, addressing him as "my son," which led to the tradition that Peter was the source for Saint Mark's Gospel.

Mark may have indirectly identified himself in his Gospel. In the scene that describes Christ's arrest, a teenage boy wearing only a loincloth has followed the Lord and the apostles to the garden of Gethsemane. As the soldiers bind Jesus, the boy turns to run; one of the soldiers reaches out to grab him, but catches the loincloth instead. The boy runs off into the night, naked.

According to tradition, on Easter Sunday in the year 68 Mark was arrested by Roman soldiers who tied a noose around his neck and dragged him through the streets of Alexandria until he died of strangulation.

Saint Mark is the patron saint of lions, lawyers, notaries, and prisoners. He is one of the patron saints of Venice and Egypt. Feast day: April 25.

**Saint Martha.** At least since the twelfth century the relics of Saint Martha have been venerated in Tarascon in Provence. Today her bones lie in an ancient sarcophagus in the crypt of the Tarascon's Collegiate Church of St. Martha.

The Gospels of Saint Luke and Saint John tell us that Martha, her sister Mary, and their brother Lazarus were close friends of Our Lord. During one of Christ's visits to their home in Bethany, Martha rushed about the house, preparing the table, cooking the meal, trying to make everything perfect, while her sister Mary sat at Jesus's feet listening to him. Frustrated, Martha said, "Lord, do you not care that my sister has left me to serve alone? Tell her then to help me." Our Lord answered, "Martha, Martha, you are anxious and troubled about many things; one thing is needful. Mary has chosen the good portion, which shall not be taken away from her" (Luke 10:40–42).

The next time the New Testament mentions the family of Bethany is in Saint John's Gospel, just days before Christ's Passion. Lazarus had died and Jesus came to see Martha and Mary. Martha went out to meet him and said, "Lord if you had been here, my brother would not have died." Then she adds this confession of faith: "And even now I know that whatever you ask from God, God will give you" (John 11:21–22).

With that Martha, Mary, Jesus, his apostles, and the mourners who gathered in Martha and Mary's house went to Lazarus's tomb, where Christ ordered that the stone at the mouth of the grave be rolled back. Then, in a loud voice he called, "Lazarus! Come forth!" And Martha and Mary's brother, four days dead, walked out of the tomb alive.

There is a legend that as Martha preached to a crowd beside the river Rhone a teenage boy on the opposite shore tried to swim across to hear her. He was carried away by the current and drowned. The boy's family and friends carried his body to Martha, who prayed earnestly to Christ, addressing him as "my dear guest." Leaning down she grasped the boy's hand; immediately he came back to life.

Saint Martha is the patron saint of homemakers, cooks, and servants. Feast day: July 29.


**Saint Martin de Porres (1579–1639).** The bones of Martin de Porres are kept in a silver chest in the Church of Santo Domingo in Lima, Peru. Visitors may see his cell in the adjacent monastery.

Martin's mother, Ana, was an African who had once been a slave, then became the mistress of Don Juan de Porres, a Spanish nobleman. Two or three years after Martin's birth Ana and Don Juan had a little girl. Ana and her children lived in poverty because Don Juan would not support them; he was ashamed that his children were dark-skinned like their mother. The year Martin turned seven Don Juan had a change of heart: he acknowledged his children and supported them and their mother.

Martin wanted to join the Dominicans, but the law in Peru barred Indians, Africans, and people of mixed race from the religious orders. The prior of the Dominican monastery in Lima agreed to admit Marin as a *donado,* essentially a servant, and permitted him to take the vows of a lay brother. Not all the Dominicans were pleased with having a man who was illegitimate and of mixed race in the community. They mocked and insulted Martin openly.

Outside the priory Martin was developing a reputation as a saint. It was said that he had healed a priest whose legs were infected with gangrene. A Peruvian merchant who fell ill in Mexico cried aloud, "Oh, Brother Martin! If only you were here to care for me." A moment later Martin entered the sick man's room.

On one occasion Martin saw an elderly beggar lying in the street, his body covered with ulcers. Martin took him back to the monastery and laid him in his own bed. He did the same for an Indian who had been stabbed and was bleeding to death. It was said that he fed 160 poor every day and gave alms generously once a week—although no one knew where he got the stores of food or the supply of coins for these acts of charity.

Saint Martin de Porres is the patron saint of African Americans, racial harmony, barbers, hoteliers, public schools, and the poor. He is invoked against mice and rats. Saint Martin is also one of the patron saints of Peru. Feast day: November 3.


**Saint Martin of Tours (c. 316–397).** The bishops of Tours who succeeded Martin erected a small chapel over his grave in Tours, but the chapel could not accommodate the throngs of pilgrims who came to pray at the tomb. In 466 construction of a grand basilica was begun; this was succeeded by several larger churches. In 1562 a mob of Huguenots attacked the church, destroying its works of art, including the tomb of Saint Martin, and scattering his bones. Catholics recovered some of the saint's relics and returned them to his battered shrine, but during the French Revolution the church was leveled and the tomb vanished. It was rediscovered in 1860, when construction of a new shrine-church began. The tomb with its fragmentary relics lies in the crypt of the new basilica of St. Martin in Tours. His cloak, which he divided with a poor beggar, was preserved by the Frankish kings, but the relic was lost centuries ago.

Martin, the son of a pagan family, was studying to be a Christian when he was called up for military service in the Roman army. During the years he served in the legions, his conversion remained incomplete, but he did become a Roman officer. One winter when Martin and his men were quartered in Amiens, his cohort presented him with a magnificent cloak of thick red wool. As he rode through the city Martin saw a poor man, dressed in rags, shivering violently in the cold. Martin drew his sword, cut his cloak in half, and gave the piece to the stranger. That night Jesus Christ appeared to Martin wearing half of the cloak. "Look," Christ said to the angels attending him, "Martin, who is not yet baptized, has wrapped me in his own cloak."

Once Martin had served his time in the army he traveled to Poitiers, where the bishop, Saint Hilary, completed his religious education and baptized him.

Martin became a priest and the bishop of Tours. He founded an abbey at Ligugé and divided his diocese into parishes. He was an active bishop who traveled into western France to bring Christianity to a region that worshipped the Roman gods, or the gods of the Druids, or both.

He is considered one of the founders of the Church in France, and one of the greatest bishops of the period following the age of persecution.

Saint Martin of Tours is the patron saint of equestrians, cavalry, soldiers, winemakers, hoteliers, panhandlers, horses, and geese. He is invoked against alcoholism. Saint Martin is one of the patron saints of the Pontifical Swiss Guards and of France. Feast day: November 11.


**Saint Martura (first century?).** In the summer of 1844 Father Clemens Hammer, pastor of St. Mary's Church in Cincinnati, Ohio, returned from a trip to Europe with the relics of a Roman martyr. Bishop John B. Purcell sealed the martyr's bones and a vial containing some of her blood inside the high altar of the church, where they remain today and are visible through a glass plate in the base of the altar. The bones and the vial were discovered in the Catacomb of St. Priscilla in Rome in January 1844. From the archaeological evidence gathered at the time her tomb was found, we know that she was a Christian martyr who died during the first century, but we possess no other facts about this woman. Even her true name is lost; "Martura" is Latin for "female martyr."

**Martyrs of Nagasaki (1597).** In most cases, after execution the bodies of the Japanese martyrs were burned and the ashes scattered, but some relics have survived and are safeguarded at the Twenty-six Martyrs Church in Nagasaki, Japan. Among the shrine's treasures is a portion of an arm bone from Saint James Kisai.

Saint Francis Xavier brought the faith to Japan in 1549. By 1580, 200,000 Japanese were Catholics, there were large churches at Nagasaki and Kyoto, a seminary to train Japanese men for the priesthood, a hospital on the island of Kyushu, and mission churches scattered around the country. By 1612, the number Catholics in the country had risen to 400,000 out of a population of 12 million.

Although there had been strong commercial and diplomatic ties between the Japanese and the Spanish and Portuguese, English and Dutch Protestant traders spread rumors among the Japanese upper classes that the Spanish and Portuguese planned to make Japan a colony and introduce the Inquisition. This false report led to the persecution of Christians in Japan and ultimately the closing of the country to all outsiders. The first execution took place on February 5, 1597, at Nagasaki, where twenty-six Christians, including eight European missionaries, were crucified. By 1664, tens of thousands of Japanese had given their lives for the faith.

Among the Martyrs of Nagasaki were:

**Saint Paul Miki,** thirty years old. The son of a samurai, this Jesuit seminarian was arrested shortly before his ordination day.

**Saint Anthony and Saint Louis Ibaraki,** altar boys, thirteen and twelve years old, respectively. These child martyrs died singing hymns. From his cross Anthony could see his grief-stricken mother and father among the crowd of spectators.

**Saint Peter Baptist,** fifty years old, a Spaniard and the superior of the Franciscans in Japan, he was renowned for his kindness to lepers.

**Saint Philip of Jesus,** twenty-four years old, from Mexico. On the day of his martyrdom his mother, back home in Mexico, was embroidering a new set of Mass vestments for him.

**Saint Pablo Suzuki,** forty-nine years old, was a lay catechist and also administrator of St. Joseph's Hospital in Kyoto.

**Saint James Kisai,** sixty-four years old, was a Jesuit lay brother who ran the guesthouse at the Jesuit residence.

Saint Peter Baptist is one of the patron saints of Japan. Saint Philip de Jesus is one of the patron saints of Mexico City. Saint Gonsalv Garcia is one of the patron saints of Mumbai, India. Feast day of the Martyrs of Nagasaki: February 5.

**Martyrs of Uganda (1885–1887).** Relics of these twenty-two martyrs are venerated at the Uganda Martyrs Shrine in Namugongo, Uganda. The shrine's altar stands on the spot where Saint Charles Lwanga was martyred, and small shrines and monuments have been erected on the site where the other saints suffered.

Between 1885 and 1887, at least forty-five Ugandan Catholics and Anglicans were executed by the despotic king Mwanga II. Some were victims of Mwanga's hatred of Ugandan Christians; others were killed because they rebuffed the king's homosexual advances. Pope Paul VI canonized the twenty-two Ugandan Catholic martyrs in 1964. Among the Catholic martyrs of Uganda were:

**Saint Joseph Mukasa,** twenty-five years old, was the king's majordomo, or chief of his household, and the first Catholic murdered by Mwanga. He rebuked Mwanga for ordering the death of English Anglican missionary James Hannington, for his heavy drinking, and for his advances toward the boys who served as royal pages. Mwanga ordered James to be beheaded.

**Saint Charles Lwanga,** twenty-one years old, was a servant of Mwanga and became the spokesman for the martyrs. He was burned alive.

**Saint James Buzabalaio's** father was Mwanga's royal bark-cloth maker. James was a warrior in the king's army. He was burned alive.

**Saint Kizito,** a fourteen-year-old page, was the youngest of the martyrs. He was burned with Saint Charles Lwanga and eleven other martyrs.

The martyrs are among the patron saints of Uganda. Saint Charles Lwanga is the patron saint of African Catholic Youth Action, converts, and victims of torture. Feast day: June 3.

**Saint Mary Magdalene (first century).** The cave where Mary is said to have passed the final years of her life as a hermit, known as La Sainte-Baume, is located in Provence. The large cavern is now a church and contains a reliquary of the saint's femur and a few strands of her hair. Tradition tells us that about the year 1000 the relics of Saint Mary Magdalene were moved from the tomb near La Sainte-Baume to the Abbey of Vézelay. In the sixteenth century, when the Wars of Religion raged in France, Huguenots occupied the abbey church, burned the saint's relics, and used the church as a stable. In 1876 the archbishop of Sens, Victor-Felix Bernadou, gave a relic of Saint Mary Magdalene to the church at Vézelay so that pilgrimages to the shrine might be revived. The relic is displayed in a glass and gilt reliquary in the crypt.

A great deal of confusion surrounds Mary Magdalene. Generally,

This silver gilt reliquary, made in 1645, once contained a foot of Saint Mary Magdalene. The reliquary, without the relic, is displayed in Rome's Museo Nazionale. Museo Nazionale, Rome, Italy/The Bridgeman Art Library

she is thought to have been a fallen woman, even a prostitute, whom Jesus brought to repentance. But none of the Gospels makes such an assertion. It was Pope Saint Gregory the Great, writing in the sixth century, who conflated Mary of Bethany, Mary Magdalene, and the sinful woman in Saint Luke's Gospel who poured scented oil over Jesus, then washed his feet with her tears and dried them with her hair. In later years the woman taken in adultery has also been identified as Mary Magdalene.

In fact, the Gospels say only that Christ drove seven demons from Mary Magdalene. There is no hint that she was sexually promiscuous. After the exorcism, Mary joined the other women who followed Christ. With the Blessed Mother and Saint John she followed Jesus to Calvary, stood at the foot of the cross as he died, and remained behind to weep outside the tomb where his body lay. On the first Easter morning, Mary Magdalene was the first of the disciples to see the Risen Christ.

A medieval legend tells us that Mary Magdalene, Martha, Lazarus, and Maximinus (a disciple of Jesus) carried the Gospel to southern France, where they all died.

Saint Mary Magdalene is the patron saint of hairdressers, perfume makers, pharmacists, reformed prostitutes, penitent women, and contemplatives. Feast day: July 22.

**Saint Mary MacKillop (1842–1909).** The remains of Mary MacKillop lie in a marble tomb in the Mary MacKillop Memorial Chapel in North Sydney, Australia. Nearby is Saint Mary's home, Alma Cottage, and a museum that displays many of her personal belongings.

Mary MacKillop's parents emigrated to Australia from Scotland. The family was Catholic. In her early twenties Mary met Father Julian Tenison Woods, a parish priest from South Australia who wanted to a found a new order of nuns who would teach school, nurse in hospitals, and operate charitable institutions for the vast number of poor immigrants who were arriving in Australia daily. In 1866 Mary became the first member and the first mother superior of the new order, known as the Sisters of Saint Joseph of the Sacred Heart; she took the name Sister Mary of the Cross. Within a year 30 Australian women had joined. By 1869, twenty-seven-year-old Mother Mary was superior of 127 nuns who operated seventeen schools and charitable institutions.

The *Rule of Life* Mother Mary and Father Tenison-Woods drew up called for the independence of the sisters from local bishops; the nuns were to be governed by their mother superior, and if an issue could not be resolved within the order they would appeal to Rome. Such independence of action was virtually unheard of for nuns or laywomen in nineteenth-century society. A nun was expected to submit to the authority of her bishop, just as a laywoman was expected to submit to authority of her husband or father.

Bishop Laurence Shiel of Adelaide, who had given his approval to the Sisters of St. Joseph, had second thoughts and insisted that they acknowledge him as the head of their order. When Mother Mary objected, Bishop Shiel ordered her to leave Adelaide for a new assignment; she said she would not go without seeing the bishop first. Instead of meeting with Mother Mary, Bishop Shiel excommunicated her for "disobedience and rebellion." Within days forty-seven of the forty-nine nuns at the Adelaide convent had left, finding shelter in the homes of friends, while sympathetic priests filed an appeal with Rome. Five months later, as he lay on his deathbed, Bishop Shiel lifted the excommunication.

In an effort to forestall such an event from happening again, Mother Mary traveled to Rome, where she was received in a private audience by Blessed Pope Pius IX. The Holy Father gave his approval to the sisters' independence from local bishops; nonetheless, almost every bishop in Australia continued to try to assert control over the order. Mother Mary fought back, on at least two occasions withdrawing her sisters from dioceses where the bishops had been especially belligerent.

In spite of these difficulties, the Sisters of St. Joseph flourished. By the end of Mother Mary's life there were approximately 750 sisters in Australia and New Zealand, operating dozens of institutions, and teaching 12,000 children. Mother Mary MacKillop was canonized by Pope Benedict XVI in 2010; she is Australia's first saint.

Saint Mary MacKillop is the patron saint of the diocese of Wagga Wagga and is one of the patron saints of Australia. Feast day: August 8.


**Saints Marys of the Sea (first century).** In 1448 King Rene discovered the relics of Saint Mary Cleophas, Saint Mary Salome, and Saint Sara below the floor of the Fortress Church in the town of Saintes-Maries-de-la-Mer in the south of France. Radicals burned the relics during the French Revolution, but Catholics recovered some fragments, and these are venerated in the Fortress Church today.

Mary Cleophas and Mary Salome were disciples of Christ who visited his tomb with Mary Magdalene on Easter morning. Legend says that they, along with Mary Magdalene, Martha, Lazarus, and another disciple named Maximin arrived in the South of France by boat to preach the Gospel. Sara was their Egyptian servant. Devotion to the Three Saints Marys is popular in Provence. Devotion to Saint Sara is especially strong among Gypsies, or Roma.

The Three Saints Marys are among the patron saints of Provence. Saint Sara is the patron saint of Gypsies. Feast day of Saint Sara: May 24; of Saints Mary Cleophas and Mary Salome: October 22.

**Saint Matthias (first century).** In 326 Saint Helen, mother of Constantine, Rome's first Christian emperor, went on pilgrimage to the Holy Land. She is said to have believed that Matthias died in Jerusalem, stoned by the Jews and then beheaded, and she is said to have found his grave and then sent the remains to the Christians of Trier in Germany, an ancient Roman colony where she had lived for several years with her son before he was successful in asserting his claim to the imperial crown in Rome.

The basilica of St. Matthias in Trier preserves his relics. For many centuries they were lost, but the monks of the Abbey of St. Matthias rediscovered them in 1127 during the construction of a new church.

Christians in the Repulic of Georgia insist that Matthias's relics lie in a grave in the ruins of a Roman fortress, Gonio-Apsaros. The claim cannot be verified because the Georgian government has not given permission for an excavation of the site.

Saint Matthias is the thirteenth apostle. In the New Testament, the Acts of the Apostles tells us that after Christ's Ascension into Heaven, Peter addressed the remaining apostles and suggested that someone ought to be chosen to replace Judas, who not only had betrayed the Lord but in his despair had hanged himself. Two candidates were put forward, the disciples Joseph Barsabbas and Matthias. The eleven apostles cast lots, and Matthias was chosen.

That is all we know of him. Saint Matthias is never mentioned again in the New Testament, and all other references to him in other texts are the work of legend.

It is said that he preached to cannibals in Ethiopia, to pagans in Colchis in what is now Georgia, and to the residents of Jerusalem. All three places claim that he was martyred and buried there.

Saint Matthias is the patron saint of alcoholics. Feast day: May 14.

**Saint Matthew (first century).** According to tradition, in 954 the relics of Saint Matthew were translated from their tomb in Ethiopia to the city of Salerno in Italy. The relics are enshrined in the crypt of the Cathedral of St. Matthew.

Although generally described as a tax collector, Matthew was in fact an extortionist. The Romans hired local individuals to collect taxes, with the understanding that the collectors could squeeze as much additional cash as they were able from the taxpayers, as long as Caesar received the revenue that was due him. The people of Judea regarded these freelance tax collectors as especially loathsome, since they not only collaborated with the Romans but also preyed upon their fellow Jews. That is why in the Gospels we often find tax collectors lumped together with prostitutes and other shameless public sinners.

While Matthew was collecting taxes in Capernaum, Jesus stood at the door of the customs house and said to him, "Follow me." To everyone's astonishment Matthew left his accounts and piles of coins on the table and walked out the door after Jesus.

Matthew's Gospel tells us the story of Christ's birth, the coming of the Magi, King Herod's massacre of the Holy Innocents, the Holy Family's flight into Egypt, the Sermon on the Mount, and the suicide of Judas.

According to tradition, Matthew preached in Ethiopia, where he was hacked to death with a sword as he said Mass.

Saint Matthew is the patron saint of accountants, bankers,

stockbrokers, tax collectors, and anyone else involved in the finance professions. Feast day: September 21.

**Saint Maurice (died c. 287).** The relics of Saint Maurice and other members of the Theban Legion are venerated in the Abbey of St. Maurice d'Agaune in Switzerland, near the site of their martyrdom. A portion of the saint's bones are preserved in the Royal Chapel in Turin, Italy. Displayed in Turin's Royal Armory is a sword, which is said to have been used to behead Saint Maurice (the sword has been dated to the thirteenth century). A sword that is said to have belonged to Saint Maurice is displayed in the Weltliche Treasury in Vienna, Austria.

Maurice was *primicerius,* or chief officer, of a legion of Christians recruited from the area around Thebes in Upper Egypt. (A Roman legion numbered 6,600 men). Emperor Marcus Valerius Maximianus Herculius sent them to Switzerland to put down a revolt among Gallic tribes. Before battle the emperor assembled the army to participate in sacrifices to the Roman gods; the Theban Legion refused to take part in the worship of false gods.

Maximianus ordered a decimation, in which one man in every ten was killed. This did not shake the Christians' resolve, so Maximianus ordered a second decimation. When the legionnaires still refused to sacrifice to the gods, the emperor unleashed his troops on them, and Maurice and all his surviving men were massacred.

Saint Maurice is the patron saint of soldiers, especially infantry-men, and armies. He is one of the patron saints of the Pontifical Swiss Guards, Austria, and Sardinia. Feast day: September 22.

**Saint Maximilian Kolbe (1894–1941).** The body of Maximilian Kolbe was cremated and dumped in a mass grave at Auschwitz. However, the cell in Auschwitz where he died has survived, and some of his personal belongings are preserved at the Basilica of St. Mary Immaculate in Niepokalanów, Poland.

Maximilian Kolbe's father fought for Poland's independence from Russia; in 1914 he was captured by the Russians and hanged as a traitor. Kolbe's mother later became a Benedictine nun, and Maximilian and his brother Alphonsus entered the priesthood.

Maximilian joined the Franciscans, and after receiving his doctorate in philosophy and theology in Rome he returned to Poland, where he started the Immaculata movement, which used the latest technology to spread the Gospel. His monastery published extremely successful magazines and newspapers (the magazine had a monthly ciculation of 750,000). And the Immaculata radio programs were among the most popular in Poland. Because of Maximilian's zeal, by 1939 the monastery complex housed eight hundred men.

In 1939, when the Nazis invaded Poland, Maximilian's monastery sheltered two thousand Polish Jews and a thousand Polish Christians. For this "crime" the Nazis arrested the refugees, shut down the monastery, scattered the monks, and sent Maximilian to Auschwitz.

In July 1941 a prisoner escaped the camp. In retaliation the Nazis selected ten prisoners at random for execution. One of the ten, Francis Gajowniczek, broke down, weeping for his wife and children. Father Maximilian stepped forward and volunteered to take Gajowniczek's place. The officer in charge accepted the exchange, and the men were marched to the punishment bunker, where they were left to starve to death. On August 14 Father Maximilian was still alive, so he was given a lethal injection of carbonic acid.

Saint Maximilian Kolbe is the patron saint of political prisoners. He is invoked against drug addiction. Feast day: August 14.

## Saint Melania, or Melanie, the Younger (c. 383–439).

This saint's relics are preserved in St. Melania's Monastery on the Mount of Olives in Jerusalem.

Melania was a Roman aristocrat, a member of the ancient Valerii family; her grandmother, Melania the Elder, is venerated as a saint.

The younger Melania wanted to enter a convent, but to please her parents she married. She and her husband had two children who died young. This tragedy rekindled her desire to become a nun. She convinced her husband, Pinianus, that they should live chastely, as brother and sister.

From that point on she lived in a manner that was highly unconventional for a Roman patrician. She and Pinianus created in their home an informal religious community that included their slaves. With Melania's mother they traveled to North Africa, where they befriended Saint Augustine and his boyhood friend Saint Alypius. They moved on to the Holy Land, where they met Saint Jerome. In Jerusalem Melania's mother and husband died. Rather than return to Rome, she founded a convent of nuns on the Mount of Olives; typically the foundress of a convent became its abbess, but Melania declined the honor, preferring to live as an ordinary nun.

During the Nestorian controversy she traveled to Constantinople to defend orthodox doctrine regarding the divine motherhood of the Blessed Virgin Mary. Then Melania escorted the empress Eudoxia on her pilgrimage to the Holy Land.

Devotion to Saint Melania flourished in the East from the time of her death, but she did not become popular in the West until the early twentieth century, when Cardinal Mariano Rampolla published her biography.

Saint Melania is the patron saint of exiles. Feast day: December 31.

**Saint Mina, Mena, or Menas (died c. 300).** For almost three hundred years the tomb of Saint Mina was the spiritual heart of the City of St. Mina in Egypt's Western Desert near Alexandria. Arab invaders destroyed the city in the seventh century, but the relics of Saint Mina were saved and lie today in the modern Monastery of St. Mina, which stands close to the ancient ruins of the City of St. Mina.

Mina was an Egyptian Christian who as a teenager was first a camel driver, then a recruit in the Roman army, then a runaway in the desert, where he escaped Emperor Diocletian's persecution of the Church.

After a time in solitude, he found his courage again, returned to the nearest city, and entered the arena on the day Christians were being martyred. He proclaimed to the crowd that he was a Christian too. The magistrate sentenced him to a gruesome death: his hands were lopped off, his eyes gouged out, and then he was beheaded.

In 1943 when Allied troops defeated the Nazis at the battle of El Alamein, the Coptic Orthodox patriarch of Alexandria declared that Egypt had been saved from German occupation through the intercession of Saint Mina.

Saint Mina is the patron saint of peddlers and traveling salesmen. Feast day: November 11.

**Blessed Miguel Pro (1891–1927).** The bones of Blessed Miguel are enshrined in a silver chest in the Church of the Holy Family in the Colonia Roma district of Mexico City.

Early in the twentieth century the government of Mexico became intensely hostile to the Catholic Church—this in a country where the overwhelming majority of the population was Catholic. Encouraged by Mexico's president, Plutarco Elías Calles, the governors of the states enacted new legislation that called for Catholic churches to be destroyed, all priests to marry, and the death penalty to be imposed on any priest who said Mass, any nun who kept her vows, and any Catholic layman or laywoman who sheltered a priest or kept the Blessed Sacrament in his or her home to protect it from profanation.

While the Church in Mexico was fighting for survival, Father Miguel Pro, S.J., was completing his studies in Belgium. A more timid man would have remained in Europe, but Father Pro returned home and immediately began a clandestine ministry to Catholics in Mexico City. Disguised as a mechanic or as an ordinary civilian taking his dog for a walk, he stopped at a house or an apartment to say Mass, hear confessions, baptize infants, marry couples, and anoint the dying.

Father Pro was arrested by accident. His brother had sold his car to a man who made an attempt on the life of a Mexican general. The police traced the car back to its original owners and arrested Miguel and his brother Humberto. Although it became apparent that the Pros were not involved in the assassination attempt, their Catholic activities were enough to win them a death sentence.

Father Pro was marched before a firing squad in the courtyard of the police headquarters. He blessed the firing squad and the spectators. Then he extended his arms like Christ on the cross and cried, "Viva Cristo Rey!" (Long live Christ the King!) The soldiers fired and Father Pro fell dead. A few minutes later Humberto was also executed.

Blessed Miguel Pro is the patron saint of the falsely accused. Feast day: November 23.

**Saint Miniato, or Minias (died c. 250).** The relics of the martyr lie in the crypt of the Church of St. Miniato al Monte, located on a hilltop high above the city of Florence.

Miniato was a Roman soldier in Florence who spoke of his Christian faith to his comrades and attempted to convert them. During Emperor Decius's persecution of the Church he was arrested and beheaded at the site of the present-day Piazza della Signoria. He was Florence's first Christian martyr.

Christians buried him on a hill across the Arno River from the city. In later centuries a beautiful Romanesque church was built over the site of his grave.

Feast day: October 25.

**Saint Monica (c. 332–387).** Monica's family buried her in Ostia, the city where she died. By the sixth century her relics had been moved to the crypt of Ostia's Church of St. Aurea, but subsequently were lost. The saint's sarcophagus, with her skeleton intact, was discovered by chance in 1430. Pope Martin V had the relics brought to Rome and deposited in a chapel in the Church of St. Augustine. In 1945 two boys playing beside the Church of St. Aurea dug up a fragment of the original fourth-century inscription from Saint Monica's tomb.

Monica came from a family of Berber Catholics in Thagaste, modern-day Souk Ahras, Algeria. Her husband, Patrictius, had no religion, but he did not object to Monica raising their two sons and one daughter as Catholics.

Of her three children, Augustine was Monica's favorite. She nursed him herself rather than turning him over to a wet nurse as was customary among well-to-do families at the time. He grew up to be an intelligent boy who went to study at the university in Carthage—one of the finest schools in the Roman Empire. Before he left, Monica urged him to keep away from women, but as Augustine recalled in his *Confessions,* he ignored his mother's advice; he was, he said, "in the mood to be seduced."

Soon after arriving in Carthage, Augustine took a mistress (he never mentions her name), and a year later they had a son whom they named Adeodatus. Then Augustine compounded his mother's sorrow by renouncing the Catholic faith and joining the Manicheans, a sect that believed that there was a constant struggle between a good realm and an evil one.

In tears, Monica called on a bishop who had once been a Manichean and begged him to bring her son back to the Church. The bishop replied that it would do no good; Augustine was in the first flush of enthusiasm for his new religion and would not listen to any argument against it. Monica persisted, making such a nuisance of herself that the bishop lost his temper. "Go away from me!" he cried. At once, to make up for shouting at a distraught mother, he tried to console Monica. "Do not worry," he said. "It is not possible that the son of so many tears should be lost forever."

The bishop was correct, but seventeen years would pass before

Augustine was ready to return to the Catholic faith. By then he and his family, including Monica, were living in Milan, where Augustine taught philosophy at the local academy. The city's bishop was Saint Ambrose, a man as well educated and sophisticated as Augustine. To please Monica, Augustine occasionally accompanied her to Mass to hear Ambrose preach, and he was impressed by what he heard. With Adeodatus he took instruction from Ambrose; on the night of the Easter Vigil, 387, Ambrose baptized Augustine and his son.

Monica was euphoric. Her prayers had been answered. But a few weeks later she fell ill. On her deathbed she told Augustine, Adeodatus, and her son Navigius, "Lay this body anywhere, do not worry about this. I have only one request, that wherever you are you remember me at the altar of the Lord."

Saint Monica is the patron saint of lapsed Catholics and of parents whose children prove to be disappointing. Feast day: August 27.

**Saint Moses the Black (330–405).** The relics of Saint Moses are venerated in the Church of the Virgin Mary at the Paromeos Monastery in northern Egypt's Nitrian Desert, known today as Wadi el Natrun.

Tall, muscular, and violent, Moses was a natural-born leader of a gang of bandits. They preyed on travelers and especially caravans crossing the Egyptian desert. The governor of the province would send out detachments of troops to eliminate the bandits, but Moses and his men always killed all the soldiers. Finally the governor sent an entire army into the desert. The bandits scattered, and Moses took refuge in the one place the governor would never look for him: the Monastery of Petra in the Skete desert.

The monks could tell Moses was not a pilgrim, but they assigned him a cell, shared their meals with him, and treated him kindly. In the months that Moses lived among the monks he was transformed. He confessed to the abbot, Saint Isidore, and asked to be admitted to the community.

Monastic life was not easy for Moses. Controlling his violent impulses, living without wine, and abstaining from meat were all a challenge. And celibacy was especially difficult. He was ready to leave the monastery when Abbot Isidore said, "This is only the beginning. That is why the demons have attacked you so vehemently, trying to force you back into your old habits. But if you endure, the demons will get discouraged and leave you alone." Moses persevered and in time became a model monk, although he was always a bit rough around the edges.

Moses was seventy-five when a warning reached the monks that Berber bandits were coming to loot the monastery. The entire community escaped, but Moses and seven of his brother monks remained behind. The Berbers killed them all.

Saint Moses the Black is one of the patron saints of Africa. Feast day: August 28.

**Saint Mungo or Kentigern (c. 518–603).** The relics of Saint Mungo survived the Reformation in Scotland. They still lie beneath an altar in the crypt of Glasgow Cathedral.

According to tradition, Mungo's mother, a married woman, became pregnant by her lover. The outraged husband threw her off a cliff into the Firth of Forth, but she survived the fall, swam to shore, and gave birth to a healthy son whom she named Kentigern. Saint Serf, the abbot of a local monastery, offered mother and child a home and raised the boy as his own son, even giving him a nickname—Mungo, Scots Gaelic for "dear boy."

Like his foster father, Kentigern became a monk and eventually was consecrated bishop of what is now Glasgow. A host of legends grew up about him: that he restored to life Saint Serf's dead pet robin; that on a frigid night he kindled a fire with ice-covered branches. He was beloved by the Scots, who did not destroy his relics during their Reformation.

Saint Mungo is the patron saint of salmon and is one of the patron saints of Glasgow. Feast day: January 13.

**Saint Nicholas (died c. 350).** About the year 1085 the Seljuk Turks conquered the portion of modern-day Turkey where the city of Myra is located. Christians feared the Turks would desecrate the tomb of Saint Nicholas in Myra's cathedral. The city governments of Venice and Bari both sent ships to Myra to collect the saint's relics and bring them to safety in their city, but the Barese reached Myra first. Bari erected a grand basilica for Saint Nicholas's relics, and they are still venerated there. Myra's cathedral and the original tomb of Saint Nicholas have also survived.

Saint Nicholas, bishop of Myra, was imprisoned during Diocletian's persecution of the Church. He is said to have attended the Council of Nicaea, where he slapped Arius across the face for daring to deny the divinity of Christ.

The stories that have come down to us about Nicholas are almost certainly legends: that he saved three impoverished young women from a life of prostitution by throwing bags of gold through an open window of their house; that he raised from the dead three boys a wicked innkeeper had butchered to serve to his guests; that he appeared on the deck of a sinking ship and brought it safely to port. Nonetheless, these legends portray Nicholas as a man of great compassion, which accounts for his tremendous popularity over the last seventeen hundred years.

Saint Nicholas is the patron saint of children, unmarried women, prisoners, penitent thieves, sailors, fishermen, pawnbrokers, pilgrims, the poor, and the Greek Catholic Church in America. He is one of the patron saints of Greece, Russia, Sicily, Amsterdam, Limerick, Liverpool, and Naples. Feast day: December 6.

**Saint Nicholas of Flüe (1417–1487).** The body of Nicholas of Flüe lies inside his parish church in Sachseln, Switzerland. His original grave slab as well as the one that replaced it about a century later are both preserved. In a glass case inside the church is one of the robes Nicholas wore during the years he lived as a hermit. The church also displays the icon of Saint Nicholas, known as "the

Book of Meditation," before which he prayed daily. In Sachseln pilgrims will find the house where Saint Nicholas was born and the house he built for his wife and family. His hermitage and chapel still stand in Ranft Gorge.

Nicholas and his wife, Dorothy Wissling, lived with their ten children in the village of Sachseln. They were prosperous farmers, but Nicholas was frequently called away to fight in a series of wars that plagued Switzerland in the fifteenth century.

Among his neighbors he had a reputation for sound judgment and unshakable integrity; Nicholas was often called upon to settle disputes in the village, and eventually he was named local magistrate.

The year he and Dorothy celebrated twenty-five years of marriage, Nicholas sat down with his family and revealed to them his desire to leave home and live the rest of his life as a hermit. Reluctantly, Dorothy and the children conceded to his wishes. He walked to the Ranft Gorge nearby where he planned to erect a hut, but the local people knew Nicholas and insisted on building him a sturdy cabin and a stone chapel. The bishop of Constance, who was also an admirer of Nicholas, sent his auxiliary to consecrate the chapel and assigned a priest to serve as Nicholas's chaplain.

In 1481 several Swiss cantons were attempting to form a political union, but the negotiations went badly and there was a real threat that civil war might erupt in the country. Some of the delegates suggested that Nicholas of Flüe be called from his hermitage to settle the matter. Nicholas came to the conference where, after hearing the various points of view, he suggested an arrangement that pleased all the representatives. Then he returned to Ranft Gorge.

Nicholas died in his cabin, with Dorothy, his children and grandchildren, and his chaplain at his bedside.

Saint Nicholas of Flüe is the patron saint of peacemakers, large families, magistrates, and separated spouses; he is also one of the patron saints of Switzerland and of the Pontifical Swiss Guards. Feast day: March 21.

**Noah's Ark.** Genesis tells us that once the great flood subsided, Noah's ark came to rest in "the mountains of Ararat." A long-standing tradition identifies the peak on which the ark ran aground as Agri Dagh in eastern Turkey. In the twentieth and twenty-first centuries, individuals and groups have come forward, claiming to have seen the ark from the air or actually visited the remains of the big boat. An Armenian named George Hagopian told how in 1905 his uncle led him to the summit of Mount Ararat where he saw the ark. It is said that in 1916 a Russian expedition reached the ark, explored its interior, and filed a report, with photographs—all of which documentation disappeared during the Russian Revolution. In the 1950s and 1960s a French adventurer, Fernand Navarra, returned from Turkey with fragments of wood that he said he had taken from the ark; carbon dating indicated the wood dated from 600 to 800 AD. In 2010 a group of Chinese and Turkish explorers announced that they were "99.9 percent" certain that they had found Noah's ark, and they had photographs to prove it. This claim was later exposed as a hoax.

In Armenia, the Cathedral Museum of the Mother See of Holy Etchmiadzin displays a reliquary that contains what is said to be wood from Noah's Ark. In the fourth century Patriarch Saint Hakob (Jacob) began to climb Mount Ararat to visit the ark. One night as he slept an angel descended from heaven to present him with a relic of the Ark and a command from God to leave the Ark undisturbed and climb down the mountain. When Hakob awoke his head was resting on the reliquary.

**North American Martyrs (1642–1649).** In the 1640s the Iroquois launched a campaign to exterminate their archrivals, the Hurons. They attacked Huron villages, indiscriminately slaughtering men, women, and children. The Iroquois were especially eager to kill or capture French Jesuit missionary priests, whom they regarded as sorcerers. On the night of March 16, 1649, during an attack on the Huron village of St.-Louis, the Iroquois captured two

Jesuits, Father Gabriel Lalemant and Father John de Brébeuf. The Iroquois considered de Brébeuf a real prize, since the French and the Hurons respected and revered him above all other missionaries in Canada. Alerted by refugees from St.-Louis, a party of French and Hurons tried to rescue Fathers de Brébeuf and Lalemant from the Iroquois, but they arrived too late. Nonetheless, they did drive off the Iroquois, and they were able to bring the mangled bodies of the martyrs back to the mission of Sainte-Marie Among the Hurons for burial. The rescuers also brought along portions of the stakes to which the martyrs had been tied for torture.

For months the Iroquois harassed Sainte-Marie until in the spring of 1650 the Jesuits, their assistants, and the Huron and Wendat Indians packed their belongings, including the relics of Fathers de Brébeuf and Lalemant, set fire to the mission, and fled to the safety of Quebec.

In December 1649 French and Christian Hurons found the body of Father Charles Garnier among the ruins of the mission of St. Matthias; they buried Father Garnier in his chapel. During the evacuation of Sainte-Marie, Father Garnier's relics were also exhumed and taken to Quebec.

The relics of the three martyrs remained in Quebec until 1926, when the Martyrs' Shrine was erected at Midland, Ontario, near the site of Sainte-Marie. The relics were translated to the church, where they continue to be venerated today.

During excavations at the site of Sainte-Marie in 1954, the Jesuit archaeologist Father Denis Hegarty discovered the original graves of Saints John de Brébeuf and Gabriel Lalemant, including nails from their coffins and the lead identification plate that had been nailed to Saint John de Brébeuf's coffin. These relics are preserved in the Archives of the Martyrs' Shrine along with the remnants of the torture stakes.

There are no remains of the other five North American Martyrs. The Mohawks dumped the bodies of Saints René Goupil, Isaac Jogues, and John de La Lande into the Mohawk River; they were never recovered. Iroquois warriors threw the body of Saint

Antoine Daniel into his burning chapel, where it was completely consumed; French and Hurons who searched the ruined mission found no trace of the martyr. The Indian who murdered Saint Noël Chabanel tossed his body into a river; it was never recovered.

**Saint René Goupil (1608–1642).** A trained surgeon, René Goupil volunteered for the Jesuit mission in Canada. He was assigned to the hospital in Quebec, where he worked for two years until Father Isaac Jogues recruited him for his mission among the Hurons. En route the entire party was captured by the Mohawks, who tortured and enslaved Goupil and Father Jogues. René Goupil was killed by a Mohawk warrior because he had made the sign of the cross on a Mohawk child.

**Saint Isaac Jogues (1607–1646).** Father Jogues's Jesuit superiors assigned him to the flourishing mission of Sainte-Marie Among the Hurons. In 1642 Jogues, Goupil, another Frenchman, and twenty Hurons were captured by the Mohawks. During torture Jogues lost his left thumb and half of his right index finger. With the help of Dutch colonists, Father Jogues escaped the Mohawks and went home to France. But he asked his superiors to be permitted to return to Canada. In 1648 Father Jogues was sent to the Mohawks to negotiate a treaty. In spite of the peaceful nature of his mission, he was murdered at Ossernenon, near modern-day Auriesville, New York.

**Saint John de La Lande (?–1646).** John de La Lande, a layman, came to Canada as a teenager and volunteered to serve the Jesuits as a lay missionary. He was sent with Father Jogues on the peace mission to the Mohawks. After Father Jogues's martyrdom, de La Lande tried to recover the body. A Mohawk warrior struck him in the head with a tomahawk, killing him instantly.

**Saint Antoine Daniel (1601–1648).** While studying at the Jesuit novitiate in Rouen, Antoine Daniel met a Christian Huron. The Indian's stories of the work of the Jesuits in Canada inspired Daniel to request an assignment in New France. He proved to be a great success as a missionary, converting hundreds of Hurons. In 1648 an Iroquois war party attacked Father Daniel's mission village. He was cut down in a hail of enemy arrows and gunfire.

**Saint John de Brébeuf (1593–1649).** The leader of the Jesuit missionaries in Canada, John de Brébeuf was a man of great physical strength, courage, and unshakable faith. To assist future missionaries he compiled a French-Huron dictionary. For the Indians he wrote a catechism and even a Christmas carol in Huron. He and Saint Gabriel Lalemant were captured together by the Iroquois and horribly tortured to death.

**Saint Gabriel Lalemant (1610–1649).** Two of Father Gabriel's uncles, Fathers Charles and Jerome Lalemant, were Jesuit missionaries in Canada. Gabriel was assigned to assist Father de Brébeuf at the Huron mission of St.-Louis, which is where they were captured by the Iroquois. He watched as the Iroquois tortured Father de Brébeuf to death; then the Indians turned on Father Gabriel. They prolonged his torment for fifteen hours.

**Saint Charles Garnier (1606–1649).** When Charles Garnier petitioned his superiors to send him to Canada, his father protested so forcefully that the Jesuits decided to keep the newly ordained priest in France. It took a year for Father Garnier to convince his father to let him go; once he had his father's permission, the Jesuits granted Father Garnier's request. He worked among the Petuns and was living among them at the village of Etarita when the Iroquois attacked. Father Garnier was scalped alive then killed while trying to assist a dying Petun man.

**Saint Noël Chabanel (1613–1649).** Father Chabanel taught rhetoric at the Jesuit college in Toulouse, but he felt called to the Huron mission. Once he arrived in Canada, however, he was overwhelmed by what was required of him. The Jesuits lived among the Indians, and Father Chabanel could not bear the filthy lodges; Indian food nauseated him; he was never at ease with their customs; and he never gained fluency in the Huron language. His superiors would have sent him home to France, but Father Chabanel believed that would be a betrayal of his vocation, so he made a solemn vow to God to remain among the Hurons. The day after Father Garnier's martyrdom, Father Chabanel was traveling alone through the forest, trying to reach the mission of St.-Matthias. He met a Huron, a former Christian, who offered to help him, but who robbed and killed the priest instead.

The North American Martyrs are among the patron saints of Canada. Saint René Goupil is the patron saint of anesthesiologists. Saint Isaac Jogues is one of the patron saints of the Americas. Feast day: October 19; September 26 in Canada.

**Saint Odilia (fourth century).** In the spring of 1287 Saint Odilia appeared three times to John of Eppa, a French lay brother of the Crosier order, bearing a message that God had appointed her the patron saint of the Crosiers and instructing him to go to a certain garden in Cologne, Germany, where he would find her relics. Brother John and his companions found the relics, as Saint Odilia had promised, and carried them to the Crosiers' motherhouse in Huy, Belgium. They remained there until 1796, when partisans of the French Revolution attacked and burned the motherhouse. A priest rescued the relics of Saint Odilia and concealed them in a church in Kerniel, Belgium. In 1949 Saint Odilia's relics were returned to the Crosiers and enshrined in their monastery at Diest, Belgium. In 1952 one of the saint's bones was given to the Crosiers in Onamia, Minnesota; the relic is venerated in the National Shrine of St. Odilia.

All we know of Saint Odilia is that she was one of the virgin companions of Saint Ursula martyred by the Huns in Cologne.

Saint Odilia is the patron saint of the Crosiers and is invoked against eye ailments. Feast day: July 18.

**Saint Olaf of Norway (c. 995–1030).** After the battle of Stikle-stad, Bishop Grimkell collected King Olaf's body from the field and buried it in the Church of St. Clement in Nidaros (present-day Trondheim). In 1070 the relics were transferred to a splendid shrine in the new Nidaros Cathedral, where they remained until 1584, when the cathedral's Lutheran clergy moved the bones to an unmarked grave within the church. Saint Olaf's relics have never been found.

As a teenager Olaf was a Viking who raided cities and towns in the Baltic, England, and Normandy. But at age eighteen, for reasons that have not come down to us, Olaf converted to Christianity and was baptized in Rouen, France. Then he returned to Norway to assert his claim as king.

Olaf made Nidaros his capital and built a church there in honor of Saint Clement. He urged all his people to convert to the Christian faith, but not all Norwegians were willing to give up their Norse gods. For that matter, not all Norwegians were willing to accept Olaf as their rightful king. Hoping to take advantage of unrest in Norway, the king of Sweden allied himself with some Norwegian chieftains and tried to depose Olaf. The coup failed, and in the aftermath Olaf fell back on traditional Viking methods to punish the rebels and followers of the old gods: hanging, mutilation, or confiscation of property. Perhaps because Viking society was based on strength and violence, Olaf's violent methods worked; by 1030 virtually all of Norway was at least nominally Christian.

But Olaf still had political rivals, and in 1030 he met them in battle at a place called Stiklestad. Three enemy warriors attacked Olaf at once, hacking him to death. After the battle, wounded men who touched the king's blood were healed, and a blind man who wiped his eyes with Olaf's blood had his sight restored. On the strength of the miracles, Bishop Grimkell proclaimed Olaf a saint and martyr.

Saint Olaf is the patron saint of kings and of Norway. Feast day: July 29.

**Saint Oliver Plunkett (1629–1681).** Most of the bones of Saint Oliver Plunkett are enshrined in the monastic church of Downside Abbey in England. His skull is preserved in a reliquary at St. Peter's Church in Drogheda, Ireland.

As archbishop of Armagh, Plunkett attempted to restore the Catholic Church in Ireland. He established new chapels to replace the Catholic churches that had been either destroyed or confiscated by the Protestant Church of Ireland. In Drogheda he opened a school for boys and a theology school for seminarians and priests; he assigned both institutions to the Jesuits. He organized missions to Catholics in remote parts of Ireland and the islands of Scotland. And he traveled a great deal through Ireland, bringing the Mass and the sacraments to tens of thousands of Catholics.

In 1679 Archbishop Plunkett was falsely accused of plotting to bring an army of 20,000 French troops into the country to free Ireland from English rule. He was sent to Dundalk for trial, but the grand jury rejected the evidence as fraudulent. A second trial in London was ordered, and this time the archbishop was convicted of propagating the Catholic faith in Ireland, "than which," the Chief Justice declared, "there is not anything more displeasing to God or more pernicious to mankind in the world."

Archbishop Plunkett was sentenced to be hanged, drawn, and quartered at Tyburn; he was the last Catholic martyr to suffer there.

Saint Oliver Plunkett is one of the patron saints of the archdiocese of Armagh, Ireland. Feast day: July 1.

**Saint Oswald (604–642).** The skull of Saint Oswald was one of the sacred treasures of Lindisfarne Abbey. It survived the disastrous Viking raid of 793, and when the monks decided to flee to a place of safety on the mainland, they took the saint's skull with them, placing it inside the coffin of Lindisfarne's greatest saint, Saint Cuthbert. Saint Oswald's skull was venerated in Durham Cathedral along with the relics of Saint Cuthbert until 1538, when

Henry VIII's commissioners destroyed the shrine and buried Saint Cuthbert, along with Saint Oswald's skull, in an unmarked grave behind the cathedral's high altar. Those relics are still there below a modern tombstone that bears the inscription CUTHBERTUS. The rest of the relics of Saint Oswald were destroyed during the Reformation.

Oswald was heir to the crown of Northumbria, but the kings of Wales and East Anglia challenged his title. In 635, at a place outside Hexham, Oswald met his enemies. The night before, Saint Columba appeared to Oswald, promising him victory. Early the next day Oswald erected a large wooden cross on a knoll above the field. That day Oswald's men scattered their enemies. Convinced that they owed their victory to God, the men of Northumbria named the place of battle Heavenfield.

For seven years Oswald labored to strengthen and unify his kingdom, and to bring his people to the Christian faith. In August 642 he went to war again, this time against a pagan king named Penda. At Maserfield near the Welsh border, Oswald fell; Penda himself hacked off Oswald's limbs. Christians collected the saintly king's remains and buried them in Bardney Abbey near Lincoln.

Feast day: August 5.


**Our Lady of Guadalupe (1531).** Since 1976 the tilma, or cloak, bearing the miraculous image of Our Lady of Guadalupe has been enshrined over the high altar of the massive modern Basilica of Our Lady of Guadalupe at the summit of Tepeyac Hill outside Mexico City. The old basilica where the image was venerated beginning in the sixteenth century still stands and is open to pilgrims and visitors. For more information see the entry for Saint Juan Diego.

Our Lady of Guadalupe is one of the patronesses of Mexico and the Americas. She is the patroness of the right-to-life movement. Feast day: December 12.

**Our Lady's Cincture or Belt.** The Jacobite Syrian Orthodox Church in Homs, Syria, claims to possess the cincture of the Blessed Virgin, as does the cathedral in Prato, Italy, where the Renaissance masters Donatello and Michelozzo created an outdoor pulpit from which the relic could be displayed to large crowds. The relic is kept in the altar of the cathedral's Chapel of the Sacred Cincture. The Cathedral of Arras in France, the Church of Our Lady of the Founders in Constantinople, and the Cathedral of Tortosa, Spain, also have claimed to possess Our Lady's cincture. The relic in Arras disappeared during the French Revolution when radicals destroyed the cathedral. The relic in Constantinople was lost either during the sack of the city in 1204, or during the Turk's conquest in 1453. The relic in Tortosa has survived.

According to legend, all the apostles returned to Jerusalem to see the Blessed Virgin Mary one last time before she died. Saint Thomas, who had to come from India, arrived late: by the time he reached Jerusalem, Mary had died and been buried. He arrived to find the apostles gathered around Mary's tomb, but when Thomas glanced down he saw the tomb was empty. His fellow apostles assured Thomas that Mary had been assumed into heaven, body and soul, but Thomas would not believe them. At that moment Our Lady dropped her cincture from heaven to prove to Thomas that what the apostles told him was true.

Feast days: The bishop of Prato displays Our Lady's Cincture on Easter, May 1, August 15, September 8, and Christmas Day.

**Our Lady's Veil (earliest date of veneration 876).** Tradition says that Charlemagne received the Veil of the Blessed Virgin Mary from the Byzantine emperor Constantine Porphyrogenitus and the empress Helena. In 876 Charlemagne's descendant, King Charles the Bald, presented the relic to the bishop of Chartres. It has been venerated in the cathedral ever since. The relic is displayed in a large glass case supported by gilded angels.

**Saint Padre Pio (1887–1968).** Following a Requiem Mass attended by over 100,000 mourners, the body of Padre Pio Forgione was buried in the crypt of the Church of Our Lady of Grace in San Giovanni Rotondo in Italy. In 2008 the body was exhumed for display in the Padre Pio Pilgrimage Church. It was dressed in a fresh brown habit of the Capuchin order, a white stole embroidered with gold threads was draped over the shoulders, and a wooden cross was placed in its hands. Finally, a silicon mask was placed over the saint's face to conceal marks of decomposition. The relics lie in a large crystal casket in the crypt of the church.

Padre Pio stood at the center of one of the religious phenomena of the twentieth century. From 1918 until shortly before his death in 1968 he bore on his body the stigmata, the wounds Christ received on the cross. There are stories of bilocation, in which witnesses saw Padre Pio at two places at the same time; of levitation; of miraculous healings. On one occasion a Polish bishop, Karol Wojtyla (the future Pope John Paul II), asked Padre Pio to pray for a friend suffering from cancer; Padre Pio interceded for her, and the woman was inexplicably cured of the disease.

Crowds mobbed the Church of Our Lady of Grace to see Padre Pio say Mass. Long lines of penitents waited outside his confessional; it was said that he would reveal sins the penitent was too ashamed to confess.

In 1956, with the approval of his Capuchin superiors, Padre Pio founded a hospital near his friary in San Giovanni Rotondo, Italy. Today the House for the Relief of Suffering treats 60,000 patients annually.

In 2002, when Pope John Paul II canonized Padre Pio, a crowd estimated at 300,000 attended the ceremony, filling St. Peter's Square and spilling down the long, broad boulevard that leads to the Vatican.

Saint Padre Pio is invoked to make a good confession. He is the patron saint of confessors, civil defense workers, and Catholic teenagers. Feast day: September 23.

**Saint Patrick (c. 390–461?).** The body of Saint Patrick lies buried beneath a large stone in the cemetery of Downpatrick Cathedral in Northern Ireland. There were other relics of the saint, but not all have survived; during the Reformation, Saint Patrick's crosier was burned in a public ceremony in Dublin. A copy of the four Gospels, said to have belonged to Patrick, is preserved in the Royal Irish Academy. A reliquary containing the saint's lower jaw is venerated in the Church of St. Colman and St. Patrick in Derriaghy. And a reliquary said to contain one of Patrick's teeth is displayed at the National Museum in Dublin, which also displays the Shrine of Saint Patrick's Bell.

At age sixteen Patrick was kidnapped from his home on the west coast of Britain by Irish raiders and sold into slavery in Ireland.

The Annals of Ulster records that in 552 Saint Columba opened Saint Patrick's grave and removed his bell, which was subsequently encased in this gold filigree reliquary. It is preserved today in the National Museum of Ireland in Dublin. Erich Lessing/Art Resource, NY

Although he had been raised a Catholic—his father was a deacon, his grandfather had been a priest—Patrick did not believe in God. But alone in the hills with his master's sheep, underfed and poorly clothed, Patrick turned to God.

After six years as a slave he heard a supernatural voice say, "See, your ship is ready." Patrick ran to the coast, where he found a ship about to sail, and although he had no money for the passage, the sailors took him aboard.

Patrick returned to his parents and after a time traveled to Gaul (modern-day France) to study for the priesthood. He had had a vision in which he heard Irish voices calling to him, "We beg you, holy youth, come and walk among us once more!" A desire to establish the Catholic faith in Ireland became the great goal of his life.

In the 430s Patrick, newly consecrated a bishop, sailed to Ireland. It is said that Patrick converted all the Irish; this is inaccurate. He brought into the Church tens of thousands, perhaps hundreds of thousands of souls, and he was delighted by the large numbers of men and women who asked to become monks and nuns, but his mission was confined largely to northern and eastern Ireland. Nonetheless, in Ireland Patrick laid the foundation for one of the most vibrant Christian nations in Europe, where piety, learning, and especially the monastic life thrived.

Saint Patrick is the patron saint of Ireland and the Irish. He is the patron saint of many dioceses and archdioceses, including Armagh; New York; Boston; Auckland, New Zealand; Melbourne, Australia; Cape Town, South Africa; and Poona, India. He is invoked against snakes. Feast day: March 17.

**Saint Paul (died c. 64).** On Sunday June 28, 2009, the eve of the feast of Saints Peter and Paul, Pope Benedict XVI announced that after several years of study Vatican archaeologists felt confident that the remains enshrined in a sarcophagus beneath the high altar of Rome's Basilica of St. Paul Outside the Walls are indeed the relics of the apostle Paul. The pope was quoted as saying, "Small fragments of bone were carbon dated by experts who knew nothing about their provenance and results showed they were from someone who lived between the 1st and 2nd century. This seems to confirm the unanimous and uncontested tradition that these are the mortal remains of Paul the Apostle."

The stump of column upon which Saint Paul was beheaded is preserved in the Church of St. Paul at the Abbey of Tre Fontane, or Three Fountains, built on the site of his martyrdom. Also in the church are three springs, or fountains, which bubbled up from the three spots where the head of the apostle bounced on the ground. In the Roman Forum is the Mamertine Prison, where Paul and Peter were incarcerated. On Malta is a cave chapel said to be the place where Paul took refuge after he was shipwrecked on the island.

Saul of Tarsus was studying with the renowned Rabbi Gamaliel in Jerusalem at the time of Jesus's trial and death, but it is not known if Saul witnessed Christ's Passion. He was involved in the execution of Saint Stephen; he guarded the cloaks of the men who stoned to death the first Christian martyr.

A fervent Jew and committed enemy of the Christians, Saul was riding to Damascus to arrest Christians there when a dazzling light blinded him and threw him from his horse. Lying in the dust of the road he heard the voice of Christ say, "Saul! Saul! Why do you persecute me?" Saul's men led him into Damascus where a Christian named Ananias visited him, restored his sight, and baptized him.

Saul's conversion (he was now know as Paul) made many Christians suspicious, including the apostles in Jerusalem. He was accepted only after Saint Barnabas, a respected disciple, vouched for the authenticity of Paul's conversion.

Paul became renowned for his missionary journeys throughout the Mediterranean and his epistles, or letters, to the Christian congregations he founded. The letters elucidate doctrine, warn against straying from the faith, and settle disputes within the congregations. They also reveal Paul as a theological genius who made Christianity accessible to Gentiles by blending the teachings of

Jesus Christ with the principles of Greek philosophy. In fact, no theologian in the history of the Church has been as influential as Saint Paul.

During Nero's persecution of Christians, Paul was beheaded at a place called Aquae Salviae, now the Abbey of Tre Fontane, or the Three Fountains. Over his grave on the Via Ostia the Emperor Constantine built the Basilica of St. Paul Outside the Walls.

Feast days: The Conversion of Saint Paul on January 25; Saints Peter and Paul, June 29; Basilicas of Sts. Peter and Paul, November 18.

**Saint Paul of the Cross (1694–1775).** The tomb of Saint Paul of the Cross is found in Rome's Church of Sts. John and Paul.

Paul Danei regarded the sufferings and death of Christ—known as the Passion—as the greatest example of God's love for humanity. In 1720 he began to found a community of priests and brothers who would encourage devotion to the Passion, bring that love to every person they met, and revive religious fervor through excellent preaching. The Passionists, as the order came to be known, developed a reputation for bringing about conversions and renewed religious zeal through their spiritual retreats and parish missions.

Saint Paul of the Cross once wrote of the Passion, "In this, the holiest of all schools, true wisdom is learned, for it was there that all the saints became wise."

Saint Paul of the Cross is the patron saint of the town of Ovada, Italy. Feast day: October 19.

**Saints Paula (347–404) and Eustochium (c. 369–c. 419).** Mother and daughter were buried together by Saint Jerome in one of the caves beneath Bethlehem's Church of the Nativity, near the grotto where Jesus Christ was born.

Paula and Eustochium were among a group of Roman patrician women who took Saint Jerome as their spiritual director. When

Jerome left Rome for the Holy Land to complete his Latin translation of the Bible, Paula and Eustochium joined him. Paula had inherited a large fortune from her family and her husband, which she used to found a monastery for men, a convent for women, and a hostel for pilgrims in Bethlehem. As she was fluent in Greek, she also assisted Jerome in translating Greek biblical texts. After her death, Saint Jerome wrote an account of Paula's life.

Eustochium became Jerome's secretary and succeeded her mother as abbess of the convent in Bethlehem.

Saint Paula is the patron saint of widows. Feast day of Saint Paula: January 26. Feast day of Saint Eustochium: September 28.

**Saint Peregrine Laziosi (1260–1345).** Peregrine Laziosi was buried in a church dedicated to Saint Agnes in Forli. After Peregrine was beatified in 1702, the Servites built a chapel where his remains could be venerated by the faithful. This chapel was later expanded into the grand baroque Sanctuary of St. Peregrine in Forli. The relics of the saint, dressed in the habit of a Servite, lie in a crystal casket above the altar of a side chapel. From the sanctuary, pilgrims have access to what is known as the Fourteenth Century Room, which preserves the fresco of the crucified Christ before which Peregrine prayed and was healed of cancer.

In his late teens Peregrine Laziosi was a hotheaded partisan of the Holy Roman Emperor. In fact, most of the citizens of Forli, Peregrine's hometown, were pro-emperor and anti-pope. Hoping to effect a reconciliation, Pope Martin V sent Saint Philip Benizi to talk sense to the people of Forli. Thanks to young men like Peregrine, Saint Philip's outdoor meeting with the Forlians degenerated into a street fight.

During the brawl Peregrine grabbed Saint Philip and struck him across the face. Philip turned his head so Peregrine could strike a blow on his other cheek. Shamed and humiliated, Peregrine ran from the piazza.

Soon thereafter Peregrine traveled to the headquarters of Saint

Philip's order, the Servites, and asked to be admitted. He was accepted, ordained a priest, and developed a reputation as a gentle, patient confessor.

When Peregrine developed cancer in his right leg, a physician declared that amputation was the only safe treatment. The night before surgery Peregrine limped to the chapter room to pray before a life-size crucifix. Eventually he dozed off. In his sleep he saw Christ come down from the cross and touch the cancerous leg. When Peregrine awoke, the cancer was gone.

Saint Peregrine Lasiozi is invoked against cancer, AIDS, open wounds, and skin diseases. Feast day: May 1.

**Saints Perpetua and Felicity (died 203).** In the fourth century, after three centuries of persecution ended, the Christians of Carthage erected a basilica over the tombs of the martyrs Saint Perpetua and Saint Felicity. In the seventh century, when Muslim Arabs conquered the city, the relics were lost, although the Church of Notre Dame in Vierzon, France, claims to have some, perhaps all, of the remains of Saint Perpetua. The saints' dungeon beneath the Carthage arena has been found by archaeologists and is now a chapel dedicated to their memory.

One of the treasures of early Christian literature is Perpetua's diary, written during her imprisonment for the faith. She was twenty-two years old, a patrician, a wife, and the mother of an infant boy. She was arrested with Felicity, her slave, who was pregnant and near term. Felicity gave birth in prison and gave her daughter up for adoption to a Christian family.

The diary concludes with a detailed, eyewitness account of the martyrdom of the two women and their companions. No one knows who completed it, although there is a tradition that it was the work of the martyrs' contemporary, the great Christian author Tertullian.

Saint Perpetua is the patron saint of expectant mothers. Saint Perpetua and Saint Felicity are both the patron saints of cattle and ranchers. Feast day: March 7.

**Saint Peter (died c. 64).** Peter, the prince of the apostles, was crucified head downward in the Circus, or Arena, of Nero on the Vatican Hill. Christians recovered his body and buried it in a nearby cemetery. By about the year 160 a small mausoleum had been erected over Peter's grave. About the year 326 the emperor Constantine erected a large basilica on the Vatican Hill, with the high altar positioned above Saint Peter's grave. But over succeeding centuries the location of the grave became forgotten; this was especially the case after 1505, when Pope Julius II resolved to tear down Constantine's dilapidated basilica and replace it with a new church.

In 1939 workmen were digging a grave for Pope Pius XI in the grottoes under Saint Peter's when one of them felt his shovel cut into a void rather than dirt. Shining a flashlight throughout the hole, the work crew saw the interior of a second-century mausoleum. Further exploration revealed an entire Roman necropolis, covered over by Constantine and perfectly preserved. Directly beneath the high altar of Saint Peter's, archaeologists found a simple tomb containing the bones of a robust elderly man. Scratched into the tomb wall were countless prayers and petitions, as well as the inscription PETER IS WITHIN.

In all the lists of the apostles found in the New Testament, Saint Peter's name always appears first. His given name was Simon, but Christ renamed him Petros, Peter, Greek for "rock," the rock upon which the Lord would build his Church. In Matthew 16:18–19 we find Christ establishing the papacy by giving to Peter spiritual authority on earth and in heaven.

In spite of his exalted place in Christian history, the Gospels and the Acts of the Apostles reveal that Peter was an impulsive man, prone to human weakness. He wanted to walk on water, and he did so until fear overcame him and he sank. He vowed to die with Jesus, until it seemed that his life was in danger; then he denied Christ three times—and within the Lord's hearing. Perhaps to exorcize the memory of that shameful night, the risen Christ three times asked Peter, "Do you love me?" Peter, humiliated, declared, "Lord, you know all things; you know that I love you." At which point

In 1939, directly beneath this shrine in the crypt of Rome's Basilica of St. Peter, an excavation crew discovered the actual tomb of Saint Peter. Scala/ Art Resource, NY

Christ confirmed Peter's pre-eminence among the apostles, commanding him, "Feed my lambs, feed my sheep." (John 21:17–19)

During the debate over whether Gentile converts to Christianity should be circumcised and keep the Jewish kosher laws, Peter, at heart a traditionalist, waffled. Saint Paul was incensed, believing that the Jewish law had been superseded by the Gospel. Furthermore, the circumcision and kosher laws made potential Gentile converts think twice about accepting Christianity.

Peter preached first in Jerusalem, where he delivered the first Christian sermon on the first Pentecost. He traveled to Antioch and made that city his headquarters before moving on to Rome, where he and Saint Paul established the Church and were martyred, according to tradition, on the same day.

Saint Peter is the patron saint of the Catholic Church, the papacy, fishermen, locksmiths, and boat builders. He is the patron saint of many cities and dioceses, including Rome, London, and St. Petersburg, Russia. Feast day: June 29.

**Saint Peter Claver (1581–1654).** The skeleton of Saint Peter Claver, clothed in Mass vestments, lies within a glass and gold casket beneath the high altar of the church of St. Peter Claver in Cartagena, Colombia. Beside the church is the Jesuit residence where he lived.

Peter Claver felt called to the religious life, but even after he entered the Jesuit seminary at Majorca he debated whether he was better suited to the monastic life or perhaps serving as a parish priest. It was the seminary gatekeeper, Saint Alphonsus Rodriguez, who told Claver that he should go to South America as a missionary.

Claver's Jesuit superiors assigned him to Cartagena, Colombia. There a fellow Jesuit, Father Alphonsus de Sandoval, recruited him to work with him in the slave pens. Cartagena was a major center of the slave trade, with as many as a thousand Africans being brought in every month, then sold to work in the mines, on the plantations, or in the houses of the Spanish colonists. The captives arrived desperate for food and water, and some required medical attention; all of them were terrified by what had already happened to them and dreaded what was to come.

Father Claver devoted his life to caring for the slaves. Every time a slave ship docked, Father Claver hurried to the slave pens with food, water, and medicine. Through interpreters he tried to console the slaves, and he taught them the basics of the Catholic faith, baptizing as many as he could. Those Africans who were sold to families in Cartagena or to owners of neighboring plantations were visited regularly by Father Claver, who said Mass, administered the sacraments, and worked to increase their knowledge of the faith. He also tried to protect the slaves from harsh masters. The slaves became his parishioners.

Father Claver's dedication to the African slaves irritated many of the colonists, including some of his fellow Jesuits. In his final illness, only one African slave stayed with Father Claver, nursing him around the clock. When word spread through Cartagena that Peter Claver had died, a large crowd of slaves forced their way into the Jesuit residence to see his face one last time.

Saint Peter Claver is the patron saint of interracial justice, the African missions, and African Americans. He is invoked against slavery and is one of the patron saints of Colombia. Feast day: September 9.


**Saint Peter of Verona, also known as Saint Peter Martyr (c. 1205–1252).** Saint Peter's relics lie in a magnificent white marble Gothic tomb in the Portinari Chapel of the Basilica of St. Eustorgius in Milan, Italy.

Peter's parents were Cathars, members of a sect that taught that anything physical was evil, including the Mass and the sacraments, and that the Christian God was Satan. As a young man he turned away from the Cathars and became a Catholic. After hearing Saint Dominic preach, Peter joined the Dominicans.

Peter was intelligent and eloquent, and given his familiarity with Cathar doctrine, he was an especially effective defender of Catholicism. The pope appointed him inquisitor of northern Italy, instructing him to bring Cathars back to the Catholic Church and granting him authority to correct Catholic priests and monks who were not living up to their vows.

Peter proved to be such an effective preacher that leaders of the Cathars in northern Italy came to regard him as a serious threat. On April 6, 1252, a band of Cathars ambushed and murdered Peter and a fellow Dominican friar. One of the assassins, a man named Carino, repented his part in the murder, renounced Catharism, returned to the Catholic faith, and became a Dominican. In and around the town of Forli there is a local devotion to him under the title of Blessed Carino.

Saint Peter of Verona is the patron saint of the Holy Office of the Inquisition, known today as the Congregation for the Doctrine of the Faith. Feast day: April 29.

**Saint Peter's Chains.** In 438 Empress Eudoxia made a pilgrimage to Jerusalem, where she acquired the chains that had bound Saint Peter when he was a prisoner of King Herod Agrippa I (see Acts of the Apostles 12). She brought the chains to Rome and presented them to Pope Saint Leo the Great. The Christians of Rome venerated the chains that had bound Saint Peter when he was in the Mamertine Prison awaiting execution. According to legend, as Pope Leo compared the two chains they miraculously fused together. The chains are displayed in a glass and gilded chest in the Church of St. Peter ad Vincola in Rome. Two links of the chain are preserved in the Treasury of the Cathedral of St. Peter in Trier, Germany.

Feast day: August 1.

**Saint Peter's Chair.** At the rear of Rome's Basilica of St. Peter, below a stained-glass window depicting the Holy Spirit, stands an elaborate shrine designed by Gianlorenzo Bernini. Above the altar four giant bronze statues of Saints Augustine, Ambrose, Athansius, and John Chrysostom support a large throne. Inside this throne is a wooden throne, parts of which are thought to have belonged to Saint Peter. In fact, tradition claims that those fragments come from the chair in which he sat when he celebrated his first Mass in Rome and first instructed the Roman Christians.

Feast day: February 22.

**Saint Petronilla (first century).** The Altar of St. Petronilla in St. Peter's Basilica in Rome preserves the relics of this virgin martyr. In 750 her relics were taken from a grave in the Catacombs

Gian Lorenzo Bernini made this massive shrine for the Cathedra, or Throne, of Saint Peter. Inside the shrine is a wooden chair from which, it is said, Peter instructed the first Christians of Rome. SCALA/ART RESOURCE, NY

of St. Domitilla near the Appian Way and enshrined in the Old Basilica of St. Peter.

Legend claims that Petronilla was the daughter of Saint Peter. But it is more likely that she was his spiritual daughter, converted by him. Petronilla was one of several Roman women who cared for the apostle. She was martyred in the first century, perhaps during Nero's persecution of the Church.

For many centuries French Catholics have been devoted to Saint Petronilla, because France is known as "the eldest daughter of the Church" and the saint is said to be the daughter of Saint Peter. Every year on Saint Petronilla's feast day French citizens in Rome gather at this altar for Mass.

Saint Petronilla is the patron saint of mountain travelers and of the dauphins of France. Feast day: May 31.

**Saint Philip Howard (1557–1595).** After ten years' imprisonment Philip Howard died of natural causes in the Tower of London. He was buried in the Tower's Chapel of St. Peter ad Vincula. In 1624 his widow petitioned King James I to permit her to bury Philip's remains among the tombs of his ancestors in the Fitzalan Chapel at Arundel Castle. The king granted her request. In 1971 when Philip Howard was canonized, his relics were moved from the castle chapel to the Arundel Cathedral, which was rededicated to Our Lady and Saint Philip Howard.

The son of the duke of Norfolk, Philip Howard grew up spoiled, arrogant, selfish, and religiously indifferent. He had been educated as a Catholic while Mary I was queen of England, but when she was succeeded by her Protestant half sister Elizabeth I, the Howards dismissed Philip's Catholic tutors and had him raised an Anglican.

At age twelve Philip married Anne Dacre, but they spent little time together: Philip went off to the university at Cambridge and then to Queen Elizabeth's court. He frequented gambling houses and brothels, accepted bribes, surrounded himself with sycophants, and ran up enormous debts. At one point he stated publicly that he doubted he was truly married to Anne. Philip's outraged grandfather and aunt cut him out of their wills, while Anne tried to bear the humiliation as best she could.

In 1581 Philip joined other members of the royal court at the Tower of London, where a panel of Anglican theologians were set to debate a prisoner, the Jesuit priest Father Edmund Campion. The Anglicans had books, notes, and clerks to assist them; Father Campion, who was still recovering from torture on the rack, had no resources except his memory. In spite of these disabilities Father Campion defended the Catholic position so well that the debate was called to a halt in order to protect the reputations of the Jesuit's opponents.

The debate touched Philip Howard's conscience. While Father Campion prepared for martyrdom, Philip reconciled with his wife and together they sought a way to escape England and find refuge in some English Catholic colony on the Continent, but someone betrayed them. In 1585 Philip was imprisoned in the Tower and fined £10,000. In 1589 he was tried and sentenced to death for treason, but the sentence was never carried out. Queen Elizabeth left him to die in prison.

He was permitted books and paper, so he studied and wrote letters to Anne, his young son, and his friends. He was permitted to leave his cell, under guard, to get some exercise outdoors. He was forbidden any religious image, so he incised a crucifix into the wall of his cell.

In 1595, after ten years of imprisonment, Philip fell ill with dysentery. He appealed to Queen Elizabeth to let a Catholic priest hear his confession and bring him the Last Rites, to let him see Anne and his son, or at least to permit him to see his brothers. The queen refused all of his requests.

Not long before he died Philip wrote to Anne, "I call God to witness, it is no small grief unto me that I cannot make recompense in this world for the wrongs I have done you; for if it had pleased God to have granted me longer life, I doubt not but that you should have found me as good a husband . . . by his grace, as you have found me bad before. . . . [God] knows that which is past is a nail in my conscience."

Saint Philip Howard is the patron saint of victims of betrayal and of spouses in difficult marriages. Feast day: October 19.

**Saint Philip Neri (1515–1595).** The relics of Saint Philip Neri lie beneath the altar of a side chapel in Rome's Chiesa Nuova. His rooms in the residence adjacent to the church are intact but are rarely open to visitors.

Philip Neri grew up in Florence, where his friendly, outgoing nature made him a favorite with children and adults. When he was eighteen a childless relative, a well-to-do businessman, offered Philip an apprenticeship with the intention of making Philip his heir, but Philip did not stay long. He felt drawn to Rome, where he found work tutoring the sons of a fellow Florentine.

In Rome Philip became increasingly devout: he prayed for hours on end, fasted often, and studied theology and philosophy at the universities. Rome in the 1530s was far from a holy city. The shameful life of Pope Alexander VI was a recent memory. The high living and low morals of cardinals and other members of the Curia were well known, and many parish priests imitated them. Countless Romans had become indifferent to their faith.

Philip began as a lay missionary, making conversation in shops and piazzas and other places where people gathered to talk. His charm and good humor made it easy for him to ingratiate himself with strangers, and eventually the conversation would turn to the subject of religion. Rather than carp on the failings of churchmen, Neri reminded his new friends of the ideals of the Catholic faith and the Gospel's power to change lives. "Well, brothers," he would say, "when shall we begin to do good?" And by doing good he meant not only returning to the Mass and the sacraments but also volunteering in one of Rome's hospitals or some other charitable institution.

Not until 1551 was Philip finally ordained a priest. He kept up his street corner conversations, but he also spent long hours in the confessional. Other priests joined him, and in time they became the Congregation of the Oratory, named for the little chapel they maintained. Philip became the best-loved priest in Rome; cardinals and even popes sought his advice. Led by Philip and his fellow Oratorians, Rome experienced a religious revival.

Saint Philip Neri is the patron saint of the United States Army Special Forces, and he is one of the patron saints of Rome. Feast day: May 26.

**Saint Philip the Apostle (died c. 80).** In the sixth century the relics of Saint Philip along with those of the Saint James the Lesser were brought from their tombs in Asia Minor to Rome, where Pope John III erected a new church dedicated to the Twelve Apostles. Over the centuries, as the church was rebuilt and repaired, the location of the saints' shrine was forgotten; the saints' remains were rediscovered early in the nineteenth century. Since 1837 the bones of Saint Philip have been enshrined in the same marble chest as the bones of Saint James, in the crypt of the Church of the Holy Apostles.

Philip was from Bethsaida in Galilee; he had several daughters, but we do not know if his wife was living at the time Philip became one of Christ's apostles. Philip recruited his friend Nathanial, also known as Bartholomew, to come meet the Messiah and become an apostle.

After Christ's ascension into heaven, Philip preached in Asia Minor (modern-day Turkey). He was about eighty years old when he was martyred by being nailed to a cross.

Saint Philip the Apostle is the patron saint of hatmakers and pastry chefs, and he is one of the patron saints of Uruguay and Luxembourg. Feast day: May 3.

**Saint Philomena (died third century).** In 1802 excavators working in Rome's Catacomb of St. Priscilla found an intact tomb covered with three funeral tiles. The tiles were out of order, but when correctly arranged they read PAX TECUM FILUMENA, or "Peace be with you, Philomena." A palm, the Christian symbol of martyrdom, was inscribed on one tile, and inside the tomb was the skeleton of a young woman and a broken vial thought to contain blood, another indication that the deceased was a Christian martyr. The relics of Saint Philomena, as she came to be called, were granted to the bishop of Nola, Bartolomeo de Caesare, who enshrined them in the Church of Our Lady of Grace in Mugnano del Cardinale, where they are still venerated.

Aside from the name of this young Christian and the fact of her martyrdom, we know nothing else about her. Early in the 1830s a Dominican nun in Naples, Italy, Sister Maria Luisa de Gesù, claimed to have received a vision of Saint Philomena in which the saint revealed the story of her life and death.

Surprisingly, devotion to this obscure saint spread rapidly throughout the Catholic world, and many saints attributed miracles to Philomena's intercession, including Saint John Mary Vianney, Saint John Neumann, Saint Damien de Veuster, Saint Peter Julian Eymard, Saint Madeleine Sophie Barat, Blessed Bartolo Longo, Blessed Anna Maria Taigi, and Venerable Pauline Jaricot. In 1837 Pope Gregory XVI approved public devotion to Saint Philomena, and successive popes encouraged devotion to her.

By 1961 some historians were casting doubts on the interpretation of the archaeological evidence, arguing that there was no reason to believe that Philomena had been a martyr. The Congregation of Rites responded by removing Philomena's feast day from the liturgical calendar, but it did not take the next step of ordering that her shrine in Mugnano be dismantled and her bones buried. As a result, Saint Philomena remains in a kind of limbo: Mass may not be celebrated in her honor, but devotion to her is permitted.

Saint Philomena is the patron saint of infants, children, teenagers, the Children of Mary, prisoners, priests, test takers, the poor, the sick, the Living Rosary, and impossible causes. She is invoked against financial troubles, infertility, and mental illness. Feast day: August 11.

**Blessed Pier Giorgio Frassati (1901–1925).** Pier Giorgio's family buried him in the Frassati tomb in Turin's Pollone Cemetery. In

1981, as part of his beatification, his remains were translated to a tomb in the Cathedral of Turin.

Photographs of Pier Giorgio Frassati show us a handsome young man with broad shoulders, dark hair, dark eyes, and a strong chin. His was a natural athlete whose favorite sports were hiking, mountain climbing, and skiing. He could be reckless, boisterous, and impulsive; once, when police attacked antifascism demonstrators, Pier Giorgio grabbed a banner pole and struck one of the officers over the head. He spent that night in jail.

At age seventeen Pier Giorgio joined the Saint Vincent de Paul Society, an organization dedicated to helping the needy. Pier Giorgio's acts of charity were intensely personal. He found an affordable apartment for a homeless woman. He persuaded a factory foreman to give a job to an ex-convict. So many people appealed to him for help that he began to record the requests in a little notebook so he would not forget anyone.

In the summer of 1925 Pier Giorgio fell ill. His doctor told him he had an especially virulent, fatal strain of polio. One of his last acts was to pass his notebook to his sister Luciana so his friends would not be forgotten. Within days of the diagnosis, Pier Giorgio was dead.

In 1990, at Pier Giorgio Frassati's beatification ceremony, Pope John Paul II praised the new blessed as "the man of the eight Beatitudes" and urged young Catholics to imitate him.

Blessed Pier Giorgio Frassati is the patron saint of athletes and World Youth Day. Feast day: July 4.


**The Pillar of the Scourging.** Two churches claim to possess the pillar to which Christ was bound when he was scourged before his crucifixion. One is found in the Chapel of the Derision, also known as the Chapel of the Crowning with Thorns, in the Church of the Holy Sepulcher in Jerusalem. The other is in the Basilica of Santa Prassede in Rome. The Santa Prassede relic is carved from a beautiful piece of black and white jasper and is very small, not even two feet high. It is enshrined in a glass and bronze tabernacle near the Chapel of San Zeno on the right side of the church. It was brought there from Constantinople in 1223 by Cardinal Giovanni Colonna. A portion of this pillar is preserved in the Treasury of the Basilica of St. Mark in Venice.

**Pittsburgh's St. Anthony Chapel Relics (chapel opened 1892).** Father Suitbert Godfrey Mollinger, an immigrant priest from Belgium, built this chapel in Pittsburgh, Pennsylvania, to house his impressive collection of relics. The collection includes the complete skeleton of Saint Demetrius, the skulls of Saints Macharius, Stephana, and Theodore, the skulls of several of the companions martyred with Saint Ursula, and Saint Anthony of Padua's tooth. With over five thousand relics, St. Anthony's Chapel possesses the largest collection of sacred relics in the United States.

**Saint Pius V (1504–1572).** The body of Pope Pius V lies in a glass and marble casket in the Chapel of the Blessed Sacrament in Rome's Basilica of St. Mary Major.

It fell to Pope Pius to enact the reforms of the Catholic Counter-Reformation set forth by the Council of Trent. He authorized publication of revised editions of the missal and the breviary, and the compilation of a new catechism, which was written specifically to define, explain, and defend Catholic doctrine and religious practices that had come under fire from Protestants and other critics of the Church.

As Turkish military power swept acoss the eastern Mediteranean, Pius organized the Holy League, a naval alliance drawn from several Catholic nations. At the battle of Lepanto in 1571, the Holy League enjoyed a decisive victory, destroying the Turkish navy and saving Western Europe from an Ottoman invasion by sea.

Feast day: April 30.

**Blessed Pius IX (1792–1878).** The body of the pope lies in a glass and marble chest beneath a side altar in Rome's Basilica of St. Lawrence Outside the Walls.

Pius IX reigned for thirty-two years—the longest pontificate after that of Saint Peter. He was also the last pontiff who was also a secular ruler. For more than a thousand years the popes had ruled the Papal States, a large territory that covered most of central Italy. Pope Pius's reign coincided with a political movement to unite the several petty principalities and dukedoms of Italy into a single nation. Pius IX resisted the unification of Italy, but on September 20, 1870, the Italian army entered Rome and the pope was forced to accept the fact that the Papal States were abolished.

During Pius's reign the Catholic Church experienced a tremendous revival in Great Britain and Ireland, while also experiencing tremendous growth in the United States. Pius re-established the hierarchy in England, Scotland, and Wales, and created new dioceses and archdioceses in America, particularly in the West.

But in Italy and Prussia anticlerical governments shut down Catholic schools, expelled members of religious orders, and exiled or imprisoned bishops who protested such actions. To protect the rights of Catholics and the freedom of the Church, Pius negotiated more than a dozen concordats with hostile governments.

After centuries of debate among theologians, in 1854 Pius defined the Immaculate Conception of the Blessed Virgin Mary as a doctrine of the Church. In 1869 he called the First Vatican Council, where the doctrine of papal infallibility in matters of faith and morals was defined.

Feast day: February 7.

**Saint Pius X (1835–1914).** The body of Saint Pius X is enshrined in St. Peter's Basilica beneath the altar of the Presentation of the Blessed Virgin Mary. The body is dressed in papal robes, and the hands and face are covered with silver.

The future pope's father was the postman in a small village

outside Venice. As bishop, Giuseppe Sarto encouraged priests and seminarians to study the theology of Saint Thomas Aquinas (he distributed copies of the *Summa theologica* to clerics who couldn't afford to buy one), and he revived Gregorian chant in the churches of his diocese.

As pope, Pius X fostered renewed devotion to the Blessed Sacrament. At the time children were twelve or fourteen years old when they made their First Holy Communion; Pope Pius lowered the age to seven. Many priests and bishops were of the opinion that few of the laity were worthy to receive Holy Communion more than a few times a year; Pius X encouraged frequent, even daily Communion.

He insisted that all Catholic church choirs must be trained to sing Gregorian chant, the ancient liturgical music of the Church. He called for clear, understandable sermons for adults and published a new, accessible catechism for children.

Pope Pius X was a vigorous opponent of an intellectual trend known as modernism, which rejected authority, religious doctrine, standards of right and wrong, and tradition, embracing in their place whatever ideas were new and fashionable, no matter how destructive they might be to the Church or society.

Pope Saint Pius X is the patron saint of First Communicants and of pilgrims. Feast day: August 21.


**Saints Praxedes and Pudentiana (second century).** In an ancient sarcophagus in the Basilica of Santa Prassede in Rome are the relics of these two sisters. Also buried with them is a sponge with which, it is said, they collected the blood of the martyrs. What is thought to be their home lies beneath the nearby Church of St. Pudenziana.

Saint Praxedes is the patron saint of unmarried women. Feast day of Saint Praxedes: July 21. Feast day of Saint Pudentiana: May 19.

**Saint Priscilla (first century).** The saint's relics were moved from her tomb in the Catacomb of St. Priscilla to the Church of St. Prisca in Rome. A portion of her house survives adjacent to the catacomb.

Priscilla was a Roman patrician, the wife of the consul Manlius Acilius Glabrio, and the mother the senator Pudens. The family was baptized by Saints Peter and Paul, and there is an ancient legend in Rome that Saint Peter stayed at the family's villa. Glabrio and Pudens were martyred during Emperor Domitian's persecution of the Church; it is not certain if Saint Priscilla was also a martyr.

Feast day: January 18.

**Saints Processus and Martinian (first century).** The relics of these two martyrs are preserved in a porphyry urn within the altar dedicated to them in the Basilica of St. Peter.

Processus and Martinian were jailers at the Mamertine Prison where Saint Peter and Saint Paul were incarcerated. The apostles converted and baptized the two men. Shortly afterward Processus and Martinian were martyred.

Saints Processus and Martinian are the patron saints of prison guards. Feast day: July 2.

**Saint Radegund (c. 518–587).** In 1562 Huguenot vandals broke into the shrine of Saint Radegund and burned some of her relics. Those relics that survived lie in a raised stone sarcophagus in the Romanesque crypt of the Church of St. Radegund in Poitiers, France.

Radegund's father, the king of Thuringia, was assassinated when she was a child. Clotaire I, king of the Franks, avenged the death of his fellow monarch and took Radegund into his palace; when she was twelve he married her. It was an unhappy match: in spite of his marriage, Clotaire never gave up his half a dozen mistresses. When Clotaire murdered Radegund's brother, she left her husband and entered a convent. Clotaire did not try to bring her back, perhaps because they had no children.

Radegund founded a convent in Poitiers that became a center of piety and learning. The Christian poet Venantius Fortunatus and the Christian historian Gregory of Tours were among her closest friends. When she died, Gregory said the Requiem Mass and Venantius wrote her biography.

Saint Radegund is the patron saint of Jesus College at Cambridge University in England, and of the city of Poitiers. She is invoked against drowning, skin diseases, ulcers, and fever. Feast day: August 13.

**Saint Richard the King (died 722).** The relics of Saint Richard lie inside a Roman sarcophagus in the Trenta Chapel of the Basilica of San Frediano in Lucca, Italy.

In the eighth century England was divided into several petty kingdoms; Richard may have been king of Wessex. He was the father of three saints, Willibald, Winebald, and Walburga, all of whom became Benedictines and missionaries to Germany. While on pilgrimage to Rome, Richard fell ill in Lucca and died there. Visitors to his tomb reported miraculous cures, so he was venerated as a saint.

Feast day: February 7.

**Blesseds Richard Whiting (?–1539), John Thorne (?–1539), and Roger James (?–1539).** Since they were convicted of treason, the bodies of Abbot Whiting and two of his monks were hacked into four pieces and displayed in various parts of England. Their heads were mounted on pikes before their vacant abbey. The skulls of the martyrs lie buried in some forgotten spot on the grounds of

Glastonbury Abbey. The abbey museum displays Blessed Richard Whiting's seal.

In 1534 Richard Whiting, abbot of Glastonbury Abbey, followed the example of virtually every other cleric in England and acknowledged King Henry VIII as Supreme Head of the Church in England. But in 1539, when the king's commissioners came to seize all the abbey's property and expel the monks, Abbot Whiting resisted. Joining him were the abbey's treasurer, Brother John Thorne, and the abbey's sacristan, Brother Roger James. They were tried and convicted of treason. On the day of their execution the three monks were dragged on a single hurdle to the summit of Glastonbury Tor, overlooking the empty abbey. There the three monks were hanged, drawn, and quartered.

Feast day: November 15.

**Saint Rita of Cascia (1381–1457).** In 1946 a new sanctuary was built in Cascia to house the relics of Saint Rita. Her body, dressed in the habit of an Augustinian nun, lies inside a glass casket under a gilded canopy in the Basilica of St. Rita.

Rita's husband was a violent, short-tempered man who was killed in one of the petty feuds that ravaged Italian society in the Middle Ages. Rita tried to dissuade her sons from seeking vengeance, but they were adamant, so she prayed to God to take their lives before they could commit the sin of murder. Both young men fell ill and died, but not before they repented of having intended to carry out the vendetta.

Rita entered a convent of Augustinian nuns, where she received an unusual form of stigmata—a wound in her forehead, like that made by a sharp thorn. It was painful and so unsightly that her superiors permitted Rita to live as a kind of recluse within the convent. She tended the convent garden and sometimes nursed patients in the infirmary. As for the stigmata wound, it healed in 1450 after Rita made a pilgrimage to Rome during the Holy Year.

Saint Rita of Cascia is the patron saint of lost causes, widows, victims of abuse, the sick, and the wounded. She is invoked against troubled marriages, loneliness, and infertility. She is the patron saint of Cascia. Feast day: May 22.


**Saint Robert Bellarmine (1542–1621).** The relics of Saint Robert Bellarmine lie in a side altar in Rome's Church of St. Ignatius.

In 1599, when Pope Clement VIII created Robert Bellarmine a cardinal, he said of him, "The Church of God has not his equal in learning."

At age eighteen Bellarmine joined the Jesuits, and he owed his intellectual training to them. After his ordination to the priesthood Father Bellarmine specialized in explaining and defending Catholic doctrine and religious practices—a vital skill during the Reformation and Counter-Reformation era.

In 1588 he was appointed spiritual director of the Roman College, the Jesuit seminary in Rome, where he guided the spiritual development of Saint Aloysius Gonzaga.

Shortly after he was made a cardinal, Bellarmine was appointed archbishop of Capua, where he worked to implement the reforms of the Council of Trent: improving the education and training of seminarians; correcting religious orders of men and women who had drifted away from the principles of their founders; sending out holy, well-instructed priests among the people of the archdiocese to teach the essentials of the Catholic faith. To assist these priests he wrote a guide on how to teach the catechism, as well as a short catechism suitable for children.

Saint Robert Bellarmine is the patron saint of catechists and canon lawyers. Feast day: September 17.


**Saint Rocco (1350–1380).** The relics of Saint Rocco lie in the church dedicated to him in Venice. In 1478 a charitable confraternity was founded at Saint Rocco's church to assist poor families of the parish with gifts of cash and food. Over the centuries at least two popes have been members of the confraternity, Saint Pius X and Blessed John XXIII.

Rocco was a French nobleman who at age twenty set out on a life as a perpetual pilgrim. In Italy he entered a town where the bubonic plague was raging. While many of the inhabitants fled, Rocco stayed to nurse the sick. When he discovered a plague sore on his leg, he hurried into a nearby forest to die before he could infect anyone else. It is said that every day God sent him a dog with a loaf of bread in his mouth. The bread nourished Rocco and he survived the plague. When he returned home to Montpellier in France, no one recognized him and he was imprisoned as a spy. He remained in prison until his death, five years later.

Saint Rocco is the patron saint of dogs, pilgrims, invalids, and the falsely accused. He is invoked against plague and epidemics. Feast day: August 16.


**Saint Rosalia (died c. 1160).** It is said that in 1624, when Palermo was being ravaged by a deadly plague, Saint Rosalia appeared to a hunter, told him where to find her remains, and requested that they be carried in a procession through the city. As the saint's bones were brought into Palermo, the plague abated. Today the relics of Saint Rosalia are kept in a silver chest in the Chapel of St. Rosalia in the Cathedral of Palermo, Sicily.

Rosalia was the daughter of Sinibald, a Sicilian nobleman; her mother claimed descent from Charlemagne. She may have been a nun of the Order of St. Basil before she began her life as a hermit. She lived in a cave at Bivona and then at Monte Pellegrino near Palermo. At her death, the local people sealed the entrance to the cave, making it her tomb, where her body remained for nearly five hundred years until it was moved to Palermo's cathedral.

Saint Rosalia is one of the patron saints of Palermo and the island of Sicily. Feast days: September 4 and July 15 (Translation of Saint Rosalia's Relics).

**Saint Rose of Lima (1586–1617).** The relics of Saint Rose are enshrined in the Church of St. Dominic in Lima. On the site of her birthplace is the Sanctuary of St. Rose of Lima; her hermitage still stands in the garden.

Rose was this saint's nickname. She was baptized Isabel, but an Incan housemaid declared that the baby was as lovely "as a rose," and the name stuck.

Rose Flores de Oliva was of mixed Spanish and Incan descent. Her parents were well-to-do and expected that Rose would further improve the family fortunes by making a good marriage. But Rose refused to marry; she intended to become a nun. Her mother and father refused to permit her to enter the cloister. The impasse between her and her parents dragged on for ten years until the family arrived at a compromise: Rose would join the Third Order of Dominicans, which would grant her the privilege of taking the vows of a nun and wearing the habit of a nun, but living at home.

Rose's brothers built a cottage for her in the family garden, and her parents permitted her to open a clinic in one room of the house. The sick who came to Rose's clinic reported that she healed everyone she touched. When a fleet of pirate ships suddenly turned away from Lima, the citizens attributed their deliverance to Rose's prayers. In Lima, Rose was regarded as a local saint.

Belief in Rose's sanctity was so widespread that immediately after her death the bishops of Peru opened the process that led to her canonization in 1671. She was the first Catholic in the Americas to be declared a saint.

Saint Rose of Lima is the patron saint of gardeners, florists, and embroiderers. She is invoked against vanity. She is one of the patron saints of Lima, Peru; South America; Central America; the New World; the West Indies; the Philippines; and India. Feast day: August 23.

**Saint Rose of Viterbo (1234–1252).** Upon Rose's death her body was sealed inside a glass casket; under these air-tight conditions, her remains mummified naturally. The mummy of Saint Rose is displayed in the Church of St. Rose in Viterbo, Italy. In 2010 an Italian paleoanthropologist, Ruggero D'Anastasio, of the Gabriele d'Annunzio University in Chieti, led a team of scientists in examining Saint Rose's heart (which had been removed from her body in 1921). D'Anastasio and his colleagues found a mass inside the heart consistent with an embolism or blood clot; they concluded that this was the cause of Saint Rose's untimely death.

In the thirteenth century most of Europe, and Italy especially, was torn between partisans who asserted that the supreme authority in Europe lay in the hands of Frederick II, the Holy Roman Emperor, and supporters of the papacy who affirmed that the spiritual authority of the pope superseded the power of kings and emperors.

Many of the citizens of Viterbo had aligned themselves with the emperor, but twelve-year-old Rose went out to the piazzas and street corners and urged her neighbors to support the pope. For three years Viterbo witnessed a war of words between supporters of the pope and the emperor, until the prefect of Viterbo (who supported the emperor) banished Rose and her parents from the city.

From her place of exile in papal territory, Rose predicted that Frederick II was about to die, and he did, on December 13, 1250. Taking this as a sign from God, the citizens of Viterbo invited Rose and her parents to return home. Two years later Rose died suddenly of what was at the time an undiagnosed illness.

Saint Rose of Viterbo is the patron saint of exiles and is one of the patron saints of Viterbo. Feast day: September 4.

**Saint Rose Philippine Duchesne (1769–1852).** In 1855 the Sacred Heart nuns exhumed the body of Mother Duchesne and entombed it in an octagonal red brick shrine dedicated to Our Lady of the Pillar. In 1951 Mother Duchesne's relics were translated to a marble sarcophagus in an alcove of the chapel of the Shrine of St. Rose Philippine Duchesne in St. Charles, Missouri.

In 1818 Sister Rose Philippine Duchesne, a nun of the Society of the Sacred Heart, led several of her sisters to America to establish their order in the New World. She opened a school in St. Charles, Missouri, and a much more ambitious complex in Florissant, Missouri, that included an orphange, a school for Indian children, a boarding school, and a novitiate for her order.

Rose's dream was to work as a missionary among the Indians, but there were so many demands on her as an administrator that it was not until 1841, when she was seventy-two years old, that she was able to travel west to Kansas to work among the Potawatomi tribe. She opened a school for Potawatomi girls and worked as a nurse at the mission infirmary, but Rose's work among the Indians was limited because she never became fluent in the Potawatomi language. In 1842 Rose's superiors recalled her; she spent the last years of her life at the Sacred Heart nuns' convent in St. Charles.

Saint Rose Philippine Duchesne is the patron of Catholics who suffer unjust opposition from Church authorities. Feast day: November 17.

**Saint Sabina (second century?).** The relics of the martyr lie beneath the high altar in the Basilica of St. Sabina in Rome. The church was built over her house.

According to tradition, Sabina was a wealthy patrician who was converted to Christianity by her slave, Saint Serapia. Mistress and maid were martyred during Emperor Hadrian's persecution of Christians.

Feast day: August 29.

**Saint Scholastica (c. 480–c. 543).** The bones of Saint Scholastica lie in the crypt of the abbey church at Monte Cassino, Italy, on the opposite side of the sanctuary from the relics of her twin brother, Saint Benedict.

About the time Benedict established the order of Benedictine monks, Scholastica founded the first convent of Benedictine nuns. The two religious houses were nearby, and once a year sister and brother, accompanied by nuns and monks, met at a guesthouse halfway between their convent and monastery. At one such meeting Scholastica had a premonition that it would be their last. As Benedict rose to leave, she begged him to stay longer. He reminded her of the rule that monks and nuns must be back in their houses before dark. As he turned to go, Scholastica bowed her head and prayed. Immediately a terrible storm erupted over the house.

"What have you done?" Benedict asked his sister.

"You denied my request," Scholastica replied. "God has granted it."

The storm raged until dawn, and the twins and their companions conversed happily all through the night.

Several days later Benedict saw a white dove flying into the clouds; he understood it as a sign from God that Scholastica was dead.

Saint Scholastica is the patron saint of nuns and of children who suffer convulsions. She is invoked against storms. Feast day: February 10.

**Saint Sebastian (died c. 300).** One of the most recognized saints on the calendar, Saint Sebastian is typically portrayed as a handsome young man, nearly naked, tied to a tree, his muscular body stuck through with arrows. Sebastian was a member of the Praetorian Guard, an elite military unit dedicated to protecting the emperor of Rome. He kept his Christian faith secret. When Emperor Diocletian unleashed an empire-wide persecution of Christians, Sebastian used his rank as a Praetorian to visit and assist imprisoned Christians. His activities were discovered, and the emperor sentenced him to be shot to death with arrows.

Although left for dead, Sebastian survived the ordeal and was nursed back to health by a Roman Christian, Irene, who had come to claim his body and take it away for burial. Once his strength had returned, Sebastian confronted Diocletian, reviling him for his cruelty to Christians who were no threat to the empire. Diocletian had Sebastian beaten to death on the spot and his body dumped into the Cloaca Magna, Rome's main sewer. Christians recovered the body and buried it in the catacombs along the Appian Way.

About the year 350 a basilica was erected over the catacomb, and Saint Sebastian's body was enshrined in the church. The catacomb is open to visitors, and guides point out the location of Sebastian's original tomb.

Saint Sebastian is the patron saint of athletes, archers, and soldiers and is invoked against epidemics. Feast day: January 20.

**Saint Sergius of Radonezh (c. 1314–1392).** The relics of Saint Sergius are venerated in the church of the Monastery of the Holy Trinity he founded at a place outside Moscow known ever since as Sergiyev Posad, or Sergius' Village.

Sergius's parents were impoverished Russian nobles who were forced to abandon their fine house for a cabin in the village of Radonezh. They had three sons, two of whom—Sergius and Stephen—became monks. The brothers lived together for a time in a hermitage in the forest, until Stephen found the solitude uncongenial and moved to a monastery in Moscow. For several years Sergius was alone in the wilderness. Peasants in the region came to him for spiritual guidance, and then disciples joined him, eventually forming the Monastery of the Holy Trinity.

As the number of monks increased, Sergius sent them out across Russia to found more monasteries. It is said that in Sergius's lifetime his disciples founded four hundred new monasteries. He became renowned as a mediator, who made peace among squabbling Russian princes. In 1380, before a major battle against the Tartars, or Mongols, Prince Dmitri Ivanovich came to Holy Trinity to beg for Sergius's prayers and his blessing. As Dmitri set off, Sergius said, "Go fearless prince and believe in God's help!" Dmitri won a decisive victory at Kulikovo that led to Russia's liberation from the Tartars.

Saint Sergius became one of Russia's most beloved saints, and his Monastery of the Holy Trinity one of the most revered in the country.

Feast day: September 25.

**Saints Sergius and Bacchus (died 303).** Both saints were martyred in Syria—Bacchus in Barbalissos and Sergius at what is now Resafa. Over Sergius's tomb a large church was built and the town was renamed Sergiopolis in his honor. The great church is now in ruins and relics that were kept there have vanished. A portion of the saints' relics were sent to Constantinople, where a church was erected in their honor; these relics also have been lost. In the ninth century the Church of Sts. Sergius and Bacchus was built in Rome and a part of their relics were enshrined there, where they still remain.

Sergius and Bacchus were close friends and officers in the Roman army. They kept their Christian faith secret, but they were discovered when they were assigned as bodyguards to a Roman official and refused to join him in offering sacrifice to the Roman god Jupiter. To humiliate them, Emperor Galerius had the two men dressed in women's clothing and led in chains through the camp and the nearby town. Bacchus was beaten to death; Sergius was tortured, then beheaded. Although the account of the martyrs, *The Passion of Sergius and Bacchus,* is almost certainly fanciful, devotion to these martyrs dates back to at least the fifth century and possibly to the fourth.

Saints Sergius and Bacchus are the patron saints of desert nomads and are among the patron saints of Syria. Since the publication of the late John Boswell's controversial work *Same-Sex Unions in Premodern Europe* (1994), Saints Sergius and Bacchus have been venerated in the gay community as a saintly, heroic, romantic couple. Feast day: October 7.

**Seven Holy Maccabees (died c. 167 BC).** In 1876, archaeologists excavating in the Church of St. Peter in Vincoli in Rome discovered the relics of the Seven Holy Maccabees. The skulls of the martyrs are venerated in the Church of St. Andrew in Cologne, Germany. The relics of the Maccabees' mother, Saint Solomone, are preserved in the Greek Orthodox Patriarchal Church of St. George in Phanar, in Istanbul.

About the year 167 BC, Antiochus IV Epiphanes, ruler of what is now Israel, attempted to replace the Jewish religion with the worship of the Greek gods. Jews who refused to abandon their faith were executed. In 2 Maccabees 7 we find the story of a Jewish mother who was arrested with her seven sons and commanded to eat pork. They all refused, and one by one the boys were tortured to death. When all her sons were dead, the mother died, although the text does not say if she was martyred or died from some other cause.

Feast day: August 1.


**Shroud of Turin (earliest record to mention the Holy Shroud, c. 1353).** About the year 1353 a French knight, Geoffroy de Charney, enshrined the Holy Shroud in a church he had built on his estate at Lirey in France's Champagne region. In 1418, during the Hundred Years War, his descendant, Marguerite de Charney, fearing the Holy Shroud would be stolen or destroyed by the English, traveled with the Shroud to the palace of her relatives, the dukes of Savoy, to whom she gave the relic. Blessed Amadeus IX, duke of Savoy, rebuilt the family chapel at Chambery to receive the Shroud, locking the relic in a silver casket. In 1532 fire swept through the chapel and part of the casket melted; drops of the molten silver burned portions of the Shroud before it was rescued. The damage was repaired by the Poor Clare nuns whose convent stood nearby. In 1578 Duke Emmanuel Philibert moved the Shroud to Turin, the new capital of the dukes of Savoy. Today the relic may be found in the Chapel of the Shroud behind the high altar of the Cathedral of Turin.

Since 2000 the Shroud has been preserved in a high-tech reliquary. The cloth is displayed at its full length behind bullet-proof glass. The chamber inside the reliquary is filled with argon gas to prevent the cloth from deteriorating. A computerized monitoring system reads the temperature, humidity, and argon levels within the reliquary chamber and makes necessary adjustments.

The Shroud is a piece of linen cloth, about 172 inches long by 44 inches wide, with a 3-inch border sewn along one side. The cloth is woven in a herringbone pattern. On the Shroud, barely

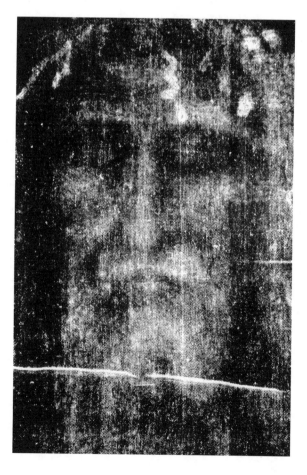

The image on the Shroud of Turin was not seen clearly until 1898, when Secondo Pia photographed the relic and saw this face on his negatives. © David Lees/corbis

discernible to the naked eye, is the image of a bearded, naked man. In addition, there are stains on the cloth that appear to correspond to head wounds, wounds on the back, and wounds to the hands, feet, and side. A much more detailed picture of the image on the cloth did not emerge until 1898, when a Turin photographer, Secondo Pia, secured permission from Church authorities to photograph the Shroud. When he produced the negatives, he saw for the first time the now-famous image imprinted on the Shroud of Turin. And so began more than a century of scientific study of the Shroud.

The tests, results, and debates are too lengthy and complex to summarize here. To date there is no consensus as to how the image was made on the cloth, nor why it was seen clearly only in a photographic negative. A carbon-14 test of the Shroud, performed in 1988, dated it to the thirteenth to fourteenth centuries, the period when it first came into the possession of the de Charney family, but given the number of repairs to the cloth, some have argued that the carbon-14 sample was not taken from the original cloth of the Shroud but from a patch sewn onto it during the Middle Ages.

Textile experts have said that the linen is consistent with fabric available in the Middle East in the first century AD. There is an ongoing debate whether the stains on the Shroud are human blood or pigment. Even microscopic dirt particles and pollen embedded in the fabric have been studied to learn if the cloth originated in the Middle East, and specifically Jerusalem (the pollen evidence suggests that the cloth did come from the Middle East).

Since the Pia photographs of 1898, several popes have stated publicly how deeply the images moved them. During his pilgrimage to Turin in 2010 to pray before the relic, Pope Benedict XVI described the Shroud as "an Icon written in blood, the blood of a man who was scourged, crowned with thorns, crucified and whose right side was pierced." But no pope has ever stated definitively whether the Shroud is authentic.

Feast day: May 4.

**Saint Sicaire (first century).** The bones of Saint Sicaire are said to have been brought from the Holy Land in 328 by Saint Helen. Eventually they passed to Charlemagne, who gave them to Brantôme Abbey in France. The relics are still there, in the abbey church, encased within a full-color doll-like reliquary statue.

Saint Sicaire is said to be one of the baby boys of Bethlehem slaughtered by order of King Herod, who hoped that in the general massacre the Christ Child would be killed. The story is found in Matthew 2:13–18.

Feast day: December 28, the feast of the Holy Innocents.

**Saint Simeon Stylites (c. 390–459).** A fragment of the pillar upon which Saint Simeon lived for thirty-seven years may be found in the ruined Church of St. Simeon Stylites, about eighteen miles from Aleppo, Syria. The saint's right hand is encased in a silver hand-shaped reliquary venerated at the Monastery of the Transfiguration of the Savior in Beroea, Greece.

In the early centuries of the Church many Christian men left society for a life of prayer and penance in the solitude of the desert. Some of these hermits adopted a way of life that strikes us as eccentric, to say the least, and among these one of the most memorable was Simeon Stylites. He had been a shepherd and became a hermit at Telanissos, Syria, where he chained himself to a rock. So many visitors sought his spiritual advice that he invented a new penance for himself: he attached a three-foot-wide wooden platform to the top of a pillar and lived there for the last thirty-seven years of his life.

If anything, his life atop the pillar drew even more visitors, including representatives from bishops and even the emperor in Constantinople. From the top of his pillar—which is said to have been sixty-six feet high—Simeon shouted down advice on spiritual and temporal matters.

Feast day: January 5.

**Saint Simon Stock (c. 1165–1265).** Saint Simon died at the Carmelite priory in Bordeaux, France, and was buried there. During the English Reformation, Henry VIII dissolved the Carmelite order in England and expelled the friars from their priories. In 1949 the Carmelites purchased the ruins of their priory at Aylesford. Soon thereafter the archbishop of Bordeaux gave to the friars the skull of Saint Simon Stock, which is enshrined in the church.

Simon Stock was the first Englishman to join the Carmelites, a new order that had begun in the Holy Land. In the Holy Land the Carmelites had been hermits; Simon convinced his companions to become friars like the Franciscans and Dominicans, a change that helped the Carmelites attract new members.

As superior general of his order, Simon established the Carmelites at the universities of Oxford, Cambridge, Paris, and Bologna.

According to tradition, the Blessed Mother with the Christ Child appeared to Simon Stock, presented him with the brown scapular, and promised that whoever repented his or her sins and wore the scapular at the hour of death would be spared the fires of hell. There are other scapulars, but the brown scapular of Our Lady of Mount Carmel, as it is known, is the most popular among Catholics.

Saint Simon Stock is one of the patron saints of Bordeaux. Feast day: May 16.

**Saint Simon the Apostle (first century).** The bones of Saint Simon lie with those of his fellow apostle Saint Jude beneath the Altar of St. Joseph in Rome's Basilica of St. Peter.

In the list of the apostles Simon is called "the Cannanite" or "the Zealot," to distinguish him from Simon Peter. There is a tradition among the Greeks that Simon was the bridegroom of the wedding at Cana, where Christ worked his first miracle, turning water into wine. Simon is said to have preached the Gospel in Persia, where he was martyred, nailed to a cross according to some stories, cut in half with a large saw according to others.

Saint Simon the Apostle is the patron saint of lumberjacks. Feast day: October 28.

**Saint Spiridon (270–348).** When the Arabs conquered the island of Cyprus, Christians took the body of Saint Spiridon to Constantinople. In 1453, when Constantinople fell to the Turks, a monk named Kalohairetis rescued the relics and brought them to Corfu, his home island. The relics are displayed in a casket in the Church of St. Spiridon.

During Emperor Diocletian's persecution of Christians, Spiridon, a shepherd, was arrested. Torturers tore out his right eye and hamstrung him; then he was sentenced to the mines in Spain. When Emperor Constantine put an end to the persecution of the Church, Spiridon returned to his wife and daughter on the island of Cyprus. After a time he decided to become a monk; his wife and daughter became nuns. In time Spiridon was consecrated bishop of Cyprus. Despite his high office he remained humble, supporting himself by tending a small flock of sheep.

Saint Spiridon is the patron saint of potters and is one of the patron saints of Corfu. Feast day: December 14.

**Saint Stanislaus (1030–1079).** The tomb of Saint Stanislaus is found in the nave of Poland's national shrine, Wawel Cathedral in Cracow. The silver casket, made about 1670, is decorated with scenes from the saint's life as well as miracles wrought after his death through his intercession. This casket replaced an older one, which had been carried off by the Swedish army during the sack of Cracow in 1655.

During his first years as bishop of Cracow, Stanislaus and the king of Poland, Boleslaw II, worked well together, particularly in founding Benedictine monasteries to assist in the conversion of the Poles. Soon, however, conflicts flared up between the two. They clashed over Church land that Boleslaw seized, over cruel punishments that he inflicted on unfaithful wives, over the king's own shameless sexual promiscuity, and his maltreatment of some of his nobles. Stung by the bishop's criticism, Boleslaw followed him outside Cracow to a chapel dedicated to Saint Michael the Archangel. There, as Stanislaus said Mass, the king drew his sword and hacked the bishop to death.

Saint Stanislaus is the patron saint of soldiers in battle, and he is one of the patron saints of Cracow and Poland. Feast day: May 8 in Cracow but April 11 elsewhere, and September 27 (the translation of Saint Stanislaus's relics).

**Saint Stanislaus Kostka (1550–1568).** The relics of Saint Stanislaus are preserved in Rome's Church of Sant' Andrea al Quirinale.

Stanislaus Kostka's parents were nominally Catholic, but he was extremely devout. Once a visitor told Stanislaus's father an off-color joke. He laughed but advised his friend not to repeat it in front of Stanislaus—"He'll faint!"

When he was in his early teens the Kostkas sent Stanislaus and his older brother Paul to the Jesuit college in Vienna. The brothers lived in a boardinghouse owned by a Lutheran who delighted in tormenting Stanislaus by saying the most scurrilous things about Catholic doctrines and Catholic religious practices. To make matters worse, most of the boys at school found Stanislaus priggish and excessively pious. And if Stanislaus did or said anything that irritated his brother, Paul beat him up.

Amid so much hostility, Stanislaus suffered a breakdown, and even believed he was dying. Paul mocked him for being overly dramatic. When Stanislaus asked his landlord to send for a priest, the man declared he would never permit the Blessed Sacrament to be carried into his house. On the verge of despair, Stanislaus turned for help to one of his favorite saints, Saint Barbara, who appeared in his room with a ciborium and gave him Holy Communion.

Stanislaus recovered and decided to join the Jesuits. He walked from Vienna to Rome, a distance of about a thousand miles. He had been in the Jesuit novitiate only a few months when he fell ill with a high fever and died; he was only eighteen.

Saint Stanislaus Kostka is the patron saint of those who wish to receive the Last Sacraments before dying. He is invoked against broken bones. Feast day: November 13.

**Saint Stephen (died c. 35).** According to tradition, in 415 a priest named Lucian received a vision instructing him to go to Caphar Gamala north of Jerusalem where he would find the relics of the first martyr. Lucian, Bishop John of Jerusalem, and a large crowd of Christians, many of them suffering from a variety of illnesses, went to the spot and unearthed the coffin of Saint Stephen. When it was opened the air was filled with a rich perfume and more than seventy of the sick and infirm in the crowd were healed instantly. In *City of God,* Saint Augustine tells us that small portions of Saint Stephen's relics were distributed to many churches, but the majority of his remains lie in the same tomb with Saint Lawrence and Saint Justin Martyr in Rome's Basilica of St. Lawrence Outside the Walls.

Stephen was a Jewish convert to Christianity and one of the first seven deacons ordained by the apostles to serve the poor, the sick, the widows, and the orphans of Jerusalem. He was a handsome young man, well spoken, with an engaging personality. He came to the attention of the Sanhedrin, the Jewish court, as a leader of the young Christian community who was zealous in converting Jews to the new religion. They ordered Stephen brought to court to question him. Filled with religious zeal while on trial, Stephen experienced a theophany and proclaimed that Jesus Christ was the Messiah the people of Israel had been waiting for and that the men of the Sanhedrin were blind to the truth: "Behold, I see the heavens opened and the Son of Man standing at the right hand of God" Acts 7:56. (Stephen's story can be found in Acts 6–8).

Shrieking with anger, the men in the court dragged Stephen

outside one of the city gates and stoned him to death. "Lord Jesus," he prayed, "receive my spirit." As he fell to the ground he prayed again, "Lord, lay not this sin to their charge."

Saint Stephen is the patron saint of deacons, stonemasons, and coffin makers. He is invoked against headache. Feast days: December 26 and August 3 (Finding of the Relics of Saint Stephen).

**Saint Stephen of Hungary (c. 935–1038).** In 1083, as part of the canonization investigation, King Stephen's body was exhumed. He right hand was found to be intact, so someone cut it off and kept it as a relic. It was held in various churches in Hungary until 1526, when it was taken to Bosnia to save it from possible destruction by the Turks who had invaded the country. In 1771 the saint's hand was returned to Hungary. It is enshrined in a gold and glass reliquary in the Basilica of St. Stephen in Budapest.

In 985 Geza, a Hungarian chief, presented himself and his ten-year-old son, Vaik, to Saint Adalbert, archbishop of Prague, and asked to be baptized. Adalbert gave the boy a new Christian name, Stephen.

Ten years later Stephen married a German princess and set about transforming pagan Hungary into a Christian nation. He wrote to Pope Sylvester II, petitioning him to recognize him as king and to grant him permission to name bishops in his realm. The pope granted both requests and sent Stephen a crown. In 1001, wearing the crown from Rome, Stephen was acclaimed the first king of Hungary.

He founded churches, monasteries, and schools across his kingdom, and trained his only son, Emeric, to be a good king and a faithful son of the Church. Emeric's death in a hunting accident in 1031 was an especially bitter blow to Stephen. He died seven years later and was buried beside his son. Stephen and Emeric were canonized in the same ceremony in 1083.

Saint Stephen is the patron saint of bricklayers and stonemasons; he is one of the patron saints of Hungary. Feast day: August 16.

**Sudarium of Oviedo (earliest date venerated in Oviedo, 1070).**
The traditional account of this relic of Jesus Christ says that it
remained in Jerusalem until 614, when the Persian king Chosroe II
conquered the Holy City. A monk named Philip took the relic and
escaped to Alexandria, Egypt. Two years later, when the Persians
invaded Egypt, Philip fled across North Africa to Spain, where
he presented the Sudarium to Saint Fulgentius, bishop of Ecija.
During the Arab invasion of Spain in 711, the relic was hidden in
an isolated mountain hermitage, Monsacro, and remained there
until 840, when Alfonso II, king of Asturias, enshrined the relic in
the Cámara Santa (the Holy Chamber) he had specially built in his
palace. The Cámara Santa is now part of the Oviedo's Cathedral of
the Holy Savior. The earliest document to mention the Sudarium
is dated March 14, 1075 (although it survives only as a thirteenth-
century copy of the original, which is lost).

The Sudarium is said to be the cloth that was wrapped around
Christ's face at the time of his burial. It is an irregular rectangle of
woven flax measuring thirty-four by twenty-one inches. Studies
of the cloth made in 1965, 1979, 1983, 1993, and 2007 have
found traces of blood and pulmonary fluid, as well as aloe, myrrh,
and pollen characteristic of plants in the Holy Land.

Feast days: The Sudarium is exposed for public veneration on
Good Friday and on September 14 (the Feast of the Exaltation
of the Holy Cross) and on September 21 (the octave of the Holy
Cross).

**Saint Susanna and Saint Gabinus (died 293).** In 330 a church
was built on the site of the house where Saint Susanna lived with
her father, Saint Gabinus. After the church was completed the relics of Susanna and Gabinus were brought from the catacombs and
reburied here. In 590 Pope Saint Gregory the Great named the
church in honor of Saint Susanna, in recognition of the Roman
people's devotion to this virgin martyr.

Susanna and her family were related to the emperor Diocletian.

Her uncle Saint Gaius would be elected pope. In 293 she received a marriage proposal from a prominent Roman general, Maxentius Galerius. Susanna refused. Suspecting that she was a Christian, the general commanded Susanna to appear in the Roman Forum and publicly sacrifice to the god Jupiter. Once again Susanna refused. The general denounced Susanna and her father to the emperor Diocletian, who ordered that she and her father be executed. Susanna was beheaded. Gabinus was imprisoned and left to starve to death.

Feast days: August 11 (Saint Susanna) and February 19 (Saint Gabinus).

**Saint Tarsicius (third century).** The body of Saint Tarsisius was buried in the Catacombs of St. Callixtus on the Appian Way outside Rome. Centuries later his relics were moved inside the city to the Church of San Silvestro in Capite. Unfortunately the exact location of the relics has been lost.

Tarsicius was an acolyte in Rome. One day after Mass had been celebrated over the tomb of one of the martyrs, the pope gave Tarsicius the Blessed Sacrament to take to Christians in prison; it was believed that the prison guards were less likely to suspect and search a boy than an adult. As he walked along the Appian Way with the Blessed Sacrament concealed under his tunic, he passed a group of men and boys who asked what he was carrying under his clothes. Pope Saint Damasus, who composed the epitaph for the boy-martyr's tomb, tells us Tarsicius refused to "surrender the Sacred Body [of Christ] to rabid dogs." The mob attacked the boy, ultimately beating him to death in the road. Once Tarsicius was dead they tore open his clothes, but they found nothing; the Blessed Sacrament had vanished.

Saint Tarsicius is the patron saint of First Communicants and altar servers. Feast day: August 15.

**Saint Teresa of Avila (1515–1582).** The majority of the relics of Saint Teresa are venerated in the Convent of St. Teresa built over her birthplace in Avila, Spain. In addition to the shrine in the church, the Chamber of Relics displays the wooden board she used as a pillow, her rosary, the cord she used to flagellate herself as penance, one of her sandals, and a finger from her right hand. The garden where she played as a child has been preserved. Her heart, said to bear a wound that corresponds with a mystical experience, as well as the saint's arm, are enshrined in the Carmelite convent at Alba de Tormes.

Teresa's early years in the Carmelite Convent of the Incarnation in Avila were pleasant: she had a suite of comfortably furnished rooms, including a private kitchen; the nuns welcomed visitors, male and female, inside the enclosure; some of the sisters had even brought their servants along. After a time, Teresa became dissatisfied with the easygoing life of the Carmelites. She longed for a return to the austere life described in the original Carmelite *Rule*; and she had become interested in contemplative prayer, something utterly alien to the nuns of the Incarnation.

Understandably, Teresa's attempt to reform her order met with forceful opposition from Carmelites who did not want to be reformed. Consequently, she founded a branch of the Carmelite order that was strict in its observance of the original *Rule*. The superior of the Carmelites in Spain encouraged her, as did King Philip II.

In addition to founding new convents, Teresa wrote mystical works that examined the interior life. In recognition of her contributions to mystical theology, in 1970 Pope Paul VI named her a Doctor of the Church.

Saint Teresa of Avila is the patron saint of members of religious orders, of those in need of grace, and of those mocked for their piety. She is invoked against all forms of illness, especially headaches. Saint Teresa is one of the patron saints of Spain. Feast days: October 15 and August 27 (the Transverberation of Saint Teresa's Heart).

**Blessed Teresa of Calcutta (1910–1997).** The body of Mother Teresa lies in a simple white marble tomb in the Mother House of the Missionaries of Charity in Calcutta, India. Near the tomb is an exhibit of Mother Teresa's personal belongings, including her crucifix and a habit she wore in life.

Mother Teresa was an Albanian Catholic who traveled to Ireland to join the Sisters of Loreto and was sent to teach at a girls' high school in Calcutta, India. In 1946 she received what she described as the "call within the call" to leave the Sisters of Loreto and devote her life to serving the poorest of the poor in Calcutta. After two years of discussion, her religious superiors permitted Mother Teresa to follow her new vocation. She took courses in medicine with an order of nursing sisters, found accommodations in the convent of the Little Sisters of the Poor in Calcutta, then, dressed in a blue-trimmed white sari, she went into the slums to help the destitute, the sick, and the dying. Several of her former students joined her, and in 1950 the archbishop of Calcutta established Mother Teresa's new order, the Missionaries of Charity.

The sisters' mission was to feed the hungry, nurse the sick, house orphans and the homeless, shelter and comfort the dying. Mother Teresa and her sisters won international attention, not to mention acclaim: in 1979 she was awarded the Nobel Peace Prize.

At the time of her death Mother Teresa's sisters numbered about four thousand; they operated 610 institutions in 123 countries. Pope John Paul II, who considered her a personal friend, said of Mother Teresa, "Traveling tirelessly the paths of the entire world, Mother Teresa has marked the history of our century: she defended life bravely; she served all human beings, always promoting their dignity and respect; she made the 'losers of life' feel the tenderness of God, the loving Father of all His creatures."

Blessed Teresa of Calcutta is one of the patron saints of World Youth Day. Feast day: September 5.

**Saint Teresa of Los Andes (1900–1920).** The relics of Saint Teresa lie in a shrine complex at Auco, Chile, near Los Andes, where she died.

Teresa grew up in a large, well-to-do, devoutly Catholic family in Santiago, Chile. She was a spiritual prodigy who began having mystical experiences at age ten, after she received her First Holy Communion. Family and friends recalled that she overflowed with love for God and her neighbor. Teresa is the first saint in Chile.

At age nineteen Teresa entered the Carmelite Convent of the Holy Spirit in Los Andes, a small town about fifty-four miles from Santiago. Six months later Sister Teresa contracted typhus and died. Like her fellow Carmelite Saint Thérèse of Lisieux, Teresa of Los Andes was virtually unknown, but accounts of her holiness and the joy she experienced serving God spread beyond the Carmelite convent to inspire millions.

Saint Teresa of Los Andes is the patron saint of young people. She is invoked against bodily ailments. Feast day: April 12. (The Carmelites celebrate her feast on July 13.)

**Saint Thecla (first century).** The relics of Saint Thecla are preserved in the Convent Church of Mar Taqla in the town of Ma'loula, Syria. Her arm is venerated in the Chapel of St. Thecla in the Cathedral of Tarragona, Spain.

The only document we possess regarding Saint Thecla is an apocryphal work from the second century, the *Acts of Paul and Thecla*. In this account Thecla is sitting at her window in Iconium (present-day Konya, Turkey), when she overhears Saint Paul preaching and is converted.

Three times the Romans tried to martyr Thecla: by burning her at the stake, by exposing her to wild beasts, and by locking her in a chamber filled with poisonous serpents. Each time she was saved by a miracle. It is said that she escaped and lived as a hermit at Ma'loula, Syria.

Saint Thecla is the patron saint of Tarragona, Spain. Feast day: September 23.

**Saint Théodore Guérin (1798–1856).** The relics of Mother Théodore Guérin lie in a wooden chest inside the Church of the Immaculate Conception at St. Mary-of-the-Woods, Indiana. The placement is temporary while a permanent shrine is constructed. The Sisters of Providence have also preserved many of Mother Guérin's personal items, some of them very humble, such as the wicker basket she used for shopping and the sabots she wore when she worked in the garden. Her childhood home in Etables-sur-Mer, France, still stands.

In 1839 the bishop of Vincennes (his diocese covered all of Indiana, eastern Illinois, and Chicago) sent a priest to France to recruit religious orders to come and establish Catholic schools and hospitals. Five Sisters of Providence, led by Sister Théodore, volunteered for the American mission. After traveling by ship, train, canal boat, steamboat, and stage coach, the nuns reached St. Mary-of-the-Woods, Indiana, in late October of 1840. There was no town, no school, no church, just a small wooden house that became their convent.

Within nine months the sisters opened an academy for girls at St. Mary's. Over the next sixteen years Mother Théodore established nine schools, opened two orphanages, and welcomed sixty-seven professed sisters, nine novices, and seven postulants into her community. Mother Théodore, like so many other tireless, dedicated pioneer sisters and priests who came from Europe to the United States, was indispensable in establishing the Catholic Church in America.

Feast day: October 3.

**Saint Thérèse of Lisieux (1873–1897).** The relics of the Little Flower are preserved in a grand basilica church in Lisieux, France.

Some of her bones are encased within a wax portrait sculpture. Others have been placed in portable reliquaries for the veneration of pilgrims. Some of the saint's bones are enshrined in the chapel of the Lisieux Carmel where Thérèse lived as a nun. The convent also has a Relic Room where many of Saint Thérèse's personal belongings are displayed. A portion of Saint Thérèse's relics have been placed in a wooden chest, which has traveled to cathedrals and churches around the world, attracting millions of the faithful.

Thérèse Martin came from a close-knit family of five sisters. Her parents were shrewd businesspeople who had made a comfortable living, sold their businesses, and enjoyed an early, carefree retirement.

Thérèse, the youngest child, was pampered and petted, but she could be willful. Nonetheless, she grew up pious and felt drawn to the austere, contemplative life of the cloistered Carmelite nuns. At age fifteen she asked her father's permission to become a Carmelite; he consented, but the superior of the convent and the bishop of Bayeux-Lisieux refused entrance to a girl so young. To distract Thérèse from her disappointment, her father took her and her sister Céline on a pilgrimage to Rome. During an audience with Pope Leo XIII, Thérèse wrapped her arms around the pope's legs and pleaded with him to let her join the Carmelites early. The Swiss Guards were obliged to pry off Thérèse's hands and carry her bodily out of the audience hall.

A few days after her sixteenth birthday, the bishop of Bayeux-Lisieux granted an exception so Thérèse could enter the Carmelite convent, where she joined two of her older sisters. In the convent Thérèse developed what she called her "Little Way," a simple yet profound type of spirituality in which she performed even the humblest tasks as if she were doing them for God. In other words, she tried to sanctify all of her actions.

During the night between Holy Thursday and Good Friday 1896, Thérèse suffered a hemorrhage, the first sign that she had contracted tuberculosis. Her dying was extremely difficult. For some unknown reason, her superior forbade the doctor to give

Thérèse painkillers. She was almost constantly harassed by her fellow Carmelites who wanted her to say something edifying to each of them before she died. Breathing became so difficult and the pain so unbearable that she almost despaired of God's mercy.

After her death the prioress decided to publish Thérèse's autobiography, *Story of a Soul,* in which she had described her "Little Way." It became an international bestseller, inspired worldwide veneration, and led to Thérèse's canonization in 1925. She remains one of the most popular saints of the Catholic Church. In 1997 Pope John Paul II made her a Doctor of the Church.

Saint Thérèse of Lisieux is the patron saint of florists, foreign missions, aviators and air crews, and AIDS patients. She is invoked against tuberculosis. Saint Thérèse is one of the patron saints of France, Australia, and Russia. Feast day: October 1.

**Saint Thomas Aquinas (c. 1225–1274).** Thomas Aquinas died at the Cistercian Abbey of Fossanova. The monks, convinced of his sanctity and unwilling to part with the relics of such a great saint, buried him in an unmarked grave inside the abbey church, intending to wait until Aquinas was canonized and then display the relics in a shrine that would attract throngs of pilgrims to the abbey. The Dominicans demanded that the remains of Aquinas be returned to them (he was a member of the Dominican order), but the Cistercians refused. In 1369, after nearly a century of tussling over the relics, Pope Urban V commanded the Cistercians of Fossanova to return the bones of Thomas Aquinas to the Dominicans (although Urban permitted the skull to be kept at the Cathedral of Priverno near Fossanova). Until the French Revolution the relics were venerated in the Dominican's priory church in Toulouse, France. When the priory appeared in danger of being looted, the Dominicans relocated the relics to the Church of St. Sernin. They remain there today, enshrined in a modern bronze chest. The room at Fossanova where Saint Thomas died has been converted into a chapel, and the site of his first grave is marked in the abbey church. Saint Thomas's birthplace in Aquino, Italy, is open to visitors.

Thomas Aquinas was a man of astonishing intellect who taught that reason works in tandem with faith to lead one to the truths of Catholic doctrine. His *Summa theologica* lays out in a clear, step-by-step fashion everything the Church believes and teaches, and why she believes it. He wrote his *Summa contra Gentiles* as a handbook for catechism teachers and preachers, to help them explain and defend the faith.

But there was more to Aquinas than intellect. He had a touch of the mystic and was a fine poet whose Latin hymns, such as *Pange lingua, Lauda Sion salvatorem,* and *Adoro Te Devote* are among the musical treasures of the Church.

Saint Thomas Aquinas is the patron saint of students, teachers, theologians, philosophers, publishers, defenders of the Catholic faith, and pencil makers. He is the patron saint of Catholic schools and colleges and is invoked for the virtue of chastity and against lightning. Feast day: January 28.


**Saint Thomas Becket (1118–1170).** After his murder in Canterbury Cathedral, the body of Archbishop Becket was buried in the cathedral crypt. In 1220 the relics were moved to a shrine behind the high altar, where they remained until 1538 when Henry VIII's commissioners stripped the shrine of is valuables and destroyed the saint's bones (legend claims the sacreligious commissioners fired the relics out of a cannon). But not all of the relics were destroyed; some of Saint Thomas's bones had been presented to distinguished visitors from the Continent, and these survived the Reformation. In the nineteenth century the bishop of Gubbio in Italy presented a piece of Saint Thomas's vestment and a bone fragment to the Roman Catholic Church of St. Thomas of Canterbury in Canterbury; in 1953 Father Thomas Becquet, prior of Chevetogne in France and a collateral descendant of the martyred archbishop, gave the same church a finger bone that his family had treasured for centuries. These relics are enshrined in St. Thomas of Canterbury's Martyrs' Chapel. In Italy, a silk chasuble believed to have belonged to Becket is preserved in Fermo Cathedral, and his miter is preserved at Anagni Cathedral.

For most of his life Thomas Becket was an unlikely candidate for sainthood. He was arrogant, selfish, emotionally detached, and ambitious, which led him to be more devoted to the service of his king, Henry II, than to his Church (in spite of Becket's rank as archdeacon). One frigid winter day in London, Henry spotted a beggar dressed in rags; Becket was wearing a magnificent new fur-lined cloak—one of many he owned. The king made the facetious suggestion that Becket, as a man of God, ought to give his cloak to the poor man. Becket flat-out refused.

In 1162 Henry arranged for Becket to be appointed archbishop of Canterbury, the highest Church office in England. Henry had every reason to expect that Becket would put the interests of his king ahead of the interests of the Church. But then something unexpected occurred: Thomas Becket was touched by grace and became a changed man. He distributed his great wealth to the poor. He did penance for a lifetime of sins. He welcomed the hungry of Canterbury to eat at his own table. And when Henry tried to extend his power into the workings of the Church courts, Becket fought him. This unforeseen opposition stunned the king, who lashed out against Becket, bringing a host of false charges against him and inciting his nobles and knights to threaten the archbishop's life.

For safety Becket fled to France, where for the next six years representatives of the archbishop, the king, and the pope tried to resolve the dispute. In 1170 Henry agreed that Becket could return to England. Back home and back in authority, Becket excommunicated several bishops who had sided with Henry against the Church. In a fit of temper Henry cried, "Will no one relieve me of this troublesome priest?"

Four of the king's knights set out for Canterbury, where they forced their way into the cathedral. Becket, about to say vespers, was at the foot of the altar stairs. The knights drew their swords and killed the archbishop in his cathedral.

The murder scandalized Europe. Two years later the pope declared Thomas Becket a saint. King Henry, fearing his people would overthrow him, did public penance for his part in the crime: he knelt at Saint Thomas's tomb while each of the cathedral's monks took turns whipping him.

Saint Thomas Becket is the patron saint of diocesan clergy. Feast day: December 29.

**Saint Thomas More (1478–1535).** Thomas More's headless body was buried in the crypt of the Chapel of St. Peter ad Vincula in the Tower of London. His head was impaled on a pike on Tower Bridge until his daughter, Margaret More Roper, retrieved it and kept it as a relic until her death in 1544. Saint Thomas's skull was buried with Margaret in the Roper family's vault in the Church of St. Dunstan, Canterbury, where it was found during an examination of the Roper vault in 1978. A crucifix, a gold and enamel figure of Saint George, a brown felt hat, and other objects that belonged to the saint are all preserved at Stonyhurst College, England. Thomas's hairshirt, which he sent from the Tower to his daughter, Margaret, is preserved in the convent of the Bridgettine nuns at Syon Abbey in South Brent, England.

Thomas More was a complicated man. He loved his wife and his large household of children and wards, but he tried every day to spend a few hours in solitude. He had a keen mind and a sharp wit. His success as a lawyer and as a trusted servant of King Henry VIII brought him wealth and status, so beneath his fine clothes he wore a prickly hairshirt to remind himself that for all his achievements he was still a sinner, and that he could lose his riches, his property, and the confidence of his king overnight. He labored to be a dutiful servant of king and country, and for his services he was appointed Chancellor of England, the highest office in the land (after the king). But in all things More's first love and his highest duty was to Almighty God and the Catholic faith.

At the time when More's career reached its pinnacle, England entered a period of crisis. Henry VIII wanted a son to succeed him, but all the male children he and his queen, Catherine of Aragon, had together died in infancy. They had a healthy daughter, Mary, but in Henry's mind she did not count; he wanted a son. At this time he became infatuated with a young woman named Anne Boleyn. Henry convinced himself that God had cursed his marriage, that he had sinned when he married Catherine because she was his late brother's widow. The pope had granted the royal couple a dispensation, but in Henry's mind that was not good enough. He wanted his marriage to Catherine annulled so he could marry Anne. The pope balked at the request, so Henry's archbishop of Canterbury pronounced the marriage null and void. All English subjects were obliged to recognize Anne as their lawful queen and her children as true heirs to the throne. But there was more: Henry declared himself Supreme Head of the Church in England and made it a crime for any English subject to profess that the pope had any authority.

From the Catholic perspective, Henry was usurping authority that Christ had given to Saint Peter and his successors. Catholics who swore to recognize the king's new title placed themselves outside the Church. A number of priests, monks, and one bishop (Saint John Fisher) would not compromise their consciences; Henry had them all executed. When Thomas More refused to recognize the title, he was imprisoned in the Tower, found guilty of treason, and beheaded. At his execution he asked the crowd of spectators to bear witness: "I die the king's good servant, but God's first."

Saint Thomas More is the patron saint of lawyers, statesmen, politicians, civil servants, widowers, and adopted children. Feast day: June 22.

**Saint Thomas the Apostle (first century).** The bones of Doubting Thomas lie in a gold casket within a white marble altar in the Basilica of St. Thomas the Apostle in Ortona, Italy. They were brought there from the city of Edessa in Mesopotamia in 1258. The Basilica of San Thome in Chennai, India, also possesses bones of Saint Thomas.

The night Christ was arrested, the apostles scattered, but by Sunday morning they had gathered behind locked doors in the room where they had celebrated the Last Supper. That first Easter evening the Risen Christ appeared to them. Thomas was away, but when he returned he found a room full of excited men. They told him Christ had risen from the dead, but he refused to believe them. "Unless I see in his hands the print of the nails, and place my finger in the mark of the nails, and place my hand in his side, I will not believe," he said, thereby earning the nickname "Doubting Thomas." A week later Christ appeared to the apostles again, and this time Thomas was in the room. To Thomas he said, "Put your finger here, and see my hands; and put out your hand, and place it in my side; do not be faithless, but believing." Thomas cried, "My Lord and my God!" (John 20:24–28).

According to tradition, Thomas preached the Gospel in India and was martyred there by a Hindu priest who ran him through with a spear.

Saint Thomas the Apostle is the patron saint of construction workers, particularly stonemasons. He is invoked against doubt and spiritual blindness. He is one of the patron saints of India, Pakistan, and Sri Lanka. Feast day: July 3.


**Three Kings, or Magi (first century).** The largest reliquary in the Western world enshrines the bones of three men said to be the Magi, or Three Kings, who followed the star to Bethlehem, where they worshipped the Infant Jesus and presented him with gifts of gold, frankincense, and myrrh.

Nicholas of Verdun (1130–1205), arguably the finest gold-smith of the twelfth century, designed part of the shrine. It measures 87 inches long, 60 inches high, and 43 inches wide. The three individual sarcophagi are wooden, but each is overlaid with gold and adorned with golden sculptures of scenes from the life of Christ, including the Adoration of the Magi, as well as sculptures of the apostles and prophets. In addition, the shrine is embellished with more than a thousand jewels, cameos, enamels, and decorative beads. The shrine is encased in a large glass box located above the high altar of the Cathedral of Cologne in Germany.

Tradition claims that during her pilgrimage to the Holy Land in 326, Saint Helen learned that the remains of the three kings were buried in Persia. She acquired the relics and took them to Constantinople. In the sixth century the Byzantine emperor Mauritius gave the relics to the city of Milan in northern Italy. In 1164, when the German Holy Roman Emperor Frederick I was waging war in northern Italy, Rainald von Dassel, the archbishop of Cologne, raised an army that enabled Frederick to capture Milan. As a token of his gratitude, Frederick presented Cologne with the relics of the Three Kings. (A portrait sculpture of Archbishop Rainald is featured on the shrine.)

The Gospel of Saint Matthew, which tells the story of the Magi, does not mention their names, but tradition calls them Balthasar, Melchior, and Caspar or Gaspar. According to tradition, one was elderly, another in the prime of life, and the third was a young man. In 2003, Bob Brier, an Egyptologist and contributing editor to *Archaeology* magazine, received permission to open the shrine of the Three Kings and photograph the skulls; he could look, but not touch. Based on the sutures of the cranium, Brier concluded that the three skulls were indeed of a young man, a mature man, and an elderly man.

The Three Kings are the patron saints of travelers. Feast day: January 6.

**Saint Timothy (died 97).** According to tradition, Saint Timothy's relics were moved from Ephesus to Constantinople, where they were enshrined in the Church of the Holy Apostles. The relics disappeared during the sack of Constantinople in 1204, although some bone fragments have survived.

A close friend and disciple of Saint Paul, Timothy received at least two letters from the great apostle, both of which are part of the New Testament. According to tradition, he was bishop of Ephesus and was stoned to death there.

Saint Timothy is invoked against stomach ailments. Feast day: January 26.

**Titulus of the Cross (first mentioned c. 382).** The Titulus is the wooden board upon which Pontius Pilate had written in Hebrew, Latin, and Greek the mocking inscription JESUS OF NAZARETH, KING OF THE JEWS. It appears that Saint Helen found it with the True Cross, for Egeria, a nun from Hispania (modern-day Spain), who made a pilgrimage to the Holy Land about the year 380, saw the Titulus displayed for public veneration, along with the True Cross, on Good Friday. At the same time there was a Titulus in Rome. Since Saint Helen divided up the relics she found in Jerusalem, it is possible that she also split the Titulus. The Jerusalem fragment vanished centuries ago, but the Roman fragment is displayed in the Basilica of the Holy Cross in Jerusalem. The Roman Titulus is made of walnut wood and measures 10 by 15.5 inches and is about 1 inch thick.

**True Cross (discovered c. 327).** Many churches throughout the world possess splinters of the True Cross. Substantial pieces of the Cross upon which Jesus Christ died are safeguarded in the treasury of the Church of the Holy Sepulcher in Jerusalem, the relic chamber of the Basilica of the Holy Cross in Jerusalem in Rome, in the Treasury of the Basilica of St. Mark in Venice, and in the Cathedral of Notre Dame in Paris, among other places. Beneath the Church of the Holy Sepulcher and accessible via the Chapel of St. Helen is the cistern where, according to tradition, Helen discovered the True Cross.

An ancient tradition affirms that in or about 327, Empress Helen, mother of Emperor Constantine, pulled down the temple of Venus that Hadrian had erected over the site of Christ's death and burial. She found the rock of Calvary and the tomb in which Joseph of Arimathea had laid the body of the Lord. And in a cistern nearby she uncovered three crosses. Unable to tell which was the Cross of Christ, she had a dying woman brought to the site and touched her with each of the crosses. The one that healed the woman was recognized as the True Cross.

In the twelfth century two tiny fragments of the True Cross were enshrined in this display case. The double-barred cross can be removed so the faithful can venerate the relic. The reliquary is displayed today at the Louvre in Paris. RÉUNION DES MUSÉES NATIONAUX/ ART RESOURCE, NY

By 347 the bishop of Jerusalem, Saint Cyril, wrote about the relics of the True Cross in Jerusalem, and other authors from the period also record that fragments of the cross were being given to churches across the Roman Empire. About 380, a Spanish nun, Egeria, went on a pilgrimage to the Holy Land. She was in Jerusalem on Good Friday, and in her account of her journey she describes in detail the exhibition of the relic of the True Cross in the Church of the Holy Sepulcher for the veneration of the faithful.

The countless tiny fragments of relics of the True Cross have led generations of skeptics to claim that if all the bits were reassembled, there would be enough timber to build Noah's Ark. In 1870 a Frenchman, Rohault de Fleury, published a book in which he recounted his attempt to catalog all existing relics of the True Cross; he included the measurements of each piece. Fleury found that taken together the extant relics were not sufficient to build a cross large enough to crucify a man.

Feast days: May 3 (Discovery of the Holy Cross) and September 14 (Exaltation, or Triumph, of the Holy Cross).


**Tyburn Convent Relics.** In 1901 a group of French nuns, Adorers of the Sacred Heart of Jesus, with their foundress Mother Mary of Saint Peter Garnier, established a convent at Tyburn in London, the site where 105 Catholic martyrs were executed between 1535 and 1681. Over the years the sisters have acquired an impressive collection of relics representing 350 Catholic martyrs of the English Reformation era. Among the relics are a fingernail of Blessed Thomas Holland, S.J.; a piece of linen and pieces of straw stained with the blood of five Jesuit priests who were martyred together—Blessed Thomas Whitbread, Blessed William Harcourt, Blessed John Fenwick, Blessed Antony Turner, and Blessed John Gavan; a piece of bone of Saint Oliver Plunkett; a portion of a finger bone of St. John Roberts, O.S.B.; a portion of vertebra and precordia of Blessed John Lockwood.

**Saint Ulrich (890–973).** Saint Ulrich's relics are enshrined in a rococo tomb in the crypt of the abbey of St. Ulrich and St. Afra in Augsburg, Germany.

For forty-eight years Ulrich served as bishop of Augsburg. Time and again he visited each parish in his diocese to ensure that Mass was being said properly, that the people were being instructed in the faith, and that the clergy were keeping their vows.

In the tenth century, Germany was the target of frequent raids from the Magyars in Hungary. To protect his people Ulrich used Church funds to improve the fortification of the city. When the Magyars attacked in 955, Augsburg's defenses held.

After Ulrich's death the bishops of Germany petitioned Pope John XV to declare him a saint (an unusual request, since at the time a bishop had the right to canonize individuals who had been members of his own diocese). In 993 Pope John made Ulrich a saint, thereby setting the precedent that would lead to canonization being reserved to the pope.

Saint Ulrich is the patron saint of pregnant women and weavers and is one of the patron saints of Augsburg. He is invoked against dizziness and rodents. Feast day: July 4.


**Saint Ursula and the 11,000 Virgins (fifth century).** The Church of St. Ursula in Cologne, Germany, possesses a remarkable room known as the Golden Chamber. For most visitors, the gold is secondary; it's the bones they notice first. The walls and ceiling of the high vaulted room are covered with human bones arranged in fanciful patterns. Set on shelves and in niches are dozens of gold and silver reliquary busts representing young women. The bones and skulls preserved inside the busts are said to be the remains of Saint Ursula and her companions, 11,000 virgins who were martyred with her.

The story of Saint Ursula was wildly popular in the Middle Ages. Ursula was a British Christian princess whose father betrothed her to the prince of a neighboring realm. Ursula, torn between giving up her virginity and disobeying her father, begged for a three-year postponement so she could go on a pilgrimage to Rome. She would take along ten virgin companions, and she and each of her attendants would be accompanied by one thousand virgins each. With the permission of her father and her fiancé, Ursula and her 11,000 ladies set sail for Italy. In Rome the presence of so many beautiful, virginal noblewomen caused a sensation. Pope Ciriacus declared that he would abdicate the papacy and joined Ursula on her return journey to Britain. Along the way the fleet of ships detoured up the Rhine to Cologne, arriving just as the city was being sacked by the Huns. Some of the Huns attacked the young women, hacking off their heads. Other marauders fired volleys of arrows at the women; Ursula was among those who were killed by Hun archers.

There are problems with the story, not least that there was no pope named Ciriacus, and the Huns never attacked Cologne.

Turning from legend to history, we find that in the fifth century a Christian named Clematius erected a church on the site of Cologne's present Church of St. Ursula to commemorate the martyrdom of eleven Christian virgins. The dedicatory stone bearing an inscription to this effect has survived and can be seen in St. Ursula's Church. Note that the inscription refers to 11, not 11,000, virgin martyrs. By the tenth century there was a tradition that 11,000 virgins had been martyred in Cologne, so in 1156, when an excavation crew working near St. Ursula's Church unearthed an enormous quantity of bones, everyone in town assumed that the bones were the relics of the 11,000 virgin martyrs.

The legend of Saint Ursula and her companions inspired great works of art, including paintings by Carpaccio and Memling. When the Italian educator Saint Angela Merici founded a new order of nuns dedicated to teaching young girls, she named her congregation the Order of St. Ursula, aka the Ursulines. And the archipelago known as the Virgin Islands was named by Christopher Columbus in honor of Saint Ursula and the 11,000 Virgins.

Saint Ursula is the patron saint of schoolgirls, teachers, Cologne, and the British Virgin Islands. Feast day: October 21.

**Saint Valentine (died c. 269).** There are at least seven martyrs named Valentine, which has led to a great deal of confusion regarding relics: all churches that possess relics of a Saint Valentine believe that they have the bones of the Roman priest whose feast day is celebrated on February 14. But the relics of that Valentine are still in Rome. They were venerated in a church dedicated to him outside Rome until the thirteenth century, when Saint Valentine's relics were moved to the Church of St. Prassede. His skull and a few other bones are thought to be in the possession of another church in Rome, St. Mary in Cosmedin.

The relics of Saint Valentine preserved in Terni, Italy, are of the bishop of the town who was martyred about the same time as the famous Valentine. The Whitefriar Street Carmelite Church in Dublin, Ireland, possesses relics of a martyred Saint Valentine that were taken from the Catacomb of St. Hippolytus in 1835 and by order of Pope Gregory XVI given to Irish Carmelite Father John Spratt, who brought the relics back to Dublin; they lie enshrined in a side altar of the Whitefriar Street Church.

In 1847 Blessed John Henry Cardinal Newman received the relics of yet another Saint Valentine from Blessed Pope Pius IX; these relics are preserved in a gold reliquary in a side altar of the Oratory in Birmingham, England. Other churches also claim to possess relics of a Saint Valentine, including the Cathedral of St. Stephen in Vienna, Austria; and the Church of Blessed John Duns Scotus in Glasgow, Scotland.

The most renowned of the Saints Valentine was a Roman priest who was martyred during Emperor Claudius II's persecution of the Church. Legend says that while in prison Valentine befriended the jailer's daughter. The day he was taken from his cell to be executed he left her a bouquet of flowers with a note that read "From your Valentine."

Saint Valentine is the patron saint of lovers, engaged couples, the happily married, and greeting card manufacturers. Feast day: February 14.

**Veronica's Veil (first venerated in Rome in the eighth century).**
Two churches claim to possess Veronica's Veil. The Basilica of St.
Peter in Rome preserves it inside one of the four massive pillars that
support the church's dome. The Capuchin friars of the Monastery
of Manoppello in Italy's Apennine Mountains claim that Veronica's
Veil is enshrined in their church. In 2006 Pope Benedict XVI visited the monastery and prayed before the Holy Veil but made no
comment about the relic. But in 1999 Father Heinrich Pfeiffer,
a professor of Christian art history at the Pontifical Gregorian
University in Rome, announced that after thirteen years of study
he had concluded that the relic in Manoppello is the authentic veil
of Saint Veronica.

The Manoppello relic is made of sheer, transparent linen,
measuring about 6.5 by 9.5 inches. It came to the Capuchins of
Manoppello in 1638, and there are theories that it is a relic that
was once kept at St. Peter's but was stolen at some point early in the
seventeenth century. Since there were many copies of Veronica's
Veil in circulation at that time, it is possible that if the Manoppello
relic is the one from St. Peter's, then the veil kept in St. Peter's
today is in fact only a copy.

Veronica is first mentioned in the *Acts of Pilate,* an apocryphal
Christian work of the fourth or fifth century, which identifies her
as the woman Jesus healed of chronic hemorrhaging. The popular Catholic devotion, the Stations of the Cross, depicts Veronica
stepping out of the hostile crowd to wipe the blood and sweat and
dirt from the face of Jesus as he carries his cross. This event is not
recorded in the Gospels; it is a traditional story that appears to be
at least fifteen hundred years old. According to this story, when
Veronica reached her home she found an image of the face of Jesus
miraculously imprinted on her veil. (The name Veronica is Greek
for "true image.")

Saint Veronica is the patron saint of photographers and laundry
workers. Feast day: On the Fifth Sunday of Lent, Passion Sunday,
Saint Veronica's Veil is taken from its shrine in St. Peter's Basilica

and carried in procession through the church. Feast of Saint Veronica: July 12.

**Saint Vibiana (third century).** In 1853 archaeologists excavating the Cemetery of Pretextanis on the Appian Way discovered an intact tomb bearing a carving of a laurel wreath and the inscription TO THE SOUL OF THE INNOCENT AND PURE VIBIANA, LAID AWAY THE DAY BEFORE THE KALENDS OF SEPTEMBER [AUGUST 31]. Inside the tomb was the skeleton of a young woman, along with a glass vial that probably contained some of her blood. The wreath was an early Christian symbol of martyrdom, and burying a martyr with a vial of the blood she or he had shed for the faith was customary in the first centuries of the Church. A subsequent examination of the young woman's bones suggested that she had died violently. In February 1854, after study of the tomb and the skeleton had been concluded, Blessed Pope Pius IX declared that Vibiana ought to be venerated by the faithful as a virgin martyr.

A few weeks later Thaddeus Amat, the newly consecrated bishop of Monterey in California, had an audience with the pope. Pius surprised Bishop Amat by presenting him with the relics of Saint Vibiana and instructing him to build a cathedral in her honor.

Initially the relics were enshrined in the Church of Our Lady of Sorrows in Santa Barbara, California. After the Cathedral of St. Vibiana was finished in Los Angeles in 1880, the relics were encased in a wax portrait sculpture and placed in a glass casket above the high altar. During renovations of the cathedral in the 1970s, the bones were removed to a solid stone sarcophagus.

Today the relics of Saint Vibiana lie in a simple marble sarcophagus in a chapel of Los Angeles's new Cathedral of Our Lady of the Angels.

Saint Vibiana is one of the patron saints of the archdiocese of Los Angeles. Feast day: September 1.

**Saint Victoria (died 304).** The complete skeleton of Saint Victoria is venerated in the chapel of the Sisters of the Precious Blood in Maria Stein, Ohio.

The daughter of an aristocratic family in North Africa, Victoria was arrested with dozens of her fellow Christians while attending Mass. Her brother, a pagan, asked the magistrate, Anulinus, to release Victoria, claiming that she was mentally unbalanced. Anulinus offered to spare Victoria if she agreed to live under her brother's supervision. Knowing that such an arrangement would require her to stop practicing the Christian faith, Victoria rejected the offer.

Anulinus, who knew Victoria's parents, pleaded with her to renounce a religion he described as "a fantasy" and save her life. Victoria disputed the notion that Christianity was a fantasy until the frustrated judge pronounced her sentence. She was taken to prison, where executioners tortured her to death. Forty-five Christians who were arrested with Victoria were also martyred by Anulinus.

Feast day: February 11.

**Saint Vincent of Saragossa (died 304).** Tradition claims that the body of the martyr was buried at Cape St. Vincent in southern Portugal. In 1173 King Alfonso Henriques translated the relics to Lisbon, where they were kept for many years in the Monastery Church of St. Vincent de Fora. Today the relics of the martyr are preserved in a mother-of-pearl-encrusted reliquary in the Cathedral of Lisbon. Castres in France and Avila in Spain also claim to possess the relics of Saint Vincent.

Vincent was a deacon in Huesca, Spain, who was arrested during Emperor Diocletian's persecution of the Church and sent to Valencia for execution. He was subjected to horrible tortures, including having his flesh torn with iron hooks and being suspended over a slow fire. At the end of the torture session he was thrown into a cell and left there to die. Vincent's courage and constancy made a lasting impression on his fellow Christians. The Christian poet Prudentius wrote his biography, and Saint Augustine preached a sermon in praise of the martyr.

Saint Vincent of Saragossa is the patron of winemakers and vinegar makers. He is one of the patron saints of Lisbon, Portugal; and Vicenza, Italy. Feast day: January 22.


**Saint Vincent de Paul (1581–1660).** The heart of Saint Vincent de Paul is enshrined in the Chapel of Our Lady of the Miraculous Medal at 140 Rue du Bac in Paris. This is the motherhouse of the Daughters of Charity, which the saint founded with St. Louise de Marillac, whose relics are also enshrined in the chapel. The body of Saint Vincent lies in the Chapel of Saint Vincent de Paul on Rue de Sevres in Paris; his bones are encased within a wax portrait sculpture of the saint.

Vincent de Paul was a peasant priest from Gascony whose goodness and intelligence attracted the attention of some of the most powerful individuals in France. Queen Marguerite of Valois made him her almoner, responsible for dispensing charity in her name. Father Pierre de Berulle (soon to be Cardinal de Berulle) and the bishop of Geneva, Saint Francis de Sales, became two of Father de Paul's closest friends. The Countess de Gondi asked Father de Paul to be her spiritual director.

Vincent de Paul could have spent his life among the upper classes, but he could not ignore the sufferings he witnessed among the poorest, most abandoned members of French society. He began by feeding the hungry and bringing medicine to the sick who could not afford a doctor. Soon he was operating soup kitchens, hospitals, shelters for abandoned babies, orphanages, and homes for the elderly; he also visited inmates in prison and slaves in the galleys. Some of Father de Paul's friends thought he took on too much, but he replied, "Charity is infinitely inventive."

Father de Paul did take on too much, but it was contrary to his nature to turn away anyone who asked for his help. He needed assistance, and he found it in Louise de Marillac, a widow who possessed energy, common sense, and great administrative skills. She recruited hardy young women from the countryside and the urban working class and organized them into a community of nuns who went into the slums to serve the poor. These women were the first Daughters of Charity.

Father de Paul and Madame de Marillac's legacy lives on not only among the Daughters of Charity but also among members of the Society of St. Vincent de Paul, a lay organization that offers hands-on, person-to-person assistance to people in need.

Saint Vincent de Paul is the patron saint of charitable organizations, volunteers, hospital workers, lepers, and prisoners. Feast day: September 27.


**Saint Vincent Ferrer (c. 1350–1419).** The saint's relics are enshrined in a chapel in the Cathedral of St. Peter in Vannes, France, the city where he died. It is said that soon after his burial, mourners brought the bodies of two newly dead to the cathedral and laid them upon Vincent's tomb; they were restored to life.

Vincent Ferrer was born in Valencia, Spain, the son of a Scottish father and a Spanish mother. He was blessed with a powerful intellect; by age twenty-one he was teaching philosophy at the University of Lleida. Three years later he was ordained a priest of the Dominican order and continued his studies in philosophy and theology, while also becoming fluent in Hebrew and mastering the art of preaching.

Vincent lived during the age of the Great Schism, when the legitimate pope in Rome was challenged by an antipope in Avignon (after 1409, there were two antipopes). Vincent traveled across Spain, France, and Italy, trying to heal the schism, even making direct appeals to one of the antipopes, Benedict, to step down. Benedict remained entrenched, until Vincent persuaded one of the antipope's staunchest allies, King Ferdinand of Aragon, to withdraw his support.

Even when he was not preaching about the schism, Vincent

drew large crowds. He pleaded with his audience to repent their sins and lead holy lives. His preaching inspired many vocations to the religious life; Vincent's brother, who was prior of the Grand Chartreuse, the motherhouse of the austere Carthusian monks, reported a large number of new postulants who attributed their vocation to Vincent.

Vincent also served as a missionary to the Jews, and he made some converts, most famously a rabbi, Paul of Burgos, who after his baptism became a priest and eventually was consecrated bishop of Cartagena. During an anti-Semitic riot in Valencia in 1391, it was Vincent who protected the Jews of his hometown from the mob.

Vincent also had a reputation as a miracle worker who healed the sick and even raised the dead. It was said that Vincent could heal an entire hospital full of patients simply by praying in front of the building.

Saint Vincent Ferrer is the patron saint of construction workers, pavers, plumbers, brickmakers, and tile makers. Feast day: April 5.

**Vietnamese Martyrs (1745–1862).** Most of the martyrs of Vietnam were buried anonymously, but some bodies were recovered, including the relics of Saint Pierre Borie and Saint John Louis Bonnard, which are enshrined in the Martyrs' Room at the headquarters of the Society of Foreign Missions in Paris. The relics of Saint Michael Dinh-Hy Ho are venerated in the Cathedral of Phu Can, Vietnam.

According to the dossier "History of the Catholic Church in Vietnam," published by the Fides Agency in Rome, between 1625 and 1886 approximately 130,000 Vietnamese Catholics and European missionaries gave their lives for the faith. In 1988 Pope John Paul II canonized a representative group of 117 martyrs. The group included 11 French and 10 Spanish missionaries, including 8 bishops; of the 96 Vietnamese martyrs, 37 were priests, 1 was a seminarian, and 58 were members of the laity. Among the most prominent martyrs are

**Saint Andrew Dung-Lac An Tran (1795–1839).** Converted to the Catholic faith in his teens, Saint Andrew became a zealous missionary after his ordination to the priesthood. He was arrested with Father Peter Thi and taken to Hanoi, where they were both brutally tortured before being beheaded.

**Saint Ignatius Delgado (1761–1838).** A Spanish Dominican who was consecrated bishop of East Tonkin, Saint Ignatius was seventy-six years old when he was arrested, locked in a small iron cage, and left hanging out in the sun to die. He succumbed to a combination of dysentery and malnutrition.

**Saint Peter Duong Van Truong (1808–1838).** Saint Peter was a lay catechist who was strangled to death after refusing to trample on a crucifix.

**Saint Joseph Marchand (1803–1835).** A French missionary, Saint Joseph suffered a horrible martyrdom: using red-hot tongs, the executioners tore bits of flesh from his body until he was dead.

**Saint Agnes Thanh Thi Le (1781–1841).** This mother of six children visited Christians in prison. Prisoners were forbidden contact with the outside world, but Saint Agnes smuggled letters for them. She was caught, imprisoned, and beaten repeatedly. She died in prison of abuse and neglect.

The Martyrs are among the patron saints of Vietnam. Feast day: November 24.

**Saint Walburga or Walpurga (710–779).** Several years after her death the remains of Saint Walburga were moved from Heidenheim Abbey to Eichstätt Abbey in Germany, which had been founded by her brother, Saint Willibald. Her relics lie in a stone sarcophagus in the abbey church.

The daughter of Saint Richard the King and the sister of two missionaries to Germany, Saint Willibald and Saint Winebald, Walburga left her Benedictine convent in Dorset, England, for Heidenheim, where she founded a convent for newly converted German women. She taught the Catholic faith to people in the region and opened a hospital for them. Heidenheim Abbey prospered, with a monastery for men and a convent for women. Walburga was elected abbess and ruled over both houses, an unusual situation in the ninth century, but a tribute to her sanctity and good sense.

Saint Walburga is the patron saint of sailors and good harvests. She is invoked against rodents, rabies, plague, famine, coughs, and storms. Feast day: February 25 and May 1 (Translation of Saint Walburga's Relics to Eichstätt).

**Saint Wenceslaus (907–929).** Originally the body of Saint Wenceslaus was buried in the church where he was murdered. It was Prince Boleslaw who, full of remorse for killing his brother, had Wenceslaus's body moved to Prague's Cathedral of St. Vitus. The saint's bones are preserved in the cathedral's St. Wenceslaus Chapel.

Wenceslaus's father, Wratislaw, was the first Christian duke of Bohemia (modern-day Czech Republic). Wenceslaus was educated and raised a devout Catholic by his grandmother, Saint Ludmilla. His mother, Dragomir, remained a pagan and supported the anti-Christian party in Bohemia, going so far as to have her mother-in-law, Ludmilla, murdered. Wenceslaus's brother, Boleslaw, feigned being a Christian, but he was a member of the anti-Christian faction too. Early one morning Boleslaw and his henchmen ambushed Wenceslaus outside a church and murdered him.

Saint Wenceslaus is the patron saint of brewers. He is one of the patron saints of Prague and the Czech Republic. Feast day: September 28.

**Blessed Widukind (died 804).** The bones of Blessed Widukind lie in the Lutheran Church of St. Dionysius in Enger, Germany.

As chief of the Saxons, Widukind was Charlemagne's foremost adversary in northern Europe. Beginning at least as early as 778, Widukind led his pagan Saxons in annual attacks on the Catholic Franks. Not until 782 did Charlemagne defeat the Saxons, but Widukind escaped, taking refuge in Denmark.

But the peace was short-lived; the Saxons rose up and murdered the priests Charlemagne had sent to convert them. In retaliation, Charlemagne executed four thousand Saxons. Widukind then came back to Germany to lead his nation and its Frisian allies against the Franks. The war lasted until 785, when Charlemagne forced Widukind to surrender, swear allegiance, and accept baptism, along with thousands of Saxon and Frisian warriors. Charlemagne served as Widukind's godfather.

A thousand-year-old legend in Germany claims that Widukind became a model Christian, founding churches and monasteries in Saxony and setting an example among his warriors of devotion to the new faith. After his death Saxons venerated their former chieftain as a saint.

Feast day: January 7.

**Saint William of York (died 1154).** After his canonization in 1227, the body of Saint William was enshrined in the choir of the York Minister. During the Reformation the shrine was dismantled and the saint's bones hidden. In the 1960s, during restoration of the crypt, workmen discovered the relics. They lie now in a stone sarcophagus in the crypt.

William Fitzherbert was an Anglo-Norman aristocrat, related

to the family of William the Conqueror. He was elected archbishop of York in 1141. In an age when bishops could be worldly,
aloof, and self-important, William set an example by being a holy,
gentle, conscientious shepherd of souls. Nonetheless, he had enemies who spread rumors that he had become archbishop by bribing
the cathedral clergy to vote for him, and he was at the center of a
political game, with the Cistercians vying for the post for their own
candidate, a man named Henry Murduc. The squabbling became
so intense that the pope, in an attempt to restore peace in York,
ordered William to resign and retire to a monastery.

In 1153, thirteen years after he had first been elected, a new
pope confirmed William as archbishop. He returned to his archdiocese and made peace with his enemies, but within a few weeks
William was dead. It is possible that he was poisoned.

Feast day: June 8.


**Saint Winifred (seventh century).** In 1536 commissioners of
Henry VIII entered Shrewsbury Abbey, stripped the shrine of Saint
Winifred of its valuables, and destroyed her relics. Catholics found
the bones of one finger and took them to Rome. The relic returned
to England in 1852 and is venerated at the Catholic shrine church
near St. Winifred's Well at Holywell in North Wales. The pool
that sprang up where Saint Winifred's head fell is still visited by
pilgrims to Holywell.

Winifred was a member of the Welsh royal family of Powys.
Her uncle, Saint Beuno, lived near her parents' house and served as
her tutor. When she was a young woman Winifred took the vows
of a nun, receiving the veil from her uncle.

One day while her family was at Mass at Beuno's chapel, a
prince named Caradog rode up to the house and asked Winifred
to bring him some water. As she handed him the cup, he made an
indecent suggestion. Winifred rebuffed him. Caradog then tried
to take Winifred by force. She broke free and ran for the chapel,
but Caradog caught up with her and with a single blow of his

sword cut off her head. Winifred fell dead at the chapel door, and Caradog stood beside the body, unrepentant.

Seeing his niece lying dead and the arrogant prince standing over her, the bloody sword still in his hand, Beuno cursed Caradog. At once, demons appeared and dragged the prince off to hell.

Beuno placed Winifred's severed head by her neck; then he and her family knelt to pray for the murdered girl. As they rose, Winifred did, too. For the rest of her life her throat bore a red mark where the sword had struck. And from the place where her head fell, a spring of clear water bubbled up.

Winifred lived for many more years. She made a pilgrimage to Rome, and when she returned, she and her mother founded a monastery and convent at Gwytherin.

Saint Winifred is the patron saint of victims of rape and of the Welsh towns of Holywell and Gwytherin and the English town of Shrewsbury. Feast day: November 3.

**Saint Wolfgang (924–994).** The saint's relics are venerated in the Church of St. Wolfgang in St. Wolfgang im Salzkammergut, Austria. The church also preserves the saint's hermitage and the ax he used to build it.

Wolfgang was one of the leading churchmen in tenth-century Germany. He made the Einsiedeln Abbey school one of the finest in the country. To bring an end to Magyar raids on German territory, Wolfgang led a band of Benedictine monks into Hungary to convert the Magyars. As bishop of Ratisbon (modern-day Regensburg), he revitalized religious life in the abbeys and convents of his diocese.

Toward the end of his life Wolfgang resigned his office and went into the forest in Salzkammergut, Austria, where he built a hermitage. It is said that he threw an ax among the trees and where it fell he built his hut and chapel.

Saint Wolfgang is the patron saint of carpenters. He is invoked against stroke, epilepsy, paralysis, and stomach ailments. He is also the patron saint of the diocese of Regensburg, Germany. Feast day: October 31.

**Saint Zeno and Companions (c. 300).** In a small crypt chapel beneath the Church of Our Lady of the Martyrs at Rome's Abbey of Tre Fontane lie the relics of Saint Zeno and his 10,204 companions.

During Emperor Diocletian's persecution of the Church these men (according to some sources they were all veterans of the Roman legions) were enslaved and put to work constructing the Baths of Diocletian. Zeno was the leader, perhaps chief officer, or spokesmen of the martyrs, all of whom were executed together. The baths on which they labored survive today in Rome as three distinct structures: the Basilica of St. Mary of the Angels and the Martyrs, the Church of St. Bernard, and the National Museum of Rome.

Feast day: July 9.

**Saint Zita (1218–1272).** The body of Saint Zita lies in a glass casket in the Basilica of San Frediano, where she attended Mass every day. The church's Angel Portal marks the place where one Christmas Eve Zita is said to have given her master's fur coat to a beggar who was an angel in disguise, come from heaven to test the charity of Christians.

Zita was only twelve when she was hired as a servant of the Fatinellis, a family of prosperous silk merchants in Lucca, Italy. She was hardworking, modest, and devout; she rose early so she could attend daily Mass at the Church of San Frediano, next door to the Fatinellis' house. When the drudgery of housework depressed her, she said a brief prayer, offering her work to God. If she had any spare time, she went to her room in the attic to pray. It is said that once, after putting bread in the oven, she went to her room where she became so caught up in prayer that she forgot about the bread.

She rushed down to the kitchen, where she found perfect loaves cooling on the table; while Zita prayed, angels had tended to the baking.

Zita never turned away a beggar who came to the kitchen door. During a famine she gave away the family's entire store of dried beans, which would have seen the Fatinellis through the crisis. Signor Fatinelli berated Zita for being a fool, then stormed into the pantry—where he found a full supply of dry beans.

Although Zita's charity exasperated the Fatinellis, they came to trust and love her. They made her the manager of their household and the governess of their children. Zita died in the Fatinelli home, where she had worked for forty-eight years.

Saint Zita is the patron saint of servants, housekeepers, and waiters and waitresses. She is invoked to find lost keys and is one of the patron saints of Lucca, Italy. Feast day: April 27.

# Bibliography

The Aachen Sanctuaries. www.aachendom.de.

Ackroyd, Peter. *The Life of Thomas More.* Doubleday, 1998.

————. *Venice: Pure City.* Nan A. Talese, 2010.

*Acta Sanctorum,* 64 vols. Antwerp, 1643.

Albin, Hugh O. *Opening of the Roper Vault in St. Dunstan's Canterbury and Thoughts on the Burial of William and Margaret Roper.* Moreana, 1979.

Anderson, Alan Orr, and Marjorie Ogilvie Anderson, eds. and trans. *Adomnan's Life of Columba.* Thomas Nelson and Sons Ltd., 1961.

Armstrong, Regis J., and Ignatius C. Brady, eds. *Francis and Clare: The Complete Works.* Paulist Press, 1982.

Barbosa, Alexandre Moniz. "Relics of St. Xavier Still a Draw." *Times of India,* December 3, 2009.

Barlow, Frank. *Thomas Becket.* University of California Press, 1986.

Bede. *The Ecclesiastical History of the English Nation,* E. P. Dutton, 1910.

Berenbaum, Michael, ed. *A Mosaic of Victims: Non-Jews Persecuted and Murdered by the Nazis.* New York University Press, 1990.

Bianchi, Lorenzo. *The Sudarium of Oviedo.* www.30giorni.it/us/articolo.asp?id=21068.

Bird, Maryanne. "Piercing an Ancient Tale: Solving the Mystery of a Christian Relic." *Time,* June 8, 2003.

Blessed Marianne Cope. http://blessedmariannecope.org.

Blessed Miguel Pro, S.J. http://puffin.creighton.edu/jesuit/pro.

The Body of St. Bernadette. www.catholicpilgrims.com/lourdes/bb_bernadette_body.htm.

*The Book of Saints,* 6th ed. Morehouse Publishing, 1989.

Bowden, Henry Sebastian. *Mementoes of the Martyrs and Confessors of*

*England and Wales.* Edited and revised by Donald Attwater. Burns and Oates, 1962.

Brophy, Don. *Catherine of Siena: A Passionate Life.* Bluebrudge, 2010.

Budge, E. A. W., trans. "The Passion of St. George." *Bibliotheca Hagiographica Orientalis,* no. 310, 1888.

Buehrle, Marie Cecilia. *Kateri of the Mohawks.* Bruce Publishing Co., 1954.

"Bulgaria, Sozopol in Euphoria over St. John the Baptist Archaeology Find." *Sofia News Agency,* www.novinite.com/view_news.php?id =118869.

Bury, J. B. *The Life of St. Patrick and His Place in History.* Book-of-the-Month Club, 1999.

Butler, Declan. "Joan of Arc's Relics Exposed as Forgery." *Nature,* April 4, 2007, www.nature.com/nature/journal/v446/n7136/fall/446593a .html.

Butler, George William. *The Curé of Ars Today: St. John Vianney.* Ignatius Press, 1988.

Camm, Dom Bede. *Forgotten Shrines: An Account of Some Old Catholic Halls and Families in England and of Relics and Memorials of the English Martyrs.* MacDonald and Evans, 1936.

Carr, John. "St. Gerard Majella." In *A Treasury of Catholic Reading.* Edited by John Chapin. Farrar, Straus and Cudahy, 1957.

Cassens, David E. "The Relics of St. Irene," stbasilthegreat.org/about/ relics/the-relics-of-st-irene.

The Cathedral and Abbey Church of St. Alban. www.stalbanscathedral .org/.

*The Catholic Encyclopedia,* 1907, www.newadvent.org.

Cross, Samuel H., ed. *Russian Primary Chronicle: Laurentian Text.* Medieval Academy of America, 1968.

D'Anastasio, Ruggero, Gianpaolo Di Silvestri, Paolo Versacci, Luigi Capasso, and Bruno Marino. "The Heart of Santa Rosa." *Lancet,* June 11, 2010.

de la Vega, Luis Lasso, Lisa Sousa et al., eds. *The Story of Guadalupe: Luis Lasso de la Vega's Huei Hamahuiçoltica of 1649.* Stanford University Press, 1998.

de Voragine, Jacobus. *The Golden Legend,* 2 vols. Princeton University Press, 1993.

Dorcy, Sister Mary Jean. *St. Dominic's Family: The Lives of Over 300 Famous Dominicans.* TAN Books, 1983.

The Ecumenical Patriarchate of Constantinople. "The Return of the Relics of St. Gregory the Theologian and St. John Chrysostom." www.patriarchate.org/patriarchate/relics.

Englebert, Omer. *The Lives of the Saints.* David McKay Co., 1951.

Essays in Honor of Oleg Grabar. *Muqarnas,* vol. 10, 1993.

Eusebius. "The Letter of the Churches of Vienna and Lyons to the Churches of Asia and Phrygia, Including the Story of the Blessed Blandina." *History of the Church,* book 5, ch. 1, 2005.

Falasca, Stefania. "The Humble Splendor of the First Witnesses: The Catacombs of Saint Callixtus in Rome." *30 Days,* no. 4, 1996.

Farmer, David Hugh, general consultant editor. *Butler's Lives of the Saints: New Full Edition,* 12 vols. Liturgical Press, 1995–2000.

Fitzgerald, Allan D., general editor. *Augustine through the Ages: An Encyclopedia.* Eerdmans, 1999.

Fraser, Antonia. *Faith and Treason: The Story of the Gunpowder Plot.* Nan A. Talese, 1996.

Furlong, Monica. *Thérèse of Lisieux.* Random House, 1987.

Graham, Edward P., trans. *Acts of the Hieromartyr Januarius, Bishop of Benevento.* St. Pachomins Orthodox Library, 1995.

Griffin, T. L., adaptor. *The Life of Philip Howard, Earl of Arundel, Saint and Martyr: Edited from the Original Mss by the Duke Of Norfolk,* www.geocities.com/griffin81au/HowardMartyr.html.

Haskins, Susan. *Mary Magdalen: Myth and Metaphor.* HarperCollins, 1993.

Hole, Christina. *English Shrines and Sanctuaries.* B. T. Batsford, 1954.

Holy Innocents. www.catholicnewsagency.com/saint.php?n=667.

Howse, Christopher. "John Henry Newman's Body Missing." *Daily Telegraph,* October 5, 2008, blogs.telegraph.co.uk/culture/christopherhowse/5374447/john_henry_newmans_body_missing.

Huysmans, J. K. *Saint Lydwina of Schiedam.* Translated by Agnes Hastings. Kegan Paul, Trench, Trubner and Co. Ltd., 1923.

Jasna Gora/Black Madonna. www.mati.com.pl/jasnagora/index.php?strona,podserwis,pol,glowny,0,0,eng,english,ant.html.

Jones, C. A. *The Life of St. Elizabeth of Hungary, Duchess of Thuringia.* Swift & Co., 1877.

Jones, Charles W. *Saint Nicholas of Myra, Bari, and Manhattan: Biography of a Legend.* University of Chicago Press, 1978.

Kalvelage, Brother Francis. M., ed. *Francis M. Kolbe: Saint of the Immaculate.* Franciscans of the Immaculate, 2001.

Kieckhefer, Richard. *Unquiet Souls: Fourteenth Century Saints and Their Religious Milieu.* University of Chicago Press, 1984.

Krakow Cathedral. www.krakow-info.com/katedra.htm.

Lecompte, Edward. *Glory of the Mohawks: The Life of the Venerable Catherine Tekakwitha.* Translated by Florence Ralston Werum. Bruce Publishing Co., 1944.

Longenecker, Rev. Dwight. "The Hand of St. Etheldreda," www.dwightlongenecker.com/Content/Pages/Articles/CatholicIssues/Ethelreda.asp.

Marguerite-Bourgeoys Museum and Notre-Dame-de-Bon-Secours Chapel. www.marguerite-bourgeoys.com/en/index.asp.

Maria Stein Center. www.mariasteincenter.org.

Martindale, C. C. *Life of St. Camillus.* Sheed and Ward, 1946.

———. *The Vocation of Aloysius Gonzaga.* B. Herder, 1927.

Martyrs of Japan. www.26martyrs.com.

Martyrs of Vietnam. www.cttdva.com/cttdvn3.htm and sites.google.com/site/vietnamesemartyrs/VietnameseMartyrs.

Mauriac, Francois. *St. Margaret of Cortona.* Translated by Bernard Frechtman. Philosophical Library, 1948.

McClory, Robert. *Faithful Dissenters: Stories of Men and Women Who Loved and Changed the Church.* Orbis Books, 2001.

McCormack, Mike. "St. Patrick's Relics." *Irish History,* 2010, www.aoh.com/pages/irish_history/2010/st_patricks_relics_030110.pdf.

McGinley, J., and H. Mursurillo, trans. *The Translation of Saint Nicholas.* Bolletino di S. Nicola, Number 10, Studi e testi, October 1980.

McLynn, Neil B. *Ambrose of Milan: Church and Court in a Christian Capital.* University of California Press, 1994.

McNabb, Vincent J. *St. Elizabeth of Portugal.* Sheed and Ward, 1938.

Michalenko, Sophia. *The Life of Faustina Kowalska: The Authorized Biography.* Charis Books, 1999.

Miravalle, Mark I. *Present Ecclesial Status of Devotion to Saint Philomena.* Franciscan University of Steubenville, 2002.

Molinari, Paolo. "Blessed Miguel Augustin Pro, Martyr for the Faith." Translated by José María Fuentes, S.J. *La Civiltà Cattolica,* vol. IV, 1988.

Musurillo, Herbert. *Acts of the Christian Martyrs.* Oxford University Press, 1972.

National Shrine of St. Andrew. www.stmaryscathedral.co.uk/standrew.html.

National Shrine of St. Elizabeth Ann Seton. www.setonshrine.org.

North American Martyrs. www.martyrs-shrine.com.

103 Korean Martyrs. Catholic Church in Korea. http://english.cbck.or.kr/Saints103.

*Our Irish Martyrs.* C & R Print, 2009.

Our Lady of Guadalupe. www.virgendeguadalupe.org.mx.

Padre Pio. www.padrepio.it.

Raffaele, Paul. "Keepers of the Lost Ark?" *Smithsonian,* December 2007.

Relics of St. Anne. www.ssadb.qc.ca/eng/2_5_relics.htm.

Ricciotti, Giuseppe. *The Age of Martyrs.* TAN Books, 1999.

Riches, Samantha. *St. George: Hero, Martyr and Myth.* Sutton Publishing, 2000.

Roberts, Alexander, and James Donaldson, eds. *The Protoevangelium of James.* Vol. 8, *Ante-Nicene Fathers.* Hendickson Publishers, 1994.

Rufus, Anneli. *Magnificent Corpses: Searching Through Europe for St. Peter's Head, St. Chiara's Heart, St. Stephen's Hand, and Other Saints' Relics.* Marlowe & Company, 1999.

"Russia's Hero Is Grand Prince Alexander Nevsky." *Kommersant,* September 24, 2008.

St. Anthony Chapel. "Mystery Priest Who Collected Huge Display

of Relics Was Himself Said to Have Powers." *Spirit Daily,* www
.spiritdaily.com//relics.htm.

St. Anthony's Chapel. www.saintanthonyschapel.org.

St. Birgitta. http://birgitta.vadstena.se.

St. Brendan the Navigator. www.moytura.com/clonfert2.htm.

"St. Catherine's: Age-Old Place of Prayer." *L'Osservatore Romano,* March
1, 2000.

St. Christopher. www.ucc.ie/milmart/Christopher.html.

St. Christopher, Holy Helper. www.kristofor.hr/english-zastitnik.html.

St. Damien de Veuster. www.fatherdamien.com.

St. Edward the Confessor. www.westminster-abbey.org/visit-us/high
lights/edward-the-confessor.

St. Maurice of Turin. www.albion-swords.com/swords/johnsson/sword-
museum-stmaurice.htm.

St. Nicholas of Flue. www.bruderklaus.com.

St. Odilia. www.crosier.org/default.cfm?PID=1.32.1.

St. Peregrine Laziosi. www.basilicasanpellegrinolaziosi.it.

St. Teresa of Los Andes. www.teresadelosandes.org.

St. Thecla. www.maaloula.net.

St. Theodore Guerin. www.spsmw.org.

St. Thomas of Canterbury Catholic Parish. www.rc.net/southwark/
canterbury/index.htm.

St. Vibiana. www.la-archdiocese.org/about/heritage/vibiana.html.

Schwertner, Thomas M. *St. Albert the Great.* Bruce Publishing Co., 1932.

Shroud of Turin. www.sindone.org/the_holy_shroud_english_/the
_shroud/00024123_The_Shroud.html.

Simon-Cahn, Annabelle. "The Fermo Chasuable of St. Thomas Becket
and Hispano-Mauresque Cosmological Silks: Some Speculations
on the Adaptive Reuse of Textiles." *Muqarnas,* vol. 10, 1993.

Sturluson, Snorri. *Heimskringla: History of the Kings of Norway.* Translated
by Lee M. Hollander. University of Texas Press, 1964.

Sullivan, Mary Louise. *Mother Cabrini: Italian Immigrant of the Century.*
Center for Migration Studies, 1992.

Sulpitius Severus. *The Life of St. Martin.* Translation and notes by
Alexander Roberts. Vol. 11, 2d series. A Select Library of Nicene

and Post-Nicene Fathers of the Christian Church. Christian Literature Company, 1894.

Thiede, Carsten Peter, and Mathew D'Ancona. *The Quest for the True Cross.* Algrave, 2000.

Trotta, Liz. *Jude: A Pilgrimage to the Saint of Last Resort.* HarperCollins, 1998.

Uganda Martyrs Shrine. www.ugandamartyrsshrine.org.ug.

Urry, William. *Thomas Becket: His Last Days.* Edited with an introduction by Peter A. Rowe. Sutton Publishing, 1999.

Walsh, John Evangelist. *The Bones of St. Peter.* Sinag-Tala, 1982.

Webb, J. F., and D. H. Farmer, trans. *The Age of Bede.* Penguin Books, 1985.

Weinstein, Donald, and Rudolph M. Bell. *Saints and Society: The Two Worlds of Western Christendom, 1000–1700.* University of Chicago Press, 1982.

Weisheipl, James A. *Friar Thomas D'Aquino: His Life, Thought, and Works.* Catholic University of America Press, 1983.

Woods, David, trans. "The Passion of St. Christopher." *Bibliotheca Hagiographica Latina Antiquae et Mediae Aetatis,* no. 1764, 1999.

# About the Author

THOMAS J. CRAUGHWELL is the author of more than twenty books on history, religion, and popular culture, including *Saints Behaving Badly* (Doubleday, 2006) and *Stealing Lincoln's Body* (Harvard University Press, 2007). He is a regular contributor to the Catholic news weekly *Our Sunday Visitor*, and has written articles for the *Wall Street Journal*, the *New York Times*, *American Spectator*, *U.S. News & World Report*, *Emmy* magazine, *National Catholic Register*, and *Inside the Vatican*. Tom has appeared on CNN, BBC, FOX, EWTN, and the Discovery Channel. In 2009 the History Channel produced a documentary based on *Stealing Lincoln's Body*. Tom writes from his home in Bethel, Connecticut.

## Also Available from Thomas J. Craughwell

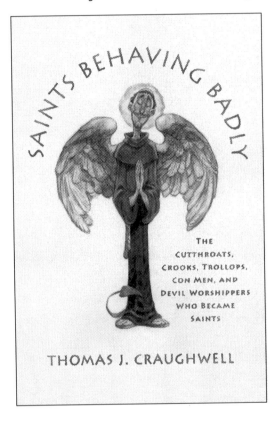

Saints are not born, they are made. And many, as *Saints Behaving Badly* reveals, were made of very rough materials indeed. The first book to lay bare the less-than-saintly behavior of thirty-two venerated holy men and women, it presents the scandalous detours they took on the road to sainthood. Written with wit and respect (each profile ends with what inspired the saint to give up his or her wicked ways) and illustrated with amusing caricatures, *Saints Behaving Badly* will entertain, inform, and ultimately inspire Catholic readers across America.

For more information or to read an excerpt, visit
www.ImageCatholicBooks.com

Printed in the United States
by Baker & Taylor Publisher Services